Understanding the Language of the Deaf World

Maureen O'Grady Hynes

Cover art designed and created by Scott M. Corollo

Interior Photos taken at Gallaudet University by Thomas N. Bland, Jr.

Printed in the United States of America

10 9 8 7 6 5 4 3 2 1

ISBN 0-536-27657-9

2006500052

MT/SD

Please visit our web site at *www.pearsoncustom.com*

PEARSON CUSTOM PUBLISHING
75 Arlington Street, Suite 300, Boston, MA 02116
A Pearson Education Company

Copyright Acknowledgments

Grateful acknowledgment is made to the following sources for permission to reprint material copyrighted or controlled by them:

"Types of Hearing Loss," by Glen R. Meier, reprinted from *audiologyawareness.com*, edited by the Audiology Awareness Campaign, 1999, Audiology Awareness Campaign.

"How to read an audiogram," reprinted from *www.jsu.edu/depart/dss/pec/resource-vr*, Postsecondary Education Consortium.

"The Glass Wall," by Lou Aymard, Ph.D., reprinted by permission of the author.

"Confronting Deafness in an Unstilled World," by Harold Orlans, reprinted from *Society 25*, no. 4, by permission of Transaction Publishers.

"Special Guest Speaker I. King Jordan," by I. King Jordan, reprinted from *Selected Proceedings of 2002 Conference of the Association of Late-Deafened Adults*, edited by L. Piper and D. Watson (2003), by permission of the Association of Late-Deafened Adults.

"Two Views of Deafness," by Chris Wixtrom, National Association of the Deaf.

"Thomas Hopkins Gallaudet: The Legacy Begins," Gallaudet University.

"Laurent Clerc, Apostle to the Deaf People of the New World," by Loida Canlas, reprinted by permission of Gallaudet University Laurent Clerc National Deaf Education Center. Copyright © 2003 by Gallaudet University Laurent Clerc National Deaf Education Center.

"The Value of the Sign Language to the Deaf," by Edward M. Gallaudet, reprinted from *Reference Handbook of the Medical Sciences* (1886), extracted from the original article, "The Language of Signs and the Combined Method of Instructing Deaf Mutes."

"Everyone Here Spoke Sign Language," by Nora Groce, Natural History Magazine, Inc.

"American Sign Language: It's Not Mouth Stuff-It's Brain Stuff," by Richard Wolkomir, reprinted from *Smithsonian*, July 1992, by permission of the author. Copyright © 1992 by Richard Wolkomir.

Introduction to *Signs Across America* (1984), by E.H. Shroyer, reprinted by permission of Gallaudet University Press.

"The Interactional Context of Deaf Mother-Infant Communication," by C.J. Erting, C. Prezioso, and M. O'Grady Hynes, reprinted from From *Gesture to Language in Hearing and Deaf Children*, edited by Virginia Volterra and Carol J. Erting (1994), by permission of Gallaudet University Press.

"Manually Coded English vs. 'Natural' Sign Languages," reprinted from *sign-language.biz*, 2006.

"Cued Speech," Maryland Cued Speech Association.

"Gestuno: International Sign Language," by Travis Rolan Jones, reprinted from *www.lifeprint.com/asl101*, November 12, 2001, by permission of Lifeprint University.

Excerpts from *International Hand Alphabet Charts*, Second Edition (1982), by Simon J. Carmel, National Association of the Deaf.

"Terminology Used to Refer to Deaf People," by Michael Schwartz (2002), Center on Human Policy/Disability Studies for Teachers, Syracuse University Press.

"Audism," by Tom Harrington, reprinted from *library.gallaudet.edu*, October 2002, Gallaudet University Library.

"Reflections of American Deaf Culture in Deaf Humor," by M.J. Bienvenu.

"Cultural Patterns of Deaf People," by Linda A. Siple, reprinted from the *Journal of Intercultural Relations* 18, no. 1 (1994), by permission of Elsevier Science.

"Inside the Deaf Community," by Barbara Kannapell, reprinted from *American Deaf Culture* (1989), Linstok Press.

"Educating Children Who Are Deaf or Hard of Hearing: Residential Life," by Judith Gilliam and Easterbrooks, reprinted from *ERIC Digest* 558 (1998).

"More Marriages Among the Deaf May have Led to Doubling of Common Form of Genetic Deafness In the US," by Walter E. Nance, Virginia Commonwealth University News Services.

"Spotlight on Bernard Bragg," National Theatre of the Deaf.

"Dance Techniques for Deaf and Hard of Hearing Dancers," reprinted from *depts.gallaudet.edu/dance*, Gallaudet University.

"Deaflympics History and Logo," reprinted from *deaflympics.com*, the International Committee of Sports for the Deaf.

"Nothing is Impossible-The Hughes Family," by Patty Hughes, National Association of the Deaf.

"The Deaf Child in Foster Care," by M. Teresa Arcari and Beth Gwinn Betman, National Association of the Deaf.

"Being Ignored Can Be Bliss: How to Use a Sign Language Interpreter," by Barbara Fink, reprinted from the *Deaf American* 34, no. 6 (1982), National Association of the Deaf.

"You're a What? Interpreter for the Deaf," by Gallaudet University Public Service Programs, Gallaudet University.

"On Guard!" by Elaine Gardner, reprinted from *Gallaudet Today,* Gallaudet University.

"As Town for Deaf Takes Shape, Debate on Isolation Re-emerges," by Monica Davey, reprinted from the *New York Times*, March 21, 2005, by permission of The New York Times Company.

"Gene Therapy Restores Hearing to Deaf Guinea Pigs," by Steven Reinberg, reprinted from *Forbes.com*, February 14, 2005, HealthDay.

Statue of Thomas Gallaudet and Alice Cogswell (Photo by Bland)

Statue of Edward Miner Gallaudet at Gallaudet University (Photo by Bland)

Gallaudet University, Washington DC (Photo by Bland)

Statue of Laurent Clerc at Gallaudet University (Photo by Bland)

BIBLIOGRAPHIES

Ear Anatomy 2001–2005 www.Enchantedlearning.com/subjects/anatomy/ear/label/label.shtml

Meier, G.R., *Types of Hearing Loss,* The Audiology Awareness Campaign, 1999, www.audiologyawareness.com/hhelp/hloss.htm

(Diagrams): How to Read an Audiogram: Everyday Sounds/ Environment Sounds www.jsu.edu/depart/dss/pec/resource-vr/audiograms.html

Cochlear Implants, www.nidcd.nih.gov/health/hearing/coch.asp#a

Aymard, L.L., *The Glass Wall* (permission obtained in the mail)

Orlans, H. (1988). *Confronting Deafness in an Unstilled World,* Society, 25 (4), 32–39.

Jordan, I.K. (2003). *Special Guest Speaker I. King Jordan.* In L. Piper & D. Watson (Eds.), Selected Proceedings of 2002 conference of the Association of Late-Deafened Adults. http://www.alda.org/aldapubs.htm http://www.uark.edu/deafrtc/publications.html

Wixtrom, C. (1988) *Two Views of Deafness,* the Deaf American, 38 (1), 21. (try at www.nad.org)

Thomas Hopkins Gallaudet: The Legacy Begins http://www.pr.gallaudet.edu/GallaudetHistory/

Laurent Clerc: Apostle to the Deaf of the New World http://clerccenter.gallaudet.edu/Literacy/MSSDLRC/clerc

Gallaudet, E.M. (1887). *The Value of the Sign Language to the Deaf.* American Annals of the Deaf, 23 (3), 1887, 141–147 http://gupress.gallaudet.edu/annals/

Groce, N. (1980). *Everyone Here Spoke Sign Language.* Natural History, 89 (6), 10–16.

Wolkomir, Richard, *American Sign Language, It's Not Mouth Stuff—It's Brain Stuff.* ff-It's Smithsonian 23.8. July 1992, 30–42.

Shroyer, E.H., 1984, *Signs Across America,* Gallaudet College Press, ISBN 0-913580-961

Erting, C.J., Prezioso and O'Grady Hynes, M. The interactional context of Deaf Mother-Infant Communication. Fourth International Symposium on Sign Language Research, Lappeenrata, Finland. July 1987.

Sign Language: *Manually Coded English vs "natural" Sign Languages.* 2006. http://www.sign-language.biz/sign/manuallycoded english.asp

Cued Speech, The Maryland Cued Speech Association, 1997. (MDCSA) an affiliate of the National Cued Speech Association, P.O. Box 9173, Silver Spring MD 20916 Amy R. Ruberi, March 1997.

Jones, T.R. (Nov. 12, 2001) *Gestuno: International Sign Language,* American Sign Language University, http://www.lifeprint.com/asl101/pages-layout/gestuno.htm

Carmel, S.J. 1975, 1982, *International Hand Alphabet Chart,* Studio Publishing Inc., Rockille, MD 20851, (ISBN 0-9600886-2-8)

Schwartz, M., 2002, Syracuse University,. *Terminology Used to Refer to Deaf People*

Audism, http://library.gallaudet.edu/dr/faq-audism.html

Bienvenu, M.J. (1989, September). *Reflections of American Deaf Culture in Deaf Humor.* TBC News, pp. 1–3

Siple, L. (1994) *Cultural Patterns of Deaf People,* The Journal of Intercultural Reviews, Volume 18 345–367. Reprinted by permission of the publisher.

Kannapell, B. (1982) *Inside the Deaf Community.* The Deaf American, 34 (4) 23–26. (try at www.nad.org) (note: The Deaf American was published by National Association of the Deaf in Silver Spring, MD)

Gilliam J., Easterbrooks S., (08/1997) *Educating Children Who Are Deaf or Hard of Hearing: Residential Life, ASL, and Deaf Culture.* ERIC Digest #558, ERIC Clearinghouse on Disabilities and Gifted Education Reston, Va., http://www.ericdigest. org/1998/life.htm

Nance, W.E. *More Marriages Among the Deaf May Have Led to Doubling of Common Form of Genetic Deafness in the U.S.* VCU News Services at 804-828-1231, Dr. Nance's article is available via email in PDF format. http://r02.webmail.aol.com/15106/aol/en-us/Mail/display-message.aspx

Spotlight on Bernard Bragg: Actor, Mime, Educator and Founder of National Theatre of the Deaf www.ntd.org/bernardbragg.html

Dance Technqiues for Deaf and Hard of Hearing Dancers, http://depts.gallaudet.edu/dance/techniques.html

Deaflympics History http://www.deaflympics.com/news/index.asp?ID=242

Deaflympics Logo http://www.deaflympics.com/about/index.asp?ID=250

Alexander Graham Bell http://en.wikipedia.org/wiki/Alexander_Graham_Bell

Milan 1880 http://www.milan1880.com/milan1880history/beforemilan1880.html

Hughes, P.(1981). *Nothing is Impossible: The Hughes Family,* The Deaf American, 34(3), 8–9. (try at www.nad.org)

Arcari, M.T., & Betman, B.G. (1986) *The Deaf Child in Foster Care.* Children Today, 15 (4), 17–21. (try at www.children-today.com)

Fink, B. (1982) *Being Ignored can be a bliss: How to use a sign language interpreter.* The DeafAmerican, 34 (6), 5–9. (Reprinted from Disabled USA, Fall 1981).

Gardner, E. On Guard! (1987. Special Issue), *Gallaudet Today*, 17, 31–38.

Davey, M. 3-21-2005 *As Town for Deaf Takes Shape, Debate on Isolation Re-emerge,* New York Times, *http://www.laurentsd.com/Newsroom/TheNewYorkTimes.htm*

Gene Therapy Restores Hearing to Deaf Guinea Pigs. Forbes. 02/14/2005. http://www.forbes.com/lifestyle/health/feeds/hscout/2005/02/14/hscout523947.html

DEDICATION TO DR. LOU AYMARD

It was exactly 33 years ago that Lou Aymard designed and taught the first continuing education course in American Sign Language at Anne Arundel Community College. Few other community colleges even knew of the American Deaf Community. Following in that history over three decades later, the College continues to respect the richness of Deaf Culture and the Language of Deaf Americans. In doing so, I was hired as the first deaf professor, to continue the tradition of bringing to its students quality educational programs in American Sign Language. The staff has been passed to the next generation.

—Maureen O'Grady Hynes

CONTENTS

AUDIOLOGY 101

1

EAR ANATOMY

Sound is collected by the pinna (the visible part of the ear) and directed through the outer ear canal. The sound makes the eardrum vibrate, which in turn causes a series of three tiny bones (the hammer, the anvil, and the stirrup) in the middle ear to vibrate. The vibration is transferred to the snail-shaped cochlea in the inner ear; the cochlea is lined with sensitive hairs which trigger the generation of nerve signals that are sent to the brain.

On average, people can hear sounds in the frequencies between 20 to 20,000 Hertz.

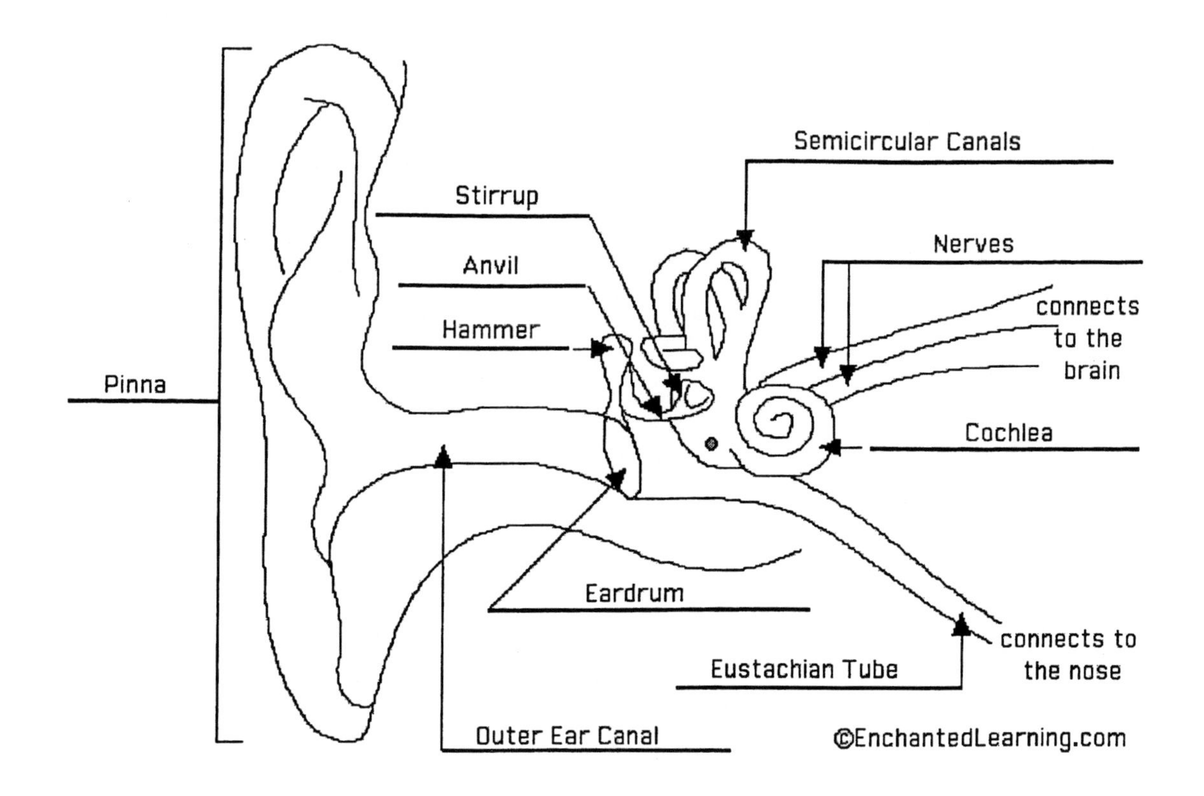

anvil—(also called the incus) a tiny bone that passes vibrations from the hammer to the stirrup.

cochlea—a spiral-shaped, fluid-filled inner ear structure; it is lined with cilia (tiny hairs) that move when vibrated and cause a nerve impulse to form.

eardrum—(also called the tympanic membrane) a thin membrane that vibrates when sound waves reach it.

Eustachian tube—a tube that connects the middle ear to the back of the nose; it equalizes the pressure between the middle ear and the air outside. When you "pop" your ears as you change altitude (going up a mountain or in an airplane), you are equalizing the air pressure in your middle ear.

hammer—(also called the malleus) a tiny bone that passes vibrations from the eardrum to the anvil.

nerves—these carry electro-chemical signals from the inner ear (the cochlea) to the brain.

outer ear canal—the tube through which sound travels to the eardrum.

pinna—(also called the auricle) the visible part of the outer ear. It collects sound and directs it into the outer ear canal

semicircular canals—three loops of fluid-filled tubes that are attached to the cochlea in the inner ear. They help us maintain our sense of balance.

stirrup—(also called the stapes) a tiny, U-shaped bone that passes vibrations from the stirrup to the cochlea. This is the smallest bone in the human body (it is 0.25 to 0.33 cm long).

2

TYPES OF HEARING LOSS

Glen R. Meier
Presented by the Audiology Awareness Campaign

Hearing loss can develop at any age and may be caused by many different factors. Most hearing losses can be categorized as either sensorineural, conductive, or a combination of both sensorineural and conductive (mixed). It is important to understand the basic anatomy of the ear and hearing mechanisms before reading about the actual types of hearing loss.

SENSORINEURAL HEARING LOSS

Sensorineural hearing losses occur when the "inner" ear or the actual hearing nerve itself becomes damaged. About 90% of all people with hearing impairment are in this category, making it the most common type of hearing impairment. Sensorineural hearing loss is often referred to as "nerve deafness." Nerve deafness is not really an accurate description because the damage most frequently occurs within the inner ear rather than the hearing nerve. Common causes of sensorineural hearing loss are aging and exposure to loud noises, but there are many other causes (viral infections, disrupted blood supply to the ear, metabolic disturbances, accident/injury, genetic predisposition, medications that are toxic to the ear, etc). Thus, "sensorineural" indicates the part of the ear that is malfunctioning and encompasses many different causes for the malfunction. This type of hearing loss is frequently not medically or surgically treatable. It is typically permanent and irreversible. However, most people with sensorineural loss find wearing hearing aids to be of significant benefit and some people with severe loss can benefit from a cochlear implant.

CONDUCTIVE HEARING LOSS

Conductive hearing losses occur when the "outer" or "middle" portions of the ear fail to work properly. Sound is blocked from being transferred to the inner ear at normal intensity. Conductive losses are often treatable with either medicine or surgery. Common causes of conductive hearing loss are fluid build up in the middle ear or wax blockage in the ear canal. Children are more likely to have a conductive hearing loss than a sensorineural hearing loss.

MIXED HEARING LOSS

Mixed hearing losses are simply combinations of the above two types of hearing loss. They can occur when a person has a permanent sensorineural hearing loss and then also develops a temporary conductive hearing loss.

This article was originally submitted by Glen R. Meier, M.S., CCC-A, FAAA and subsequently edited by AAC.

3

HOW TO READ AN AUDIOGRAM

AUDIOGRAMS

The following chart shows the levels of hearing loss as they relate to an audiogram.

Normal Hearing
can hear soft conversations
Minimal loss
16 to 25 decibel loss
will have trouble hearing faint or distant speech
Mild
26 to 40 decibel loss
will miss up to 50% of a group discussion
Moderate
41 to 55 decibel loss
conversation over 5 feet away may not
be understood
Moderate to severe
56 to 70 decibel loss
will miss 100% of speech information without
amplification
Severe
71 to 90 decibel loss
can only hear loud noises at close distances
Profound
91 decibel loss and above
depends solely on vision instead of hearing for
processing information

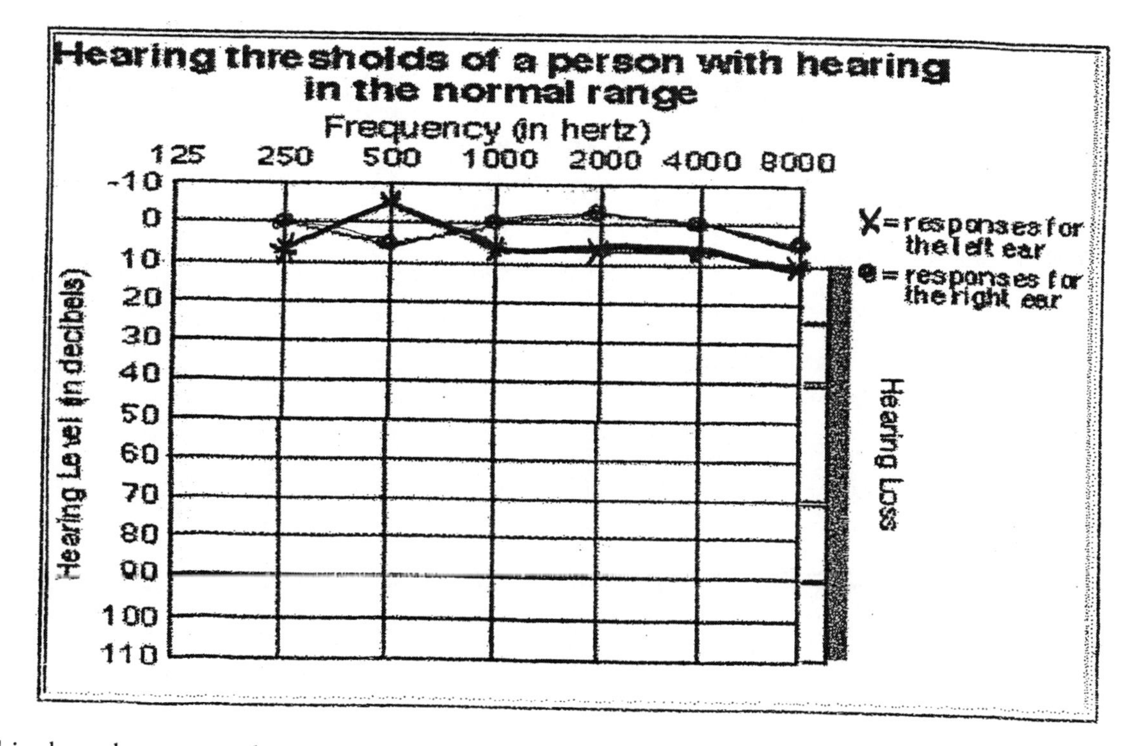

This chart shows an audiogram of a person with normal hearing.

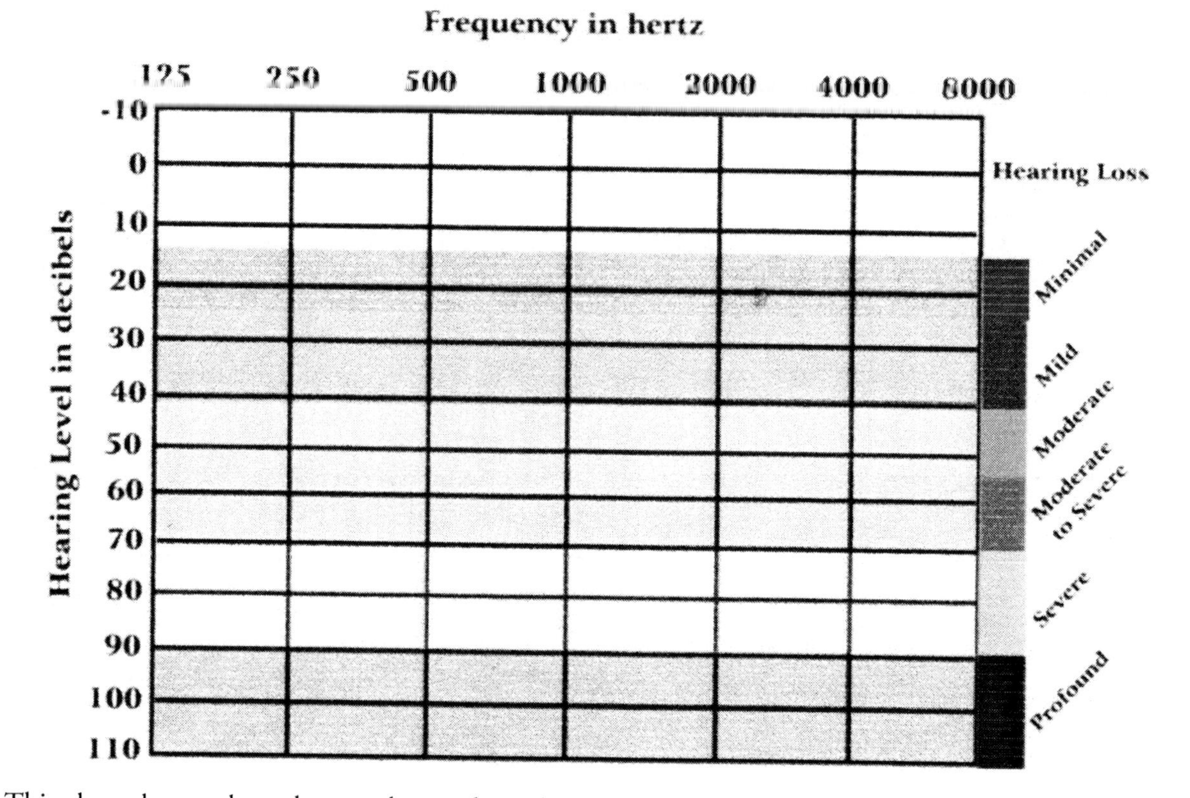

This chart shows where the speech sounds are located on an audiogram. It also shows at what dB level various sounds occur.

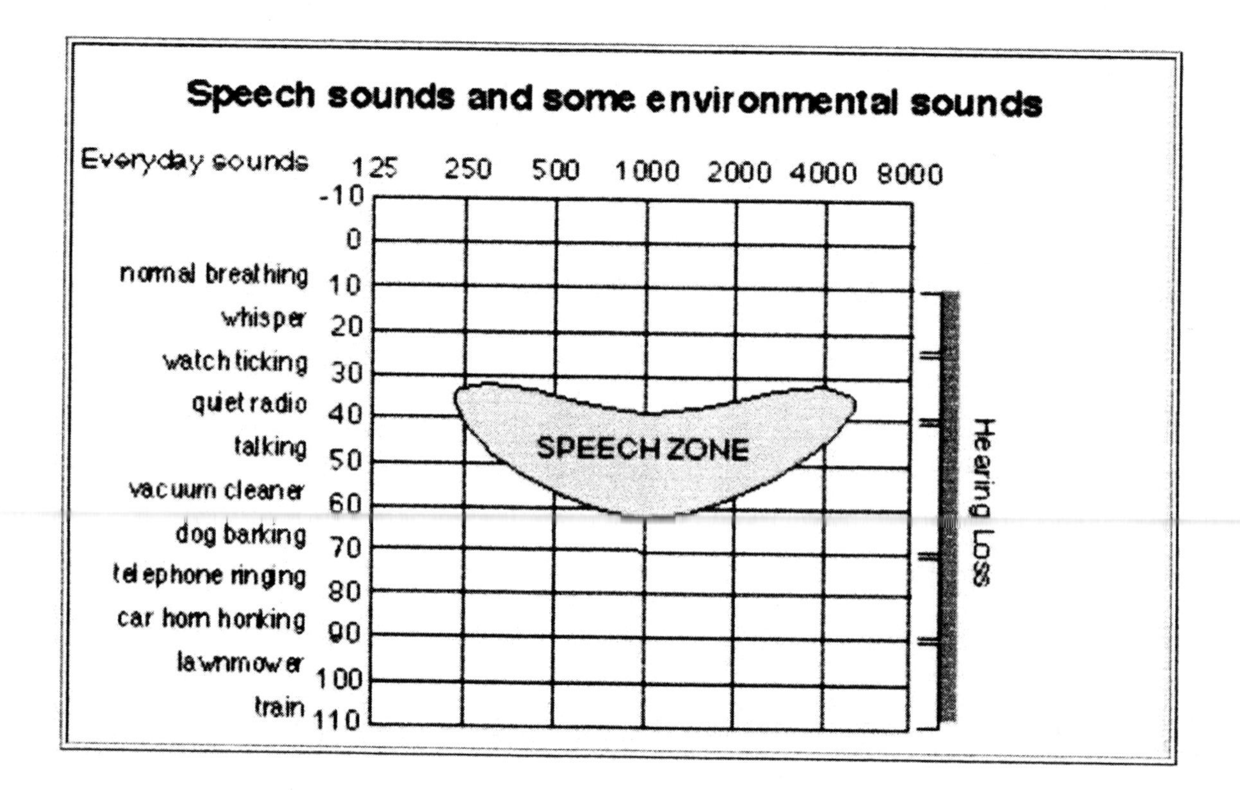

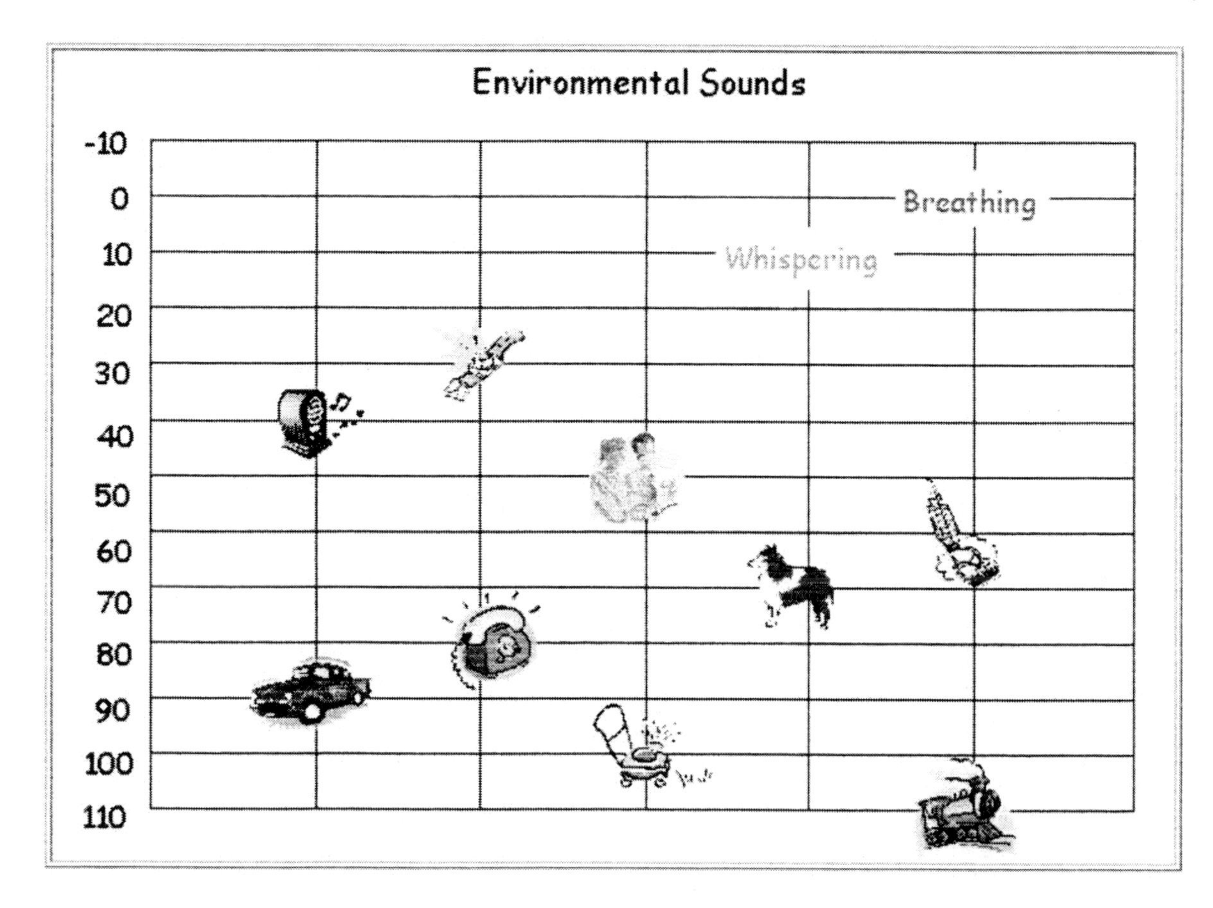

Some of the speech sounds are softer than others such as: "th" and "s". A mild hearing loss means these softer sounds can no longer be heard. A person will hear only parts of words. As the hearing loss increases so does the amount of information lost. A moderate to severe hearing loss will make most speech sounds unintelligible. A person with a profound hearing loss hears no speech sounds.

4

COCHLEAR IMPLANTS

WHAT IS A COCHLEAR IMPLANT?

A cochlear implant is a small, complex electronic device that can help to provide a sense of sound to a person who is profoundly deaf or severely hard of hearing. The implant is surgically placed under the skin behind the ear. An implant has four basic parts:

Cochlear implant.

- A *microphone,* which picks up sound from the environment;
- A *speech processor,* which selects and arranges sounds picked up by the microphone;
- A *transmitter* and *receiver/stimulator,* which receive signals from the speech processor and convert them into electric impulses;
- And *electrodes,* which collect the impulses from the stimulator and send them to the brain.

An implant does not restore or create normal hearing. Instead, under the appropriate conditions, it can give a deaf person a useful auditory understanding of the environment and help him or her to understand speech.

HOW DOES A COCHLEAR IMPLANT WORK?

A cochlear implant is very different from a hearing aid. Hearing aids amplify sound. Cochlear implants compensate for damaged or non-working parts of the inner ear. When hearing is functioning normally, complicated parts of the inner ear convert sound waves in the air into electrical impulses. These impulses are then sent to the brain, where a hearing person recognizes them as sound. A cochlear implant works in a similar manner. It electronically finds useful sounds and then sends them to the brain. Hearing through an implant may sound different from normal hearing, but it allows many people to communicate fully with oral communication in person and over the phone.

WHO GETS COCHLEAR IMPLANTS?

Different types of deaf and severely hard of hearing people choose cochlear implants. Both children and adults can be candidates for implants. According to the Food and Drug Administration 2002 data, approximately 59,000 people worldwide have received implants. In the United States, about 13,000 adults have cochlear implants and nearly 10,000 children have received them.

Adults who have lost all or most of their hearing later in life can often benefit from cochlear implants. These older candidates can often associate the sounds made through an implant with sounds they remember. This may help them to understand speech without visual cues or systems such as lipreading or sign language.

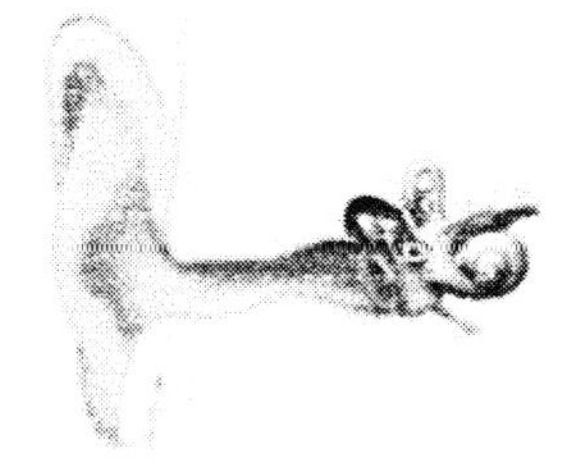

Normal ear anatomy.

Young children can also be candidates for implants. Cochlear implants, coupled with intensive post-implantation therapy, can help young children to acquire speech, language, developmental, and social skills. The best age for implantation is still being debated, but most children who receive implants are between 2 and 6 years old. Earlier implantation seems to perform better.

HOW DOES SOMEONE RECEIVE A COCHLEAR IMPLANT?

A cochlear implant is a surgical procedure. The decision to receive an implant should involve discussions with many medical specialists and an experienced surgeon. The process is expensive. Some may choose not to have a cochlear implant for a variety of personal reasons. Also, though surgical implantation is almost always safe, complications are a risk factor, just as with any kind of surgery. An additional consideration is learning to interpret the sounds created by an implant. This process takes time and practice. Speech-language pathologists and audiologists are the professionals frequently involved in this learning process. Not everyone performs at the same level with a cochlear implant. Prior to implantation, all of these factors need to be discussed.

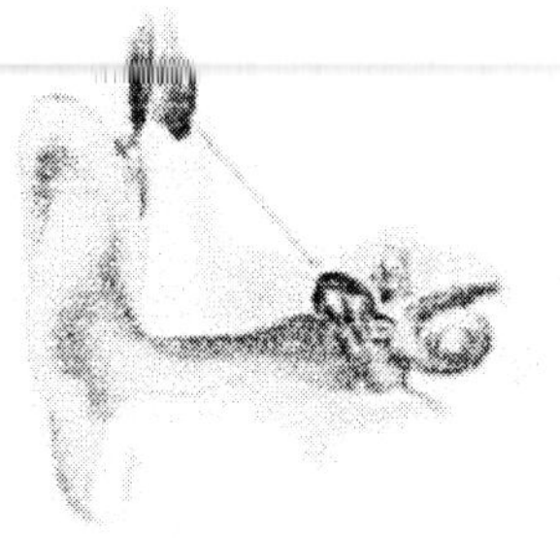

Ear with cochlear implant.

WHAT DOES THE FUTURE HOLD FOR COCHLEAR IMPLANTS?

The technology behind cochlear implants is changing rapidly. With advancements in technology and continued follow-up research with people who have already received implants, researchers are evaluating new opportunities and additional possible candidates for cochlear implants.

Related Topics

- What Are the Communication Considerations for Parents of Deaf and Hard-of-Hearing Children?
- More About Cochlear Implants . . .
- Risk of Bacterial Meningitis in Children with Cochlear Implants
- Cochlear Implant in Adults and Children, Consensus Statement
- VideoCast—Cochlear Implants: Past, Present, and Future
- Why NIDCD Does Research: Helping People with Hearing Loss (video)

UNDERSTANDING HEARING LOSS

5

THE GLASS WALL

Lou Aymard, Ph.D.

Have you ever stood behind a glass partition and watched your friends talk to each other? They gesticulate wildly. Their mouths move rapidly in animated conversation. You know the language they are using, but you are clueless about the content of the discourse. That kind of communication chasm is a common experience for deaf persons. In *Reflections on the Language and Culture of Deaf Americans,* Aymard and Winstanley (1992), describe the effect of a hearing-loss in the following way:

> Deafness has been likened to a glass wall that separates people. It is an invisible condition which has a significant impact upon human interaction. If we are denied the experience of expressing ourselves and understanding others, we become isolated cells in the society in which we live. Deafness affects more that a person's ability to hear, it influences human communication in a profound way. (p. 1)

One of life's ironies is that only seconds and a life-altering event separate you from being deaf. Jean, an attractive, competent, surgical nurse was driving to work. She entered a busy intersection near her home. The light was green. Moments later her life, as she knew it, profoundly changed. Jean sustained bilateral basal skull fractures that destroyed the functioning of both acoustic nerves and caused damage to the inner ear mechanism. Reflect upon her poignant description of the realization that she had become deaf (Mulrooney, 1972).

> The day faded into evening. My sister was back with a resident physician I knew. I was fighting nausea, exhaustion and pain. I wanted to sleep but there was something to ask. "Tom?" I said. He smiled and shook his head yes. He was talking to me, but I didn't know what he was saying. I said it very calmly, "I can't hear you." And then I realized that I was deaf. That realization was the beginning of a long journey through the paths leading to a new identity as a deafened individual. It involved learning and relearning, unbelievable isolation, barely controlled rage, the depths of depression, personal devaluation, acute sustained anxiety, frustration of the most basic human needs, and continual feelings of conflict in interpersonal relations. (p. 2)

In the latter portion of the passage, Jean aptly identifies the handicap of deafness with the words "conflict in interpersonal relations." The disability of deafness is not the inability to hear. Deafness impacts upon the most fundamental interpersonal endeavor. It impedes reciprocal human communication.

Approximately 16 million Americans have some hearing loss. This disability affects all age groups from the newborn infant to the elderly. Of these 16 million hearing-impaired persons, approximately 2 million are considered profoundly deaf. Profound deafness is a hearing loss so severe that an individual is unable to understand speech or the sounds commonly encountered daily in the environment.

The Baltimore-Washington metropolitan area is home to the second-largest population of deaf persons in the United States. If you have not encountered a deaf individual in your travels around the area, it is likely that you will. The majority of deaf high school seniors attend Gallaudet University in Washington, D.C. The classrooms at the university are designed to accommodate the visual presentation of course content and lectures are given in American Sign language. Some deaf students attend the College. Without a sign language interpreter, the deaf student does not have equal access to lectures, videotapes, films or classroom discussions in your course.

Education and accurate information can shatter the barriers of prejudice that separate people. "The Glass Wall" will be shattered only when we dispel the myths that freely circulate about Deaf Americans and their native language, the American Sign Language. Consider the following:

Myth: All deaf people read lips well and communicating with them will be easy.

Fact: English is a homophonous language. Different English words or phrases look identical when formed on the lips. For example, "bacon and eggs" and "pancakes" are almost impossible to distinguish when lip-reading. Some other factors that influence lip-reading are the ambient lighting in the room, the rapidity of speech, and facial hair. Deaf persons who have had extensive training in speech-recognition assert that only 30 percent of interpersonal dialogue is intelligible from lip-reading.

Myth: Deaf people are not sensitive to noise.

Fact: The degree, frequency and onset of a hearing loss are all critical factors in determining an individual's ability sensitivity to acoustical events. Physiological psychology studies the processing of neurosensory inputs. Neuropsychological research reveals that some types of hearing loss actually accentuate sensitivity to noise. Loud sounds become garbled and uncomfortable. Persons with residual hearing, who use hearing aids, often find loud sounds are greatly magnified by their aids and very unpleasant.

Myth: American Sign Language (ASL) is a crude gestural system and not really a language.

Fact: A considerable body of linguistic research (Lucas, 1990; Klima & Bellugi, 1979; Schlesinger & Namir, 1978) has been devoted to studying the structure of American Sign Language. ASL is an artful, manual language that molds space into meaning. It has a lexicon, grammar and syntax as do all human languages.

Myth: All deaf people use hearing aids.

Fact: Some deaf people benefit considerably from hearing aids. Other deaf individuals consider them intrusive, annoying and choose not to use them.

Myth: All deaf people are mute.

Fact: Deafness usually has little or no effect on the vocal system. Thus very few deaf people are truly mute. Some deaf persons, who have been trained in the oral method (with total emphasis on speech and lip-reading), may speak very clearly and distinctly. Congenitally deaf individuals may have been raised in a deaf family where the emphasis is exclusively on manual communication.

Myth: Fingerspelling is sign language. Sign language is fingerspelling.

Fact: Dactylology or fingerspelling is of uncertain but ancient origin. In the seventh century, the Venerable Bede wrote the essay *De Loquela per Gestum Digitorum* in which he documented three different forms of dactylology in existence at that time (Best, 1943). The American Manual Alphabet is made with 26 distinct handshapes. It is used by deaf persons to fingerspell proper nouns, acronyms and some technical terms. Deaf people don't fingerspell whole phrases and sentences. They use American Sign Language for that purpose.

Myth: All hearing losses are the same.

Fact: Understanding the various types of hearing loss and their impact upon reciprocal human communication takes time and training. The word "deafness" is glibly used to describe a wide range of hearing impairments that have very different effects on a person's ability to process sound and understand speech.

Myth: American Sign Language is ungrammatical.

Fact: Transliterations are literal translations from one language to another. They often result in ungrammatical and syntactically odd sentences. Suppose you ask your students "have any of you been to the Big Apple?" The deaf student in your class raises his hand. She signs excitedly to the sign interpreter. You are curious about what has been "said" and so you patiently wait for the English translation. The interpreter responds with the English *translation* "some time ago I visited New York." You go on to ask the student more questions or to comment further. If the interpreter *transliterated* the ASL (i.e., word for sign), imagine your surprise when you heard him say "ago, ago, touch finish me New York City." American Sign Language is no more ungrammatical than is a literal translation of a French passage, poor English.

Myth: Deaf people are less intelligent than hearing people. People with impaired hearing are "deaf and dumb."

Fact: It is astounding that thirty years ago, some curricula in school for deaf children were based on that premise. Psychological research that definitively disproved that assertion was published in several books, the most notable ones by Hans Furth (1966, 1973).

Myth: American Sign Language is iconic. All signs look exactly like the objects they represent.

Fact: Some signs do resemble the objects they represent. However, linguistic research conducted by Hoemann (1975) demonstrated that "only a small percentage of the signs in the American Sign Language lexicon have transparent meanings for persons who have had no prior experience with the language, 10 to 15 percent based on a conservative estimate and 20 to 30 percent based on a liberal estimate" (p. 161).

Celebrate the cultural diversity of your fellow Deaf Americans. Take a small, but significant step towards doing your part in shattering "The Glass Wall." In pursuit of that lofty goal, consider one of the following projects. Who knows, you may have F-U-N in the process.

1. Study the language and culture of Deaf Americans. Enroll in a sign language classes offered at your local college, church or civic group.
2. Visit Gallaudet University in Washington, D.C. Many deaf persons consider it the Deaf Cultural Mecca of the United States.

3. Purchase an American Sign Language dictionary (Costello, 1994) or a set of sign language flash cards (Hoemann, 1988). Study a few signs each day and decide for yourself if sign language is iconic.
4. Logon to the Internet and explore websites that are devoted to Deaf Culture or American Sign Language.
5. Go to a deaf theatrical performance at Gallaudet University or view a videotape from the National Association for the Deaf (NAD) about deaf culture and sign language.
6. Join the odyssey of a deaf actor. Read Bernard Bragg's autobiography, *Lessons in Laughter.*
7. Learn to use a Telecommunications Device for the Deaf (TDD).
8. Read the book *Deaf Like Me* (Spradley & Spradley, 1978). You will empathize with a hearing father's grief as he shares the experiences of discovering his daughter was born deaf. Be prepared to cry.
9. Don't miss the PBS program "For a Deaf Son." It should be available at a local library or at a video rental store.

Finally, if you have a deaf neighbor, client, or co-worker, make time in your busy schedule to visit with them. Invite them to share with you the cultural and life experiences that make them unique.

6

CONFRONTING DEAFNESS IN AN UNSTILLED WORLD

Harold Orlans

"Man was born free, and he is everywhere in chains." With this call in *The Social Contract,* Rousseau may be said to have launched the Romantic, not to mention the French, Revolution. To Rousseau, society was the enemy: convention, ostentation, the clever chatter in the salons was false; society constrained the freedom of the individual to live and speak honestly and virtuously, just as chains then constrained the residents of mental institutions. The theme of society and the individual dominates the experience of deafened adults; but to most, society is paradise lost, the false friend who betrays and ejects them from their accustomed place. As their sense of exclusion grows, they may come to feel, like Rousseau, that society is indeed the enemy and that peace can be found only in solitude.

The adjustment of adults to progressive hearing loss can be viewed as a conflict between their drive for continued sociability and their need for the relief that solitude offers from the tensions and blows that sociability now brings. I shall review some of the common feelings about and adjustments to hearing losses of varied severity and age of onset reported by some 1,500 members of *Self Help for Hard of Hearing People* (SHHH), the large American voluntary organization of hearing-impaired persons. Their accounts were obtained by a four-page questionnaire inserted in the January-February 1984 issue of *Shhh,* the bimonthly magazine distributed to all SHHH members. I will try, in part, to summarize these comments and, in part, to depict and interpret the emotional and social dynamics of increasing deafness in formerly hearing persons, as reflected in this material. All unidentified quotations in this article are drawn from these questionnaires, and each in a series of quoted passages represents a different individual.

Most quotations come from responses to five open-ended questions: "How has your hearing loss affected your personal life (e.g., family, social life, leisure activities)? How has your hearing loss affected your working life? Who and what has best helped you adjust to your hearing loss (e.g., spouse, friend, hearing aid)? What could be done to help you now? We welcome any other comments you wish to make about your hearing loss and any suggestions you have for SHHH activities or articles." Only one page was allotted to replies, but many members attached additional pages of comment; some even enclosed a copy of their audiogram.

The questionnaire was prepared jointly with Kathryn P. Meadow-Orlans, Research Scientist at Gallaudet University, in cooperation with SHHH President Rocky Stone and Vice President Patricia

Clickener. Michael Karchmer, Susan King, and other staff of the Gallaudet Research Institute undertook the computer programming and statistical analyses; the project was authorized by Raymond Trybus, Dean of the Institute, and financed by Gallaudet.

Questionnaires were received from 1,670 persons, 28 percent of the 6,000 SHHH members. Seventy respondents (audiologists, teachers, counselors, and other professionals working with hearing-impaired persons or family members of a hearing-impaired person) had normal hearing. The number and quality of responses to specific questions varied: 1,518 persons replied to the question about the effects of hearing loss on their personal life, 1,415 to the question about its effects on their work, and 1,069 offered suggestions for SHHH activities. The average age of respondents was sixty-two; 30 percent were seventy or older and only 11 percent, under forty; 62 percent (and 70 percent of those under sixty) were women. In this preponderately elderly, female population, only 22 percent were employed full-time and another 9 percent, part-time; 48 percent were retired; 18 percent classified themselves as housewives and 5 percent, as unemployed.

Most respondents had a major hearing loss. The difficulty of assessing the severity of loss by a series of graduated questions (the Gallaudet Hearing Scale) was evident; nonetheless, as estimated by this method, which a good many respondents criticized, 53 percent had a loss of 56 decibels or more and another 34 percent, of 41–55 decibels, in their better ear. Nineteen percent said that they had lost some or all of their hearing by the age of nine or earlier; and from 11–14 percent, during each succeeding decade (their teens, their twenties, and so on, up to and including their sixties).

These SHHH members are heavy users of hearing aids: 89 percent owned one or, more often, two, and most wore one or both "all the time." The remaining 11 percent included some with a small loss and some who refused to wear an aid, but most were evidently too deaf to benefit from one and some could not endure the excruciating noise.

From all the evidence provided, Kathryn Meadow-Orlans and I attempted to assess the adjustment—the degree of personal acceptance and contentment or bitterness, anger, and dissatisfaction—of each respondent. Of the 1,388 persons we ventured to classify, we judged the adjustment of 33 percent to be "poor," 31 percent as "good," and 36 percent as intermediate or average. On a five-point scale, we classified the adjustment of 7 percent as "very poor"; 26 percent, "poor"; 36 percent, "average"; 23 percent, "good"; and 8 percent, "very good." The proportion classified as "poor" was higher among women, those with a severe loss, and those who were divorced or separated as compared with those who were either living with their spouse or widowed. Relatively fewer of the oldest respondents (those over seventy) were classified as poorly adjusted: old age brought a greater degree of either peace or weariness and a disinclination or inability to protest.

UNDETECTED LOSS

Hearing loss is not only invisible, a fact often lamented as adding the burden of disclosure to that of the condition. It may go undetected by those with the loss. Adults who suffer a sudden loss are, at least, inescapably aware of that traumatic event. If awareness is the first step in the long process of adjustment, that step is thrust upon them. It would follow, as some argue, that their adjustment is earlier or, at any rate, quicker than it is for the person with a gradual loss. Both the theoretical point and the empirical facts are debatable. One can also argue that a great deal of adjustment proceeds unconsciously and that the perfect marriage between consciousness and reality exists only in the minds of some intellectuals.

Certainly, some hearing loss can go undetected at all ages: in infants and children, because they have never experienced any other kind of hearing, and in adults, because their loss is so slight it can be misinterpreted. After all, to miss a word, especially in a noisy place, is entirely normal. Who can hear anything in a disco? Many people with a "good" ear live so completely in the hearing world that they are seldom considered, and do not consider themselves, "impaired."

> If hearing impairment is the most prevalent disease [one respondent writes], I wonder why I meet so few who have it. I go to a spa, to classes, to clubs. Occasionally someone says he or she is hard of hearing, but there is either no hearing aid or a dainty behind-the-ear model and you don't even have to raise your voice. Where are all those people, in hiding?

The answer is that most have a loss that is functionally insignificant. If the line between an insignificant and a significant loss is drawn between "having difficulty only with faint speech" and "frequent difficulty with normal speech" (which the National Center for Health Statistics places between the 40 and 41 decibel levels), in 1981 roughly 3.1 million or 1.5 percent of the United States population had such "frequent difficulty," while over 11 million or 5 percent had a lesser loss in one or both ears. Thus, the population with some hearing loss fades into the hearing population much as the population with some loss of hair fades into the population with a full head of hair.

That is both the opportunity and the aggravation of adults who, as puzzling episodes, miscues, and misadventures mount, finally realize that something may be wrong with their hearing. "I couldn't figure out how the other kids heard what they did," a twenty-two-year-old girl, who evidently had some hearing loss since infancy, writes: "after high-school graduation, it 'clicked' in my mind." Similarly, a girl of twenty, also with an early loss, for many years "didn't realize how much I was missing." How can you know everything that you do not hear?

PASSING AND BLUFFING

A loss not noticed by the person who has it can also be overlooked by friends and family, who may attribute the nonresponsiveness they observe to personality, not physiology. "During school years, before I *knew,* I had a hearing loss, my friends always complained that I was stuck up and thought I was better than anyone. They said I never answered them when they spoke to me!"

Passing, or being taken, for someone with normal hearing but not normal conduct—"unfriendly, uncooperative, stupid, no personality"—is common. Indeed, it is unavoidable in casual encounters in public places, crowds, and social gatherings; for, whether a hearing aid is worn or not, few people are as alert to the presence of hearing loss as the person who has it; and the opportunity to disclose it may not arise. Thus, be it vigilant or, as the years go by, dulled and weary, the deafened person's passage through the hearing world, oblivious to much that transpires, is characteristically guarded and uncertain, hoping to avoid but necessarily encountering pitfalls, surprises, misunderstanding, error, frustrations, irritation, embarrassment, pain, puzzlement, and a simple lack of comprehension. Surprise, irritation, and puzzlement can be experienced both by the person who hears and the one who does not.

A condition that is not anticipated, that can go undetected, and, if detected, cannot be quickly, precisely, and fully known, invites further disguise:

> Have become an excellent bluffer.

> I used every cover-up known! The only ones who suspected were my children.

> I'm apt to laugh in response to [the movie] audience rather than what I've heard and comprehended.
>
> I am one of the greatest hypocrites in pretending that I can hear or understand.
>
> In most social situations I resided in my glass coffin, putting up an appearance.... I appeared pretty, neat, and smiling.
>
> I wear two "faces"—one usually has a smile and has been described as vibrant—the other is bewildered.
>
> Grin and act pleasant.
>
> Smile a lot! Look pleasant!

The anthropologist Ruth Benedict, author of *Patterns of Culture,* often wore that smile, as if to ward off or soften the annoyance that might arise from her failure to reply to what she did not hear.

The difficulties and perplexities of not understanding what one is assumed to hear, may, it is said, be relieved by a public declaration of hearing loss. That is one function of the visible hearing aid, of signing, of the pin or other symbol which is often suggested and sometimes worn, and of the individual signs and notices that deaf or deafened persons sometimes use: one woman wears a "Deaf and Bright" button; another, a pin, "I READ LIPS."

A public declaration can relieve only the misconception that one hears well; it does not explain how a conversation should proceed thereafter and exactly what will and will not be grasped. To determine that requires familiarity, frankness, and close and patient attention. The normal pace of conversation must be slowed, which does not happen in a crowd; and if it does, in a smaller group or party, the deafened person can become the center of unwanted attention.

> I . . . often resisted even to attempt conversation because of the awful result when I lost the topic, and said something irrelevant because I misunderstood. When, worse yet, the group realized I wasn't hearing and several people at once attempted to tell me what was said, resulting in a loud jumble, and me still not understanding. At this point I would "freeze," pretend [to understand], and retreat as unobtrusively as possible, figuratively licking my wounds.

NOISY GROUPS

To deafened adults, noisy places—gatherings, parties, dances, playgrounds, stores, restaurants and bars, any busy unshielded place with a hubbub of voices, traffic, machines, or music—are a hostile setting for conversation. The quieter the place, the fewer the voices, the closer and clearer the speaker, the easier is it to converse by lipreading, partial hearing, and careful speech. The hearing aid, which magnifies background noise and nearby speech alike, can be a mixed blessing when ears register only distorted sound, recruitment (the intense magnification of sound) renders loud noise unendurable, and tinnitus (a noise in the ears) adds its distressing accompaniment. Thus, the adult with a growing hearing loss tends increasingly to forsake group socializing and to see only a few people or one person at a time in a quiet location.

This tendency may be altered or delayed with a moderate loss well corrected by a hearing aid, good lipreading ability, a strong, confident personality adept at handling people, or simply persistence, a determination to continue social activity despite inescapable blunders and blows. The comments of three respondents, all relatively young women in their twenties to forties, illustrate this attitude:

I have two choices . . . to continue going out and do normal things and to try extra hard to get along . . . or . . . to stay away from people. To me there is only one choice.

My hearing aids help some, but mostly [it takes] sheer determination to not hide. Constantly reminding myself that I'm a person too and I have the right to work and enjoy life the same as anyone else. I try not to moan about my hearing loss or feel defeated. If someone isn't speaking loud enough, I say "Please speak up—I'm hearing impaired!" No apologies from me! . . . I am not going to withdraw from life because of feelings of embarrassment.

STRAINING TO SOCIALIZE

Socializing imposes a physical and emotional strain. The concentration required to diagnose the meaning of distorted, half-heard speech, other sounds, lip movements, and facial expressions is tiring; requests to repeat or to face the listener can be made just so often and shy people may not make them at all; attempts to position oneself closer to speakers and to look at their lips may make them uncomfortable and disturb the conversation.

I believe I am a source of annoyance to people who must repeat what they have said.

I am very intelligent and articulate but feel dumb when I ask to repeat and even then I don't understand what is said so I just let it pass.

If you ask people to speak up repeatedly and they don't, then you try and move your ear closer to their mouth; they draw away, as if you have a contagious disease, or else they are stymied by my staring at their lips.

Inappropriate remarks, talking too much or too little, too loudly or softly, a hearing aid that whistles or crackles or is often adjusted can upset the flow of conversation and reduce the pleasure of the occasion. When socializing is not relaxing but becomes an ordeal—"I'm terrified that someone will talk to me and terrified that no one will talk to me"—and the deafened person feels embarrassed or lost in the midst of the group, he or she may wonder if it is really worth the effort:

Seems like one can never relax when with others.

It is very stressful for me to mix with hearing people.

I have to look at people's faces and never know in what direction the next person's going to speak. I am exhausted after group meetings.

People become annoyed at having to repeat themselves, and I become embarrassed when I misunderstand what was said. . . . in such situations I often say something that had previously been stated. Many people find it amusing, and I usually laugh along with them even though I am feeling embarrassed or frustrated.

Miss "small talk" and jokes. Therefore feel left out. . . .

Discomfort, embarrassment, confusion, and loss of confidence are common. "Embarrassed times without number." "I don't always know how to handle it [misunderstanding]." "I have lost confidence and social comfort." It "has resulted in a lack of confidence, feelings of inadequacy and extreme sensitivity." "Confidence and ease have been replaced with anxiety and apprehension."

Resentment and anger can grow. "I resent very much being deaf." "I get angry over the insensitivity of people who don't understand hearing loss." "I was very anxious, frustrated, angry, embarrassed and humiliated." A married woman of fifty-five, a secretary who is apparently well adjusted, acknowledges "a great sense of anger at my situation. Actually I function very well; most people are not aware that I wear an aid. . . . But I am still angry since my loss is not my fault, and I expect consideration for this."

Feelings and concomitant behavior may swing between a determination to persevere and overcome the obstacles to social activity; anxiety or frustration, the fear or experience of failure in that effort; and withdrawal to rest and recuperate.

> I want to withdraw and have to push myself to attend social functions.
>
> Sometimes I stay at home for a while and then get up enough courage to go out and face life again and try not to let it bother me.
>
> I go between painfully shy and overcompensating aggressiveness.
>
> How [do] people weigh whether doing something is worth the energy (of trying to hear) to participate[?] . . . some people pull back too soon and maybe others frustrate themselves by doing too much.

SELECTIVE SOCIALIZING

In ventures into society, the individual becomes more selective. Smaller groups with friends who "know" are preferred to large gatherings with strangers. Visiting may be undertaken only with one's spouse or a friend, who can repeat a remark, correct a mistake, or keep one abreast of the conversation. Small parties at home, where the number of guests, seating, and lighting can be controlled, may replace attendance at large gatherings. Conversation with strangers is avoided: "I am afraid of being asked something I won't hear so I avoid eye contact and people in general whenever I can. . . . My worst times are with casual 'How are you doing?' . . . I don't relax, joke, smile, and enjoy people."

Friends who recognize the hearing problem and show patience in dealing with it are retained, while others are dropped. "I pick friends . . . I can lipread well." "I avoid people who are irritated by requests to repeat a phrase." "I catch myself avoiding . . . people with soft light voices." ". . . selected a husband because of loud voice." "Those friends who understand my problem and I enjoy a good social life. I *refuse* to let my hearing loss make me an introvert." "When choosing friends, I'm very careful. . . . My best friends understand my hearing problems. In a way, I *don't* want too many friends."

Even a small group of understanding friends can present hazards. As they turn to talk to each other, the deafened individual is left out: "In a group, the interaction they have between one another causes them to forget or choose to ignore my hearing loss." "My friends have been good to me, but at times forget my hearing problem and get me into situations . . . where I cannot function properly."

As deafness grows, socializing may be reduced to one-on-one encounters, to life within the home and family, to dependence on the spouse, or, ultimately, to utter solitude. Some may seek the company of other deafened people, which is more easily done in urban than in rural areas. Some want to learn lipreading, fingerspelling, and/or signing, partly as a means of communication and partly to meet other people with similar problems. It may be difficult to find an instructor, to get enough people together to justify a class, and also to induce a spouse or relative to learn so that there is someone with whom to practice and communicate. Also, after a lifetime spent in hearing society, most have no wish to sign. They would rather remain isolated in the society they have known than enter a new one.

PROSPECTS OF SOLITUDE

At each stage in this gradual removal from hearing society, the prospect of solitude emerges, either as a desolate state or as a condition which, if not as idyllic as Rousseau's in *Reveries of the Solitary Walker,* is at least relaxing and preferable to the constant pains of contending with people who think that you hear. Upon occasion, each feeling may prevail, as the individual struggles with himself, not knowing which course is best, perhaps not knowing the kind of person he or she has already become. As time goes by, the extrovert can become an introvert, the partygoer stays increasingly at home, and the socializer turns into a loner.

> When I had my hearing I was an outgoing person. I don't care to be with people any more.
>
> I have become more isolated, personality changes from a fun loving type to a more skeptical person, less willing to confront rejection.
>
> I avoid socializing and going out. It's too painful to sit there and be left out. . . . I'd rather stay home—alone!
>
> It's a *lonely* disease. My love of people, and being with them, diminishes daily.
>
> I tend to enjoy being with myself, because it is easier.
>
> I am least alone when I am alone. Most alone at a dinner or cocktail party.

The saddest condition portrayed in our responses is that of some very deafened elderly persons, usually but not always living alone. They desperately want some human contact but no longer know how to obtain it. Thus, a woman of seventy-three, a former public school teacher, widowed twice, now lives by herself in a city apartment. Her hearing loss began at age sixty-three; one ear is now "useless"; she wears an aid in the other but cannot make out words: "I cannot communicate with people—it takes so long—trying to comprehend, their point. . . . Learning *anything* is not easy at my age. I'm alone—no one to try to talk to, no one to say '*you are too loud!*' etc. I can't understand T.V., so I keep it on to feel that someone is with me." A man of sixty-five, recently retired from work as a draftsman, lives with a wife who is apparently considerate and understanding. His hearing loss began at twenty-eight; despite two aids, he can now barely hear loud noises: "I am very despondent and wonder if life is worth living. . . . I don't feel even a psychiatrist can help me. . . . I am ready and waiting for God to take me out of my miseries and know that when I get up to heaven I'll be able to hear." An eighty-nine-year-old woman, whose long, gradual loss started at eighteen, is now so profoundly deaf that she does not use her aid—"Too noisy. Sounds like an iron foundry." Never married, she lives alone:

My greatest need is more companionship. There is an *awfulness* about silence. If someone would just drop in once in a while—smile—say Hi! and hand me a note "I'm on my way to the store—do you need anything? Postage stamps? Could I make a phone call for you?" etc. My only female neighbor said "I could visit you oftener but I haven't time to sit down and write." Understandable, isn't it? I am days at a time without speaking a word. It is affecting my voice and I fear for my mind. I can't hear the alarm clock, telephone ring, door bell, radio, television—or the human voice. . . . HAVE SOMEONE CROSS THE THRESHOLD OF THE SHUT-IN . . . EVERY DAY.

FAMILY ACCORD AND DISCORD

As the case of the despondent husband may suggest, even a good marriage and loving family give no immunity from the pains of deafness. Deafened people can find refuge and comfort at home, where family members are sympathetic, familiar with the condition—here, at least, they do not have to announce it—and can cater to special needs. Some adults whose families have an established history of hearing loss (with either an early or late onset) seem to be among our better adjusted respondents. Living with hearing loss and expecting it themselves, members of such families may take it for granted, like poor eyesight, obesity, or other defects that "run in the family." "My hearing loss never affected my personal life because my mother taught me just what a hearing loss meant," a woman of sixty-seven, with an 80 decibel hearing level in her better ear, writes: "She was developing her hearing loss when I was born so I had no fear when I was hearing less at age twenty-five." A librarian with a moderate hearing loss, who hears fairly well with an aid, says, "five of my children have hearing loss so we all understand each other."

As other respondents attest, hearing loss in the family affords no assurance of a satisfactory adjustment. Obvious maladjustment and an inability to accept and cope with the loss can be shared by several family members and passed from parent to child. Far more information than is available would be needed to allocate responsibility for family discord. Some respondents accept primary responsibility; some blame their spouse or relatives; plainly, all parties can contribute. The same battles that are waged in public—for respect, understanding, accommodation, acceptance, and participation—can be fought at home. Familiarity can breed either sensitivity or contempt.

Respondents complain about family members' "mumbling," talking from another room or over background music, and their impatience or anger at not being understood and having to repeat what they said. Respondents acknowledge similar feelings of frustration, impatience, and anger.

My own husband talks to me from another room or with his back to me. My own mother forgets that I am deaf.

With my family it's a constant conflict between their desire to have background music and my desire to join in conversation.

I felt he [her husband] mumbled and he felt I didn't pay attention when he was talking.

After 10 years, my wife cannot make allowance for my inability to hear her from another room.

My husband gets mad because I can't hear, and I get angry because he can't remember to look at me when talking to me.

On the humorous side: My husband will sometimes *yell:* "Are you deaf?" I yell back: "YES!"

Even a spouse who is usually patient and considerate, "an in-house saint," can at times be curt and impatient. Hearing as well as deafened persons can get weary of conversation that requires close attention and careful enunciation. When family members talk to one another, deafened people can feel as left out as if they were at someone else's party. In the family as in society, good conversation with them must be one-on-one or, at least, one at a time.

> If only my family . . . would try a little harder to make me feel more comfortable—sitting one to one for instance, but they'd all rather sit around the living room and converse among themselves.
>
> My worst problem is my husband's family—they all have very tiny soft voices—a nightmare! They don't seem to speak up no matter how often I remind them, so the past year I've been practicing "not caring" what they say unless they make a point to speak clearly and directly to me—it was (is) too frustrating to rush from one side of the room to the other trying to catch every word!
>
> My family and long time friends are supportive, but it is inconvenient to include me in most communication. My pad and pencil slow them down.
>
> My large family has a reunion at Thanksgiving. I feel like an outcast. They try so hard to include me but the quick repartee is impossible.

Reflective respondents recognize that adjustment in the family is an intricate, interactive process requiring accommodations on both sides of the sound barrier. "There has been more adjustment needed for my family than me," observes a man who hears well with an aid. "They are the ones who must speak up to be heard." One woman complains that "My family always wanted me to wear my hearing aid for THEIR convenience" and another that "My parents treated me normal. I think *too* normal." It is evident that excessive sensitivity and moodiness—defining expected conduct too strictly and changing that definition too often—can be obstacles to successful adjustment in the family.

WHAT HELP DO DEAFENED ADULTS WANT?

Responses to the question, "What could be done to help you now?" evoked comments such as "new ears," "a medical cure," "give me my hearing back," "Miracle!" "some miracle to stop the progression of loss!" "Outlaw mustaches and dark or mirror sunglasses and send hard to lip-read people to Beirut!" "Nothing," "I don't really know," "a long walk on a short pier."

In a more serious vein, respondents hope for research, medical treatment, or surgery to prevent hearing loss, restore their hearing, or at least arrest further loss; and for effective relief from tinnitus. Some have had repeated operations and a few, cochlear implants; some have doctored themselves with medications, including niacin and zinc, vitamins, special diets, and dubious regimes to promote fitness, increase the flow of blood, and "clear the ears." The hearing aid receives much comment. It is "my lifesaver," "my dearest possession," "my crutch," "my friend and my enemy." "I sometimes fantasize about smashing them on the ground to relieve the frustrations they cause." The frustrations include amplified noise, distorted and "artificial" sound, feedback, the expense of purchase and maintenance, short-lived batteries, unreliable operation, and slow and unreliable repair service. Respondents would like cheaper, better, and directional aids that clarify speech, amplify only selective frequencies, and screen out background noise, loud sounds, and such noises as rustling clothing and paper; some want waterproof aids that can be worn while swimming. The volume control should work more simply, quickly, and inconspicuously. Ear molds should fit comfortably and not cause pain or tenderness, rashes, swelling, seepage, or perspiration.

Reimbursement for hearing aids under medicare and medical insurance, and the subsidization of—at least the removal of taxes on—aids, amplified telephones, and other assistive devices would help many deafened persons, especially those who are unemployed, retired, have high medical expenses, and live only on social security benefits. The better regulation of hearing-aid dealers and of audiologists who dispense only one manufacturer's products is also requested.

Most respondents use telephones with a loud ring and volume control, but some cannot obtain them or object to the added charges. The court-ordered breakup of the American Telephone and Telegraph Company has led to a proliferation of instruments, some of poor quality and not compatible with a hearing aid. Many respondents are poorly informed about such devices as the telephone switch on a hearing aid or the use of a tape recorder to play back messages or have them transcribed.

The provision and clear signposting of more amplified phones in offices, public facilities, and motel rooms is often requested. Those who cannot use a phone ask for message services or teletypewriters, especially at hospitals and police and fire stations. The increasing use of word processors and home computers that can be linked to telephone lines may soon provide broader communication, to those who can afford it, than that available with teletypewriters.

Respondents want more audio loops and infrared sound systems installed in theaters, churches, and meeting halls; visual signals and notices to augment loudspeaker announcements in airports, planes, buses, schools, and so on; more and better captioned films and television programs (and superscripts in theaters, such as those at Sydney opera house performances). The video cassette recorder offers a new way to view captioned films and educational programs.

Many hope for the elimination of noise and blaring commercials on television and the omnipresent background "music" in films, elevators, telephones, and restaurants; plainly, under a dictatorship of the deaf, juke boxes and Muzak would be extirpated. A suggestion many hearing people would welcome is the establishment of quiet sections, comparable to "no smoking" areas, in restaurants, bars, and other public places.

Half of our respondents had some assistive device besides an aid and amplified telephone: the most common were captioned television, a teletypewriter, a signal light on the doorbell or alarm clock, a vibrator alarm, and television or radio earphones. Few had an audio loop or broadcasting system. Many knew little about these and other devices, but would like to learn and to try them out. Even some severely deafened faculty at Gallaudet University, with its many special provisions for assisting the communication of deafened persons, have been surprised at how much better they can hear with a loudspeaker and loop. A service displaying a range of hearing aids, telephones, and other instruments; providing information about their quality, cost, benefits, and limitations; enabling the equipment to be examined and tried out; and helping to install and maintain it would be of significant help to deafened persons.

Stricter enforcement of laws barring employment discrimination against handicapped persons is mentioned by relatively few respondents (only a minority were working); evidently still fewer consider it likely or practicable. Although many jobs can be reorganized so that a deafened person can perform them well without having to use the telephone or talk with clients, respondents evidently feel that, because the cooperation of their employer and workmates is required, this is best done voluntarily.

Requests are made for help in finding: good, secure jobs; good audiologists, surgeons, and hearing aid dealers; instruction in lip reading, signing, and cued speech; penpals; "singles" services to locate friends and companions of the opposite sex; and tour groups and clubs for hearing-impaired persons.

Discovering SHHH and reading its bimonthly magazine have given many people comfort and help, a sense of dignity, and a feeling that they are, at last, understood and not alone. Often the magazine is also read by family members and friends, and the information in an article (for example, on how to talk to a deafened person) may be photocopied and distributed to others. Our questionnaires abound in comments such as "I can not state often enough the help your organization has been to me in adjusting to my handicap." "The SHHH organization and journals have given me much joy and encouragement, as well as information." "SHHH is a real inspiration and help." "Just knowing there are so many other people going through what I am gives me the courage to carry on with hope." Members also benefit from joining local SHHH chapters and meeting others with similar hearing problems.

Their comments also indicate that it is difficult for a single organization of volunteers, with low dues and very modest resources, to serve the needs of all hearing-impaired persons, whose conditions, circumstances, age, education, income, and interests differ so greatly. Young persons want to meet other young people; some members are, and others are not, sophisticated about technical and policy issues; some are affluent and others, poor; some do, and others do not, hear fairly well with an audio loop. A few sign but most do not and, in some chapters, conflict has developed between the two groups. Sadly, some persons go to a SHHH meeting and come away having heard, lip-read, and understood very little.

EDUCATING THE PUBLIC

Everyone, it seems, wants to inform and educate the public, their family, their friends. They want them to know how to talk to them; to understand that a hearing aid does not enable the wearer to hear normally; to realize that they are not stupid, that only their hearing, not intelligence, is impaired and that otherwise they are ordinary, normal people who, with patience, consideration, and some practical help, can function well at work and at home. Even doctors, audiologists, psychologists, the staff of retirement and nursing homes, and teachers of the deaf, some respondents say, have much to learn about dealing with hearing-impaired persons.

> Everyone talks too fast. Tell the whole world to talk slower and more distinct.
>
> Public servants, clerks, waitresses, etc., think that just because you have a hearing aid you can hear.
>
> Educate all of the people with whom I have contact—family, friends, other social groups—about the aspects of deafness that I call psychological, physiological. Most audiologists, and all doctors, that I have had need this education.

It would be splendid if everyone could be thus educated, but most unlikely. The hectic pace, the appalling noise and clatter of urban life will not stop and few people will change their normal style of conversation because three in two hundred have "frequent difficulty" hearing and one in a thousand may say so. The public will not and cannot learn everything that every sect and party, every organization and interest group, would like them to, anymore than they can buy everything that advertisers would like them to.

HELP AND SELF-HELP

Abstract knowledge is not enough for incorporating hearing-impaired persons—or those who want to be incorporated—into hearing society. Social scientists tend to make too much of abstract knowledge, the "laws" and generalizations they formulate. Personal experience, rapport, perceptiveness, patience, and sympathy are vital. Can we teach a busy, selfish, insensitive person—hearing well or poorly—to be patient, sympathetic, and sensitive? One woman writes, "My husband will never understand my loss," and another, "My husband is unbelievably understanding—he doesn't even notice when he has to repeat something three times!" Can we teach understanding and affection?

To the question, "Who and what has helped you to adjust to your hearing loss?" too many people reply, "I don't think we ever really adjust," "I shall *never* completely adjust," "I am still . . . trying to adjust." A twenty-two-year-old woman says, "God, mostly. I never have to ask Him to speak up."

In recounting the responses of SHHH members to their hearing loss, I do not mean to suggest that all deafened persons follow the same path from sociability to an unhappy or contented solitude. Certainly, many do; some—either with a mild, well-corrected loss or with a severe loss and remarkable lipreading ability and character—remain socially active; and some oscillate between the poles of sociability and solitude. One-to-one conversation is the fulcrum on which the deafened adult's adjustment hinges and a spouse or relative often serves as the indispensable partner in that adjustment.

If the spouse's commitment can be critical to a successful adjustment, so is the deafened person's resolve. "Who . . . has helped you to adjust?" A common reply is "*me!*" "myself," "my willpower," "The Lord and myself," "what there has been has been by myself" "I feel that I myself have been the best help, because no one could do that for me." Nothing can be added to that simple truth.

7

SPECIAL GUEST SPEAKER I. KING JORDAN

I. King Jordan

Jerry Barnhart: I have the honor to introduce our guest speaker. The interesting thing about this is that though he and I have never met, we have some ties. In the spring of 1988 I was a doctoral student at Gallaudet University, the year of the president protest, and had the opportunity to see this man rise from relative obscurity to lead deaf people into world prominence. At that time, I was there among several thousand other deaf people marching to the steps of the Capitol to support him. I even took part in a sit-in in the early stages of that protest at the front gates of Gallaudet, which effectively closed down the university. We watched as the police came with paddy wagons to haul us off to jail. For some reason at the last minute, they backed off and let us be. I don't know if this man had anything to do with that, but I want to thank him if he did, as it meant I did not spend the night in jail.

There is one other connection I have with this man that I feel is even more important, and that is that we both became deaf later in life. At the time I came to Gallaudet University I was just starting to emerge from the long and emotional process of becoming deaf myself. And during my time at Gallaudet, this man showed me that there is, indeed, life after deafness. He demonstrated that deaf people can rise above their disability and go on to bigger and better things. In fact, he was able to go on to bigger and better things not in spite of his deafness, but because of his deafness. And I have a feeling that if you were to ask him if he would trade his life after deafness to become hearing once more he would say: "No thanks." Please welcome Dr. I. King Jordan.

King Jordan: Jerry, you are lucky you weren't put in jail. But the reason that happened is that the police didn't know what to do. They are a very sophisticated unit that works with protests. And when the Gallaudet students began to protest, they arrived in large numbers. They opened their trunks, and they took out their mega phones. . . . and the rest is history.

I am late deafened. I became deaf at age 21. I am going to try to speak to those of you who are here as first timers. But before I do, a few disclaimers. I grew up hearing, but am now, and for most of my life have been, a deaf person. For you, that's not true yet.

Second, I have wonderful family support. My family has only known me as a deaf person. I met my wife after I became deaf. My children were born after I became deaf. So they didn't have to adjust to my deafness. They all know me as a deaf man. And that's very important distinction I think.

And third, and perhaps most important, is that where I live and work, my life is probably unique in the world. I'm very lucky. I go to work everyday. Everybody signs. I never have to worry about communication access. If something is not accessible for me, I can make it happen. You probably can't do that. I am standing here and preaching to you about what life is like as a deaf person, but comparatively my life is relatively easy. If I had not lost my hearing, I would never have become president of Gallaudet. I honestly think that if I made a list of good and bad things that have happened since becoming deaf, the good list would be very long, and the bad list very short.

As first timers you may want to hear about my personal adjustment to deafness. As I said, I grew up hearing, in a hearing family, in a regular school, in rural America. During that time I don't think that I ever met a deaf person. I never thought about deafness. Then all of a sudden I had a motorcycle accident, and became a deaf man. The doctors told me that my deafness was temporary. I was in the U.S. navy. It was 1965. They didn't know deafness, because in the military, there aren't any deaf people, and they encouraged me to believe that I should not be concerned about my hearing because I would soon become hearing again—which was exactly what I wanted to hear. I held onto that belief much, much too long. This is a textbook example of how not to adjust to deafness, for I stayed in denial for years and years. I thought of myself as a hearing person who couldn't hear. This is an important distinction. I'm not sure when I realized I was a deaf man. I went to a program at Walter Reed in 1953 for adjusting to deafness and I don't have one single memory, because I knew it wasn't for me. They put me there and I had to go. It was an order. It was for deaf and hard of hearing people, and I was, after all, a hearing person who could not hear. So I didn't pay any attention. I gained nothing.

In my family the goal was to go to college. I really wanted to go, so I went to Gallaudet. But I went as a hearing person who couldn't hear. I couldn't sign. I couldn't fingerspell. I can remember my first class, with a wonderful chemistry professor, who signed without talking at all and I went through that first class with no idea what to do. Gallaudet was a wonderful experience all in all, but I know if I had gone as a deaf person, I could have gained so much more.

I then went to the University of Tennessee graduate school—again as a hearing person who couldn't hear. It was hard. This was 1969 and the field of interpreting didn't exist. In 1969, family or friends or anyone who was willing to help you did interpreting. I went to class, and I asked people to take notes for me. That was my total support service.

I have heard some people talk about the faking it. We all do that—we smile and nod, when we really don't understand. I did a lot of pretending. And while I did have a great graduate experience, I know that if I had only insisted that people repeat and acknowledged to them that I was a deaf person it would have been far better.

My wife has a saying that finally got through to me. She said, when life gives you something to challenge you, deal with it. You have to. That is life. Maybe it's not what we want if we could choose, but it is the hand that we've been dealt, and we have to deal with it. One of our biggest challenges is that people who are not deaf, who don't really know deaf people are afraid of deafness. They're afraid of me as a deaf person. They're afraid of you. People really fear the unknown. So one of your goals should be to help people understand that deafness is really just a communication issue. It's an inconvenience. It's a pain in the neck for me, and it's a pain in the neck for them, but really that is all it is.

One of the worst things I've experienced is the notion that if we would just try harder, we could understand. One time I went to a black-tie event. We were seated around a round table and a 77-year-old man, a doctor, whom I had never met before, was talking to me, and I was watching my interpreter. And he kept telling me to look at him—over and over again. I said: "I can't look at you, I can't understand if I don't look at my interpreter. He said, "If you really looked at me and you tried, you could understand me." He is a physician, used to dealing with and helping people, and he believes that if I try harder I could understand? Sorry, it doesn't work that way. I can't understand, and trying harder won't help me understand. Now, maybe I should have been mad, and maybe I should have been rude, but instead I tried to explain to him. I don't know if he ever understood. And this happens a lot, and we need to educate people and help them understand that deafness is a communication problem and if we all work together we can find ways to get around it.

I can't put a date on when I became a deaf man. One day I was a hearing man who couldn't hear, and the next day I was a deaf man. I can't tell you exactly when that happened, but I am very glad that it did. Once I was able to acknowledge my deafness, life became easier.

My family and I became skilled signers only after I decided I was a deaf person. In graduate school, I didn't sign very much. I didn't have to sign since no one else could. But at some point that changed, and it was one of the best things that ever happened to me.

You are deaf, and I am deaf. If you're going to become deaf, it is a pretty good time right now for that to happen. Two reasons: attitudes, and technology.

Attitudes about deafness are really different than they used to be. I went to college in the '60s. In the 1960s, even at Gallaudet, when students left campus, we signed small. If you were standing in line at a movie, and you were signing to someone, you signed small; hoping people would not notice you. If someone looked, you stopped. We tried to hide our deafness. Now you see signing everywhere and people don't hide it anymore.

When I got my first hearing aid, the object was to try and hide it. You let your hair grow long so your ear mold could not be seen. Now people have brightly colored ear molds and hearing aids.

I remember getting on airplanes all those years ago and telling the flight attendant that I was deaf and seeing them roll their eyes, because I was one more problem to deal with. These days when I fly and I tell them of my deafness they are full of questions and eager to help in any way. They want to talk about it. I think that's a wonderful advancement.

During the rallies for a deaf president at Gallaudet, when the media first came to cover it, they weren't sure how to deal with deaf students. They would walk up to a deaf person who didn't speak, and pull out a microphone. The deaf person of course, would push it away. But within a day or two you could see the change as the media learned to walk up to them and put the microphone by the interpreter, while keeping the camera on the deaf person. And by the end of a week, they were cheering for the deaf students. Attitudes really started changing during that time.

The ADA opened up many wonderful opportunities for us. Those opportunities put deaf people on jobs with hearing people. The more hearing people are exposed to deafness, the more hearing people begin to understand that we are just people who can't hear, and their attitudes become positive. Right now attitudes about deafness are as good as they have ever been.

Technology: I am not an expert in this area, but I am a consumer. Technology has changed since I became deaf in ways that I can't even begin to explain. We had two telewriters when I first went to Gallaudet. You had a pen that was hooked up to a mechanical arm and you wrote, and then that was transmitted to the other machine which also had a mechanical arm, and copied what had been sent. We could send messages from one end of the campus to another, and that was the most wonderful thing. Wow! We thought it amazing that we could send a message to someone a mile away. This was when, if you were deaf and you wanted or needed to talk to someone, you drove. You couldn't use a telephone. There were not TTYs. You had to go to them. So things have really changed.

I sat down recently and tried to make a list of what I think are the most important advances technologically which impact directly on deaf people. I grouped them into three categories. One is communication—and telecommunication especially. One is entertainment, and one is hearing assistance.

First are TTYs. Then in the '80s, Gallaudet started to use text-based e-mail. I remember our old fax computer system. You couldn't send any graphics. Now you can. And you don't even have to be home to receive it. And now we have the instant messenger system. You can IM anyone in the world and have a conversation. You can buy a TV video camera and hook it up to your computer and you talk with sign to people anywhere in the world. There are two-way pagers, which are the deaf guy's version of a cell phone. I suspect that not far in the future we will have a hand held device which will give us text when someone talks to us which uses voice recognition software. And there is captioned television and, one of my favorites, the new caption telephone, or CapTel. For deafened people, relay works better when you can speak yourself using voice carry over, but this phone is a huge advancement and will allow us to make a phone call with no time lag such as we have now just like anyone else. It uses voice recognition software and is much faster and smoother. Soon you won't even know it's a deaf person that is making the call. There is also video interpreting, and video relay, which allows those that sign to talk on the phone.

I don't have to go only go to foreign films anymore. Now many theaters have first-run, open-captioned films. They do show them at off times. I don't understand why they do that, but you do get to see it with captions right there. Captioned plays, and captioned operas are also available. Interpreted plays are very common. We can see captioned movies at home or away on our laptops now, and pick what we want to see when we want to see it.

Last, hearing. Hearing aid advancement and cochlear implants are really changing very fast. Many people now use digital hearing aids. And people who get a digital say that it has changed their life. People who have successful implants tell me again and again how it has changed their life.

Remember I said deafness was an inconvenience? If you are hearing you go to the movies. If you are deaf, you can't unless it's captioned. If you are hearing, you open up your cell phone. If you are deaf, you have to have a special device. But even so, these days the inconvenience is so much less. Technology is changing the world for everybody, and the good news is that we have very good and effective advocacy groups who are refusing to allow the corporate world or the government to forget our need for access. That is really important, because technology changes so fast, that unless we are vigilent new devices may not be compatible with hearing aids or cochlear implants. Maybe we still don't have captioning on the Internet, but there are many groups fighting to make sure that we will.

I will close with a short suggestion. I said before that if you could choose to be deaf or hearing, you would probably say you would rather be hearing. But since you can't choose, then what you need to do is acknowledge your deafness. Do it more quickly than I did it. Don't wait years before you acknowledge that you are a deaf person. Last year I had the opportunity to speak in Rhode Island at the ALDA convention, and I am not sure why I said this, but I said that if you haven't acknowledged your deafness, then do yourself and your family a favor. Leave the meeting when it's over, go back to your room, look in the mirror, and say to yourself: "Okay, I am deaf." Watch yourself say it, and if you can, accept the fact that you are a deaf person. After that it's really easier. So my last two suggestions to you are be yourself, and value yourself. Deaf or not, continue to value yourself.

Gallaudet University President I. King Jordan grew up in Glen Riddle, Pennsylvania, a small town just outside of Philadelphia. After finishing high school, he enlisted in the Navy and served four years. Dr. Jordan was involved in an automobile accident when he was 21 years old, which resulted in a profound hearing loss.

Dr. Jordan earned a B.A. in psychology from Gallaudet University in 1970. Gallaudet, which is located in Washington, D.C. is the world's only university with programs and services designed specifically for students who are deaf and hard of hearing. In 1971 Dr. Jordan earned an M.A., and in 1973 he earned a Ph.D. in psychology, both from the University of Tennessee.

Upon earning his doctorate, Dr. Jordan became a faculty member of Gallaudet University in the Department of Psychology. In 1983 he became Chair of the Department of Psychology, and in 1986 he was named Dean of the College of Arts and Sciences. Dr. Jordan has made international contributions in education through a number of professional fellowships abroad. He served as a visiting research fellow at Donaldson's School for the Deaf in Edinburgh, Scotland, as an exchange scholar at the Jagiellonian University in Krakow, Poland, and as a visiting scholar and lecturer at schools in Paris, Toulouse, and Marseilles, France.

After an historic protest on the Gallaudet University campus in 1988 which catapulted the needs and accomplishments of deaf people into a national focus, the Gallaudet Board of Trustees appointed Dr. Jordan the eighth President of Gallaudet and the first deaf President since the institution was established in 1864.

Since then, I. King Jordan has served not only as an international spokesperson for deaf and hard of hearing people, but also as an advocate for persons with disabilities as well. Much sought after as a speaker, Dr. Jordan continues to challenge the American Public to examine their attitudes toward people with disabilities and to open their minds, hearts, and workplaces to people with disabilities.

This publication is available to the public in this on-line format. If you are interested in using any portion of this publication the reference is as follows:

Jordon, I.K. (2003). Special Guest Speaker I. King Jordan. In L. Piper & D. Watson (Eds.), *Selected proceedings of 2002 conference of the Association of Late-Deafened Adults.* [on-line] available:
http://www.alda.org/aldapubs.htm and
http://www.uark.edu/deafrtc/publications.html

8

TWO VIEWS OF DEAFNESS

Chris Wixtrom

1st View: Deafness as Pathology	**2nd View: Deafness as a Difference**
With this perspective, a person might:	With this perspective, a person might:
Define deafness as a *pathological condition* (a defect, or a handicap) which distinguishes *abnormal* deaf persons from normal hearing persons.	Define deafness as merely a *difference,* a *characteristic* which distinguishes *normal* deaf persons from normal hearing persons. Recognize that deaf people are a linguistic and cultural minority.
Deny, downplay or hide evidence of deafness.	Openly acknowledge deafness.
Seek a "cure" for deafness; focus on ameliorating the effects of the "auditory disability" or "impairment."	Emphasize the abilities of deaf persons.
Give much attention to the use of hearing aids and other devices that enhance auditory perception and/or focus on speech. Examples: Amplifiers, tactile and computer-aided speech devices, cue systems....	Give much attention to issues of communication access for deaf persons through visual devices and services. Examples: telecommunication devices, captioning devices, light signal devices, interpreters....
Place much emphasis on speech and speechreading ("oral" skills); avoid sign and other communication methods which are deemed "inferior."	Encourage the development of all communication modes, including—but not limited to—speech.
Promote the use of auditory-based communication modes; frown upon the use of modes which are primarily visual.	Strongly emphasize the use of vision as a positive, efficient alternative to the auditory channel.
Describe sign language as inferior to spoken language.	View sign language as equal to spoken language.
View spoken language as the most natural language for all persons, including the deaf.	View sign language as the most natural language for people who are born deaf.

1st View: Deafness as Pathology	2nd View: Deafness as a Difference
Make mastery of spoken language a central educational aim.	In education, focus on subject matter, rather than on a method of communication. Work to expand all communication skills.
Support socialization of deaf persons with hearing persons. Frown upon deaf/deaf interaction and deaf/deaf marriages.	Support socialization within the deaf community as well as within the larger community.
Regard "the normal hearing person" as the best role model.	Regard successful deaf adults as positive role models for deaf children.
Regard professional involvement with the deaf as "helping the deaf" to "overcome their handicap" and to "live in the hearing world."	Regard professional involvement with the deaf as "working with the deaf" to "provide access to the same rights and privileges that hearing people enjoy."
Neither accept nor support a separate "deaf culture."	Respect, value and support the language and culture of deaf people.

EARLY FOUNDATION OF SIGN LANGUAGE

9

THOMAS HOPKINS GALLAUDET: THE LEGACY BEGINS (1787–1851)

Thomas Hopkins Gallaudet, for whom Gallaudet University is named, was born in Philadelphia, Pa., in 1787. His family later settled in Hartford, Conn., the home of his maternal grandparents. A brilliant student during his early years, Gallaudet entered Yale University at age 14 and graduated first in his class three years later. He returned to Yale as a graduate student in 1808 after having served a law apprenticeship and studying independently. After earning a master of arts degree in 1810, Gallaudet worked as a traveling salesman. However, having been raised in a family deeply rooted in Protestantism, he felt called to the ministry. In 1812 he enrolled in the Andover Theological Seminary, graduating in 1814.

Gallaudet's goal, to serve as an itinerant preacher, was put aside when he met Alice Cogswell, the 9 years old deaf daughter of a neighbor, Dr. Mason Cogswell. Cogswell, a prominent Hartford Physician, was concerned about proper education for his daughter. He asked Gallaudet to travel to Europe to study methods for teaching deaf students, especially those of the Braidwood family in England. Gallaudet found the Braidwoods unwilling to share knowledge of their oral communication method. At the same time, he was not satisfied that the oral method produced desirable results. While still in Great Britain, he met the Abbe Sicard, head of the Institut Royal des Sourds-Muets in Paris, and two of its deaf faculty members, Laurent Clerc and Jean Massieu. Sicard invited Gallaudet to Paris to study the school's method of teaching deaf students using manual communication. Impressed with the manual method, Gallaudet studied teaching methodology under Sicard, learning sign language from Massieu and Clerc, who were both highly educated graduates of the school.

Having persuaded Clerc to accompany him, Gallaudet sailed for America. The two men toured New England and successfully raised private and public funds to found a school for deaf students in Hartford, which later became known as the American School for the Deaf.* Young Alice was one of the seven students in the United States.

Gallaudet served as principal of the school from 1817 to 1830. He resigned his position on April 6, 1830, to devote his time to writing children's books and to the ministry.

* The American School for the Deaf still educates deaf students today. It is first *permanent* school for the deaf children established in the United States.

10

LAURENT CLERC: "APOSTLE TO THE DEAF PEOPLE OF THE NEW WORLD"

Loida Canlas

THE EARLY YEARS

Louis Laurent Marie Clerc was born on December 26, 1785 in La Balme-les-Grottes, in southeastern France. He was born into an important family. From the 15th century, the males in the Clerc family had served the king through the office of Tubelion or Royal Commissary. At the time, his father, Joseph Francois, was the royal civil attorney, justice of the peace, and from 1780 to 1814 was mayor of their village. His mother's father was a magistrate in another town. Thus, his family knew and practiced law.

When he was about a year old, Clerc fell from his high chair into the kitchen fireplace. His right cheek was severely burned, a fever followed, and later, it was discovered that his senses of hearing and smell were damaged. It was never clear if this resulted from his accident or if he was born with those disabilities. His name-sign derives from the scar that remained—the middle and index fingers brushed downward across the right cheek near the mouth*. His parents tried many different treatments to restore his hearing, but none succeeded. For the next 11 years he stayed at home, exploring the village, helping take care of their cows, turkeys, and horses. He did not go to school and did not learn to write. Thus, as a deaf child, Clerc had no education nor a systematic mode of communication.

YOUNG LAURENT ENTERS SCHOOL

In 1797, when he was twelve years old, his uncle-godfather after whom he was named, Laurent Clerc, enrolled him in the Institut National des Jeune Sourds-Muets. This institution was the first public school for the deaf in the world. It was started by the priest Abbe De L'Epee, the "father of the deaf," as he was called. It became the model for hundreds of other schools that were to be established later. It was directed by the Abbe Roch-Ambroise Sicard.

His first teacher, who later became his mentor and lifelong friend, was Jean Massieu, 25 years old and deaf like him. At the time, Abbe Sicard was in prison, expected to be put to death for sympathizing with

---

**see* a demonstration at: *DeafWorldWeb*

the deposed King Louis XVI. Massieu led the school's deaf students, including Clerc, to petition the court for the release of Sicard. Because of this action, Sicard was released.

A LIFE-CHANGING EXPERIENCE

Clerc was excellent in his studies. However, an assistant teacher, the Abbe Margaron tried teaching him to pronounce words. Clerc's difficulties in pronouncing certain syllables so infuriated this teacher that one time, he gave Clerc a violent blow under his chin. This caused Clerc to accidentally bite his tongue so badly that he swore never again to learn to speak. Later, this experience would help to strengthen his belief that signing is the method of communication by which deaf students will learn.

He learned to draw and to compose in the printing office of the Institution. In 1805, just eight years later, he was chosen to become a "tutor on trial." The following year, he was hired as a teacher. His salary was about $200.00.

When Napoleon returned to Paris in March, 1815, Sicard decided that he should be away. He visited England and brought with him Massieu and Clerc. In London, they lectured and demonstrated their teaching methods. One of their lectures on July 10 was attended by the Yankee Congregationalist minister, Thomas Hopkins Gallaudet, from Hartford, Connecticut.

HOW GALLAUDET MET CLERC

Gallaudet was a neighbor of Mason Fitch Cogswell. Cogswell had taken interest in deaf education due to the deafness of his daughter, Alice, and the fact that there were no schools for the deaf in the United States at that time. As his neighbor and friend, Gallaudet became equally concerned for this cause. The two men gathered support from their friends, wealthy members of their community, and the city fathers. In due time, Gallaudet was sent by their supporters to travel in Europe to learn about teaching methods for the deaf.

Earlier, Cogswell had loaned a treatise to Gallaudet—the Theorie des Signes, written by Sicard. Now, in London, Gallaudet was introduced by a member of Parliament to Sicard himself. Sicard, in turn, introduced Gallaudet to Clerc. Clerc and the others invited Gallaudet to visit and attend daily classes in their Institution in Paris. He gladly accepted the invitation.

In 1816, Clerc had become Sicard's chief assistant, and he was teaching the highest class in the Institution. In addition to his classes with Sicard, Massieu, and Clerc, Gallaudet was also given private lessons by Clerc. Gallaudet was so impressed by Clerc that he invited this "master teacher" to go to America and help him establish a school for the deaf there.

After much discussion, the Abbe Sicard gave his permission for Clerc to leave. However, he convinced Clerc's mother that he "could not spare [Clerc]." Clerc's mother tried to dissuade him from leaving.

Clerc had been offered a teaching position in Russia. However, he declined due to financial problems. Now came Gallaudet's offer. He was only 28 years old. He knew that if he went, he might never be able to see his family again. He also knew that the work involved would be enormous. But he was greatly motivated by his empathy for Alice and other deaf Americans who were languageless and receiving no education. He was also adventurous and was intrigued by the prospect of living in a country that was not Catholic. In spite of his mother's objections, Clerc decided to go. However, Gallaudet had to sign a contract with Sicard, stating that Clerc was "on loan" only for three years in the States.

CLERC HEADS TO AMERICA

Clerc and Gallaudet left for America on board the ship Mary Augusta on June 18, 1816. The voyage lasted fifty-two days. Clerc used that time to teach Gallaudet "the method of the signs for abstract ideas." In return, he received tutoring in the English language from Gallaudet (Clerc already had a "considerable skill" in writing in English, as evidenced by his writing his journal entirely in English during this voyage). He also brought with him a French-English dictionary which was written by Massieu and published in 1808.

They arrived in Hartford on August 22, 1816. That same day, he met Alice Cogswell and communicated with her through sign associations. He found her to be a very intelligent girl who was hungry for knowledge but "virtually without a language." Clerc became more resolved to carry out the mission that he came to do.

Clerc, with Gallaudet as his interpreter, and sometimes accompanied by Dr. Cogswell, delivered many speeches and demonstrations of their teaching methods to get public, legislative, and financial support for their goals. From October 1816 to April 1817, they went to Boston, New York, Philadelphia, New Jersey, and other places. They informed the public, interviewed parents of deaf children, communicated with prospective students. They raised around $12,000 from the public. In a great show of support, the Connecticut General Assembly made history by voting an additional $5,000 for the school—the first appropriation ever for the education of handicapped people.

THE FIRST SCHOOL FOR THE DEAF IN AMERICA

On April 15, 1817, rented rooms made up their school which opened with seven students—Alice Cogswell being the first to enroll. It was originally called the Connecticut Asylum at Hartford for the Instruction of Deaf and Dumb Persons (now the American School for the Deaf). Gallaudet was the principal, and Clerc was the head teacher. A year later, poor and uneducated students filled the school. They ranged from 10 to 51 years of age.

In January, 1818, Clerc went to Washington, D.C. to gather support from Congress. He sat next to the Speaker of the House of Representatives, the Hon. Henry Clay. He was the first deaf person to ever address Congress. Later, at the White House, he was introduced to President Monroe by the French Ambassador, Mr. Hyde de Neuville. He was well-received and applauded for his work by the President, who had attended one of Sicard's demonstrations in London with Clerc and Massieu.

In the 1819–1820 session, with the help of Mr. Clay, the congressmen from Connecticut sponsored a bill granting the school with 23,000 acres of government land in the state of Alabama. President Monroe easily sanctioned the act. That land was sold for around $300,000. The proceeds were used to construct school buildings at the Asylum and start an endowment from which income could be drawn for the school.

On May 3, 1819, Clerc was married to Eliza Crocker Boardman, one of their earliest pupils from Whiteborough, New York. The wedding was held at the house of Eliza's uncle, Benjamin Prescott, Esq. The Rev. Mr. Butler officiated at the wedding. A year later, the first of their six children Elizabeth Victoria, was born. Clerc visited France in 1820. He went again in 1835, taking his son, Francis, with him. His last visit to his homeland was in 1846, with his son, Charles.

CLERC'S INFLUENCE

While Clerc taught students, he also trained future teachers and administrators—hearing or deaf. Many of their students went on to become productive deaf citizens and educated deaf leaders, spreading his teachings and making Clerc the greatest influence in the establishment of new deaf schools in the States at that time. His invitations were not limited to teaching. For example, he was invited to be the acting principal of the Pennsylvania Institution in Philadelphia from August 1821 to March 1822.

Clerc's students and trained teachers founded other schools around the nation or taught in them, using Clerc's teaching methods. The first school modeled after the Hartford Institution was established in New York; the second, in Philadelphia. Other schools were to follow in many states around the Union such as in Kentucky, Ohio, Indiana, Illinois, Tennessee, Virginia, and Quebec in Canada. In all, more than thirty residential schools were established all over the nation during Clerc's lifetime.

Clerc went on to complete 50 years of teaching (41 of those in the States), retiring in 1858, when he was 73 years old. Although retired, he continued his advocacy for deaf education, maintaining an active interest in the school, and appearing as a guest or speaker at many academic functions. In June 1864, with much difficulty due to his age of 79, Clerc came to Washington, D.C. He was the guest of honor at the inauguration of the National Deaf-Mute College, now Gallaudet University.

He never attended college, but several honorary degrees were bestowed upon him for his pioneering work in deaf education.

On July 18, 1869, Clerc passed away. He was 84 years old.

Clerc and his wife, Elizabeth, are buried at Spring Grove Cemetery in Hartford. In 1992, a deaf man, Alan Barliowek, visited the Clerc gravesites. He was appalled at the deteriorated and vandalized headstones. He started a nationwide campaign to restore the headstones. His efforts drew great support from countless individuals and organizations, including the Laurent Clerc Cultural Fund of the Gallaudet University Alumni Association. Six years later, honor was brought back to the Clercs with the unveiling of new headstones at their final resting place.

CLERC AND THE AMERICAN SIGN LANGUAGE

Clerc's mode of instruction was French signs. His students learned those signs for their studies. However, for their own use, they also borrowed or altered some of those signs and blended them with their own native sign language. As the Hartford students and teachers widely spread Clerc's teachings in his original and in their modified signs, deaf communication acquired an identifiable form. This evolved into the American Sign Language, used in education and assimilated into the personal lives of America's deaf population and its culture. Consequently, about two-thirds of today's ASL signs have French origins. Examples of words that mean the same and have the same signs in American and French are: wine = vin; woman = femme; hundred = cent; look for = chercher.

REFERENCES

Carroll, Cathryn and Harlan Lane. *Laurent Clerc: The Story of His Early Years.* Washington, D.C.: Gallaudet University Press, 1991.

Carroll, Cathyrn and Susan M. Mather. *Movers and Shakers: Deaf People Who Changed the World.* DawnSignPress. 1997.

Gannon, Jack. *Deaf Heritage: A Narrative History of Deaf America.* Maryland: National Association of the Deaf, 1981.

Golladay, Loy. "Laurent Clerc: America's Pioneer Deaf Teacher." *The Deaf American* March 1980: 3–6.

Lane, Harlan. *When the Mind Hears: A History of the Deaf.* New York: Random House, 1984.
"Laurent Clerc . . . In His Own Words." *Deaf Life Plus* December 1995:22–30.
Moore, Matthew Scott and Robert F. Panara. *Great Deaf Americans.* New York: Deaf Life Press, 1996.
Moores, Donald F. *Educating the Deaf: Psychology, Principles, and Practices.* Boston: Houghton Mifflin Company, 1987.
Parsons, Frances M. "In Search of Laurent Clerc." *Deaf Life* Dec. 1995:10–20.
Stansbury, Robin. "New Headstone for Educator Unveiled." 18 Apr. 1998: n. pag. *On-line Internet.* 20 Apr. 1998. http://www.courant.com/news/archiveapr18%2Dctnews4.stm. (editor's note: this link is no longer active)
Winzer, Margret A. *The History of Special Education: From Isolation to Integration.* Washington, D.C.: Gallaudet University Press, 1993.

WEB RESOURCES

Laurent Clerc Info Quest: Questions and Answers
Laurent Clerc Stamp Project
Laurent Clerc

11

"EVERYONE HERE SPOKE SIGN LANGUAGE"

Nora Groce

The fifth of April, 1715, had not been a good day for Judge Samuel Sewell of Boston. On his way to the island of Martha's Vineyard there had been trouble finding a boat to cross Nantucket Sound. The vessel then lay for hours without wind, and once it was across, the horses had to be pushed overboard to swim for shore on their own. Sewell and his company reached shore at dusk—cold, hungry, and in bad humor. Finding a group of local fishermen nearby, the judge engaged one of them to guide him to Edgartown and later noted in his diary: "We were ready to be offended that an Englishman . . . in the company spoke not a word to us. But," he continued by way of explanation, "it seems he is deaf and dumb."

This Englishman was indeed deaf, as were two of his seven children. His is the first recorded case of what we now know to be a form of inherited deafness that was to appear consistently within this island population for more than 250 years and affect dozens of individuals. Probably one or several of the small number of settlers who originally populated the area brought with them a trait for hereditary deafness. As long as the "gene pool" remained limited in the small island population, this trait appeared with high frequency in subsequent generations. Put another way, the founders of this isolated society had a greater likelihood of perpetuating the trait for congenital deafness than if they had been part of a larger, changing population.

Martha's Vineyard offers what I feel to be a good example of the way in which a community adapts to a hereditary disorder. Lying some five miles off the southeastern coast of Massachusetts, the island was first settled by Europeans in the early 1640s. The population, of predominantly English stock with some admixture of indigenous Wampanoag Indian, expanded rapidly, owing to a tremendously high birthrate. Families that had fifteen to twenty children were not uncommon and twenty-five to thirty not unheard of. Although several hundred households are listed in the census records of the mid-eighteenth century, only about thirty surnames are to be found, and during the next century and a half only a handful more were added to the original group of names.

After the first generation, marriage "off-island" was rare. While Vineyard men sailed around the world on whaleships, merchantmen, and fishing vessels, they almost invariably returned home to marry local girls and settle down. Women married off-island even less frequently than did the men. Contact with the mainland was said to be more sporadic than with foreign countries. In the nineteenth century, islanders claimed that more of their men had been to China than to Boston, only eighty miles away. Even today, many islanders have never been to the island of Nantucket, barely eight miles to the east.

Throughout the seventeenth, eighteenth, and nineteenth centuries, marriage patterns on the island followed the customs of any small New England community. Most of the islanders, however, could trace their descent to the same small nucleus of original settlers, indicating that although they were unaware of it, considerable "inbreeding" took place. The result was that during these two and a half centuries, within a population averaging little more than 3,100 individuals, hereditary deafness occurred at a rate many times that of the national population. For example, in the latter part of the nineteenth century, an estimated one out of every 2,730 Americans was born deaf. On Martha's Vineyard the rate was closer to one out of every 155. But even this figure does not accurately represent the distribution of deafness on the Vineyard.

Marriages were usually contracted between members of the same village, creating smaller groups *within* the island's population characterized by a higher frequency of deafness. The greatest concentration occurred in one village on the western part of the island where, by my analysis, within a population of 500, one in every twenty-five individuals was deaf. And even there the distribution was not uniform, for in one area of the village during this time period, one out of every four persons was born deaf.

The high rate of deafness on the island brought only occasional comment from island visitors over the years. Because most of the island deaf lived in the more remote areas of the island, few off-islanders were aware of their presence. Vineyarders themselves, used to a sizable deaf population, saw nothing unusual in this, and many assumed that all communities had a similar number of deaf members. Almost nothing exists in the written records to indicate who was or was not deaf, and indeed, only a passing reference made by an older islander directed my attention to the fact that there had been any deaf there at all.

While most of my information on island deafness has been obtained from the living oral history of islanders now in their seventies, eighties, and nineties, part of my genealogical data was acquired from the only other study of this deaf population. I came to know of it when an 86-year-old woman I was interviewing recalled that her mother had mentioned a "teacher of the deaf from Boston" at one time taking an interest in the island deaf. This "teacher of the deaf" turned out to be Alexander Graham Bell, who, having recently invented the telephone, turned his attention back to his lifelong interest in deafness research. Concerned with the question of heredity as it related to deafness, Bell began a major research project in the early 1880s, which was never completed.

Nineteenth-century scholars, without the benefit of Mendel's concept of unit factor inheritance (which only received widespread circulation at the turn of the century, although it had been published in the 1860s), were at a loss to explain why some but not all children of a deaf parent were themselves deaf. Selecting New England because of the older and unusually complete records available, Bell believed that by tracing back the genealogy of every family with two or more deaf children, he could establish some pattern for the inheritance of deafness. He soon found that practically every family in New England with a history of deafness was in some way connected with the early settlers of Martha's Vineyard, but he was unable to account for the fact that a deaf parent did not always have deaf children and so he abandoned the study. Although Bell never published his material, he left dozens of genealogical charts that have proved invaluable for my research—particularly because they corroborate the information I have been able to collect from the oral history of the older islanders.

Since Bell's time, scientists have found, through the construction and analysis of family pedigrees and the use of mathematical models, that congenital deafness may result from several causes: spontaneous mutations involving one or more genes; an already established dominant or recessive inheritance, as Mendel demonstrated; or factors otherwise altering normal development of the ear and its pathways to the brain. Human populations, of course, cannot be studied with the same exactness as a laboratory experiment. However, the appearance of apparently congenitally deaf individuals is far too frequent on Martha's Vineyard to be mere coincidence, and the evidence collected thus far points to a recessive mode of inheritance.

While the genetic nature of a hereditary disorder in small populations is something that both anthropologists and geneticists have studied, there is another question, rarely addressed, that is of equal importance: How does the population of a community in which a hereditary disorder exists adjust to that disorder—particularly one as prominent as deafness? In modern society the emphasis has been on having "handicapped" individuals adapt to the greater society. But the perception of a handicap, with its associated physical and social limitations, is tempered by the community in which it is found. The manner in which the deaf of Martha's Vineyard were treated provides an interesting example of how one community responded to this type of situation. "How," I asked my informants, "were the island deaf able to communicate with you when they could not speak?" "Oh," I was told, "there was no problem at all. You see, everyone here spoke sign language."

From the late seventeenth century to the early years of the twentieth, islanders, particularly those from the western section where the largest number of deaf individuals lived, maintained a bilingual speech community based on spoken English and sign language. What is of particular interest is that the use of sign language played an important role in day-to-day life.

Islanders acquired a knowledge of sign language in childhood. They were usually taught by parents, with further reinforcement coming from the surrounding community, both hearing and deaf. For example, recalling how she learned a particular sign, one elderly woman explained:

> When I was a little girl, I knew many of the signs, and the manual alphabet of course, but I didn't know how to say "Merry Christmas," and I wanted to tell Mr. M. "Merry Christmas." So I asked Mrs. M., his wife. She could hear and she showed me how. And so I wished Mr. M. "Merry Christmas"—and he was just so delighted.

This women then described how she taught her son, now in his late seventies, how to speak the language.

> When my son was perhaps three years old, I taught him to say in sign language "the little cat and dog and baby." This man, who was deaf, he used to go down to our little general store and see people come and go. One day when I went down there, I took my son there and I said to him, "Go over and say 'how-do-you-do' to Mr. T.," the deaf man. So he went right over, and then I told him to tell Mr. T. so-and-so—a cat, a dog, and whatever. And wasn't Mr. T. tickled! Oh, he was so pleased to know a little bit of a boy like that was telling him all those things, and so he just taught my son a few more words. That's how he learned. That's how we all learned.

Particularly in the western section of the island, if an immediate member of the family was not deaf, a neighbor, friend, or close relative of a friend was likely to be. Practically all my "up-island" informants above the age of seventy remembered signs, a good indication of the extent to which the language was known and used. In this section, and to a lesser extent in the other villages on the island, sign language formed an integral part of all communications. For example, all informants remembered the deaf participating freely in discussions. One remarked:

> If there were several people present and there was a deaf man or woman in the crowd, he'd take upon himself the discussion of anything, jokes or news or anything like that. They always had a part in it, they were never excluded.

As in all New England communities, gathering around the potbellied stove or on the front porch of what served as a combination general store and post office provided a focal point for stories, news, and gossip. Many of the people I have talked to distinctly remember the deaf members of the community in this situation. As one man recalled:

> We would sit around and wait for the mail to come in and just talk. And the deaf would be there, everyone would be there. And they were part of the crowd, and they were accepted. They were fishermen and farmers and everything else. And they wanted to find out the news just as much as the rest of us. And oftentimes people would tell stories and make signs at the same time so everyone could follow him together. Of course, sometimes, if there were more deaf than hearing there, everyone would speak sign language—just to be polite, you know.

The use of sign was not confined to small-group discussions. It also found its way into assembled crowds. For example, one gentleman told me:

> They would come to prayer meetings; most all of them were regular church people, you know. They would come when people offered testimonials, and they would get up in front of the audience and stand there and give a whole lecture in sign. No one translated it to the audience because everyone knew what they were saying. And if there was anyone who missed something somewhere, somebody sitting near them would be able to tell them about it.

The deaf were so integral a part of the community that at town meetings up-island, a hearing person would stand at the side of the hall and cue the deaf in sign to let them know what vote was coming up next, thus allowing them to keep right on top of things.

The participation of the deaf in all day-to-day work and play situations contrasted with the manner in which those handicapped by deafness were generally treated in the United States during the same time period.

Sign language on the island was not restricted to those occasions when deaf and hearing were together, but was used on a regular basis between the hearing as well. For example, sign language was used on boats to give commands and among fishermen out in open water to discuss their catch. I was told:

> Fishermen, hauling pots outside in the Sound or off Gay Head, when they would be heaven knows how far apart, would discuss how the luck was running—all that sort of thing. These men could talk and hear all right, but it'd be too far to yell.

Indeed, signs were used any place the distance prohibited talking in a normal voice. For example, one man remembered:

> Jim had a shop down on the shore of Tisbury Pond, and his house was a ways away, up on the high land. When Trudy, his wife, wanted to tell Jim something, she'd come to the door, blow a fish horn, and Jim would step outside. He'd say, "Excuse me, Trudy wants me for something"; then she'd make signs to tell him what she needed done.

On those occasions when speaking was out of place, such as in church, school, or at some public gatherings, the hearing communicated through signs. Such stories as the following are common: "Ben and his brother could both talk and hear, but I've seen them sitting across from each other in town meetings or in church and telling each other funny stories in sign language."

Island people frequently maintained social distance and a sense of distinct identity in the presence of tourists by exchanging comments about them in sign language. The occurrence of what linguists call code switching from speech to sign also seems to have been used in certain instances. For example, I was told:

> People would start off a sentence in speaking and then finish it off in sign language, especially if they were saying something dirty. The punch line would often be in sign language. If there was a bunch of guys standing around the general store telling a [dirty] story and a woman walked in, they'd turn away from her and finish the story in sign language.

Perhaps the following anecdote best illustrates the unique way island sign language was integral to all aspects of life:

> My mother was in the New Bedford hospital—had an operation—and father went over in his boat and lived aboard his boat and went to the hospital to see her every night. Now the surgeon, when he left him in her room, said they mustn't speak, father couldn't say a word to her. So he didn't. But they made signs for about half an hour and mother got so worked up, they had to send father out, wouldn't let him stay any longer.

Sign language or rather sign languages—for even within this country there exist a number of distinct languages and dialects—are languages in their own right, systems of communication different from the spoken languages used by hearing members of the same community. It has often been noted that American Sign Language, the sign system commonly used among the deaf in the United States today, is influenced by French Sign Language, introduced to America in 1817. The data from Martha's Vineyard, however, clearly support the hypothesis, made by the linguist James Woodward, that local sign language systems were in use in America long before this. By 1817 (the year the American School for the Deaf was founded in Hartford, Connecticut), deaf individuals on Martha's Vineyard had been actively participating in island society for well over a century. Because they were on an equal footing, both socially and economically, with the hearing members of the community, and because they held town offices, married, raised families, and left legal and personal documents, there must have existed some sort of sign language system that allowed full communication with family, friends, and neighbors.

It may prove difficult to reconstruct the original sign language system used on the island during the seventeenth and eighteenth centuries, but study of this question is currently under way. Whatever the exact nature of the original language, we know that it later grew to acquire many aspects of the more widely used American Sign Language, as increasing numbers of deaf island children were sent to the school in Hartford during the nineteenth century. This combination of the indigenous sign system with the more standardized American Sign Language seems to have produced a sign language that was, in many respects, unique to the island of Martha's Vineyard. The most common remark made by islanders who still remember the language is that they find it very difficult or are completely unable to understand the sign language spoken by off-islanders or the translations for the deaf that are beginning to be seen on television.

The use of sign language as an active system of communication lessened as the number of individuals in the community with hereditary deafness gradually disappeared, the last few dying in the 1940s and early 1950s. This decrease in the number of deaf can be attributed to a shift in marriage patterns that began in the latter part of the nineteenth century, when both hearing and deaf islanders began to marry off-islanders. The introduction of new genes into the once small gene pool has reduced the chance of a reappearance of "island deafness."

As the number of islanders born deaf dwindled, younger generations no longer took an interest in learning sign language, and the older generations rarely had the need to make use of it. Today, very few people are left who can speak the language fluently, although bits and pieces of it can be recalled by several dozen of the oldest islanders. A few signs are still kept alive among those who knew the language and on a few of their fishing boats. As one gentleman, well along in his seventies, told me recently:

> You know, strangely enough, there's still vestiges of that left in the older families around here. Instinctively you make some such movement, and it means something to you, but it doesn't mean anything to the one you're talking to.

ASL AS LANGUAGE

12

AMERICAN SIGN LANGUAGE: 'IT'S NOT MOUTH STUFF—IT'S BRAIN STUFF'

Richard Wolkomir

Research on how deaf people communicate gives them a stronger hand in our culture, and casts new light on the origin of language

In a darkened laboratory at the Salk Institute in San Diego, a deaf woman is signing. Tiny lights attached to her sleeves and fingers trace the motions of her hands, while two special video cameras whir.

Computers will process her hands' videotaped arabesques and pirouettes into mathematically precise three-dimensional images. Neurologists and linguists will study these stunning patterns for insight into how the human brain produces language.

Sign has become a scientific hot button. Only in the past 20 years have linguists realized that signed languages are unique—a speech of the hand. They offer a new way to probe how the brain generates and understands language, and throw new light on an old scientific controversy: whether language, complete with grammar, is innate in our species, or whether it is a learned behavior. The current interest in sign language has roots in the pioneering work of one renegade teacher at Gallaudet University in Washington, D.C., the world's only liberal arts university for deaf people.

When Bill Stokoe went to Gallaudet to teach English, the school enrolled him in a course in signing. But Stokoe noticed something odd: among themselves, students signed differently from his classroom teacher.

"Hand talk": a genuine language

Stokoe had been taught a sort of gestural code, each movement of the hands representing a word in English. At the time, American Sign Language (ASL) was thought to be no more than a form of pidgin English. But Stokoe believed the "hand talk" his students used looked richer. He wondered: Might deaf people actually have a genuine language? And could that language be unlike any other on Earth? It was 1955, when even deaf people dismissed their signing as "slang," Stokoe's idea was academic heresy.

It is 37 years later. Stokoe—now devoting his time to writing and editing books and journals and to producing video materials on ASL and the deaf culture—is having lunch at a café near the Gallaudet campus and explaining how he started a revolution. For decades educators fought his idea that signed languages are natural languages like English, French and Japanese. They assumed language must be based on speech, the modulation of sound. But sign language is based on the movement of hands, the modulation of space. "What I said," Stokoe explains, "is that language is not mouth stuff—it's brain stuff."

It has been a long road, from the mouth to the brain. Linguists have had to redefine language. Deaf people's self-esteem has been at stake, and so has the ticklish issue of their education.

"My own contribution was to turn around the thinking of academics," says Stokoe. "When I came to Gallaudet, the teachers were trained with two books, and the jokers who wrote them gave only a paragraph to sign language, calling it a vague system of gestures that looked like the ideas they were supposed to represent."

Deaf education in the '50s irked him. "I didn't like to see how the hearing teachers treated their deaf pupils—their expectations were low," he says. "I was amazed at how many of my students were brilliant." Meanwhile, he was reading the work of anthropological linguists like George Trager and Henry Lee Smith jr. "They said you couldn't study language without studying the culture, and when I had been at Gallaudet a short time, I realized that deaf people had a culture of their own."

When Stokoe analyzed his students' signing, he found it was like spoken languages, which combine bits of sound—each meaningless by itself—into meaningful words. Signers, following similar rules, combine individually meaningless hand and body movements into words. They choose from a palette of hand shapes, such as a fist or a pointing index finger. They also choose where to make a sign; for example, on the face or on the chest. They choose how to orient the hand and arm. And each sign has a movement—it might begin at the cheek and finish at the chin. A shaped hand executing a particular motion creates a word. A common underlying structure of both spoken and signed language is thus at the level of the smallest units that are linked to form words.

Stokoe explained his findings on the structure of ASL in a book published in 1960. "The faculty then had a special meeting and I got up and said my piece," he says. "Nobody threw eggs or old vegetables, but I was bombarded by hostility." Later, the university's president told Stokoe his research was "causing too much trouble" because his insistence that ASL was indeed a *language* threatened the English-based system for teaching the deaf. But Stokoe persisted. Five years later he came out with the first dictionary of American Sign Language based on linguistic principles. And he's been slowly winning converts ever since.

"Wherever we've found deaf people, there's sign"

Just as no one can pinpoint the origins of spoken language in prehistory, the roots of sign language remain hidden from view. What linguists do know is that sign languages have sprung up independently in many different places. Signing probably began with simple gestures, but then evolved into a true language with structured grammar. "In every place we've ever found deaf people, there's sign," says anthropological linguist Bob Johnson. But it's not the same language. "I went to a Mayan village where, out of 400 people, 13 were deaf, and they had their own Mayan Sign—I'd guess it's been maintained for thousands of years." Today at least 50 native sign languages are "spoken" worldwide, all mutually incomprehensible, from British and Israeli Sign to Chinese Sign.

Not until the 1700s, in France, did people who could hear pay serious attention to deaf people and their language. Religion had something to do with it. "They believed that without speech you couldn't go to heaven," says Johnson.

For the Abbé de l'Epée, a French priest born into a wealthy family in 1712, the issue was his own soul: he feared he would lose it unless he overcame the stigma of his privileged youth by devoting himself to the poor. In his history of the deaf, *When The Mind Hears,* Northeastern University psychologist Harlan Lane notes that, in his 50s, de l'Epée met two deaf girls on one of his forays into the Paris slums and decided to dedicate himself to their education.

The priest's problem was abstraction: he could show the girls a piece of bread and the printed French word for "bread." But how could he show them "God" or "goodness"? He decided to learn their sign language as a teaching medium. However, he attempted to impose French grammar onto the signs.

"Methodical signing," as de l'Epée called his invention, was an ugly hybrid. But he did teach his pupils to read French, opening the door to education, and today he is a hero to deaf people. As his pupils and disciples proliferated, satellite schools sprouted throughout Europe. De l'Epée died happily destitute in 1789 surrounded by his students in his Paris school, which became the National Institution for Deaf-Mutes under the new republic.

Other teachers kept de l'Epée's school alive. And one graduate, Laurent Clerc, brought the French method of teaching in sign to the United States. It was the early 1800s; in Hartford, Connecticut, the Rev. Thomas Hopkins Gallaudet was watching children at play. He noticed that one girl, Alice Cogswell, did not join in. She was deaf. Her father, a surgeon, persuaded Gallaudet to find a European teacher and create the first permanent school for the deaf in the United States. Gallaudet then traveled to England, where the "oral" method was supreme, the idea being to teach deaf children to speak. The method was almost cruel, since children born deaf—they heard no voices, including their own—could have no concept of speech. It rarely worked. Besides, the teachers said their method was "secret." And so Gallaudet visited the Institution for Deaf-Mutes in Paris and persuaded Laurent Clerc to come home with him.

During their 52-day voyage across the Atlantic, Gallaudet helped Clerc improve his English, and Clerc taught him French Sign Language. On April 15, 1817, in Hartford, they established a school that became the American School for the Deaf. Teaching in French Sign Language and a version of de l'Epée's methodical sign, Clerc trained many students who became teachers, too, and helped spread the language across the country. Clerc's French Sign was to mingle with various "home" signs that had sprung up in other places. On Martha's Vineyard, Massachusetts, for example, a large portion of the population was genetically deaf, and virtually all the islanders used an indigenous sign language, the hearing switching back and forth between speech and sign with bilingual ease. Eventually, pure French Sign would blend with such local argots and evolve into today's American Sign Language.

After Clerc died, in 1869, much of the work done since the time of de l'Epée to teach the deaf in their own language crumbled under the weight of Victorian intolerance. Anti-Signers argued that ASL let the deaf "talk" only to the deaf; they must learn to speak and to lip-read. Pro-Signers pointed out that, through sign, the deaf learned to read and write English. The Pros also noted that lipreading is a skill that few master. (Studies estimate that 93 percent of deaf schoolchildren who were either born deaf or lost their hearing in early childhood can lip-read only one in ten everyday sentences in English.) And Pros argue correctly that the arduous hours required to teach a deaf child to mimic speech should be spent on real education.

"Oralists" like Horace Mann lobbied to stop schools from teaching in ASL, then *the* method of instruction in all schools for the deaf. None was more fervent than Alexander Graham Bell, inventor of the telephone and husband of a woman who denied her own deafness. The president of the National Association of the Deaf called Bell the "most to be feared enemy of the American deaf." In 1880, at an international meeting of educators of the deaf in Milan, where deaf teachers were absent, the use of sign language in schools was proscribed.

After that, as deaf people see it, came the Dark Ages. Retired Gallaudet sociolinguist Barbara Kannapell, who is cofounder of Deafpride, a Washington, D.C. advocacy group, is the deaf daughter of deaf parents from Kentucky. Starting at age 4, she attended an "oral" school, where signing was outlawed. "Whenever the teacher turned her back to work on the blackboard, we'd sign," signs Kannapell. "If the teacher caught us using sign language, she'd use a ruler on our hands."

Kannapell has tried to see oralism from the viewpoint of hearing parents of deaf children. "They'll do anything to make their child like themselves," she signs. "But, from a deaf adult's perspective, I want *them* to learn sign, to communicate with their child."

In the 1970s, a new federal law mandated "mainstreaming." "That law was good for parents, because they could keep children home instead of sending them off to special boarding schools, but many public schools didn't know what to do with deaf kids," signs Kannapell. "Many of these children think they're the only deaf kids in the world."

Gallaudet's admissions director, James Tucker, an exuberant 32-year-old, is a product of the '70s mainstreaming. "I'd sit in the back, doing work the teacher gave me and minding my own business," he signs. "Did I like it? Hell no! I was lonely—for years I thought I was an introvert." Deaf children have a right to learn ASL and to live in an ASL-speaking community, he asserts. "We learn sign for obvious reasons—our eyes aren't broken," he signs. Tucker adds: "Deaf culture is a group of people sharing similar values, outlook and frustrations, and the main thing, of course, is sharing the same language."

Today, most teachers of deaf pupils are "hearies" who speak as they sign. "Simultaneous Communication," as it is called, is really signed English and not ASL. "It looks grotesque to the eye," signs Tucker, adding that it makes signs too "marked," a linguistic term meaning equally stressed. Hand movements can be exaggerated or poorly executed. As Tucker puts it: "We have zealous educators trying to impose weird hand shapes." Moreover, since the languages have entirely different sentence structures, the effect can be bewildering. It's like having Japanese spoken to English-speaking students with an interpreter shouting occasional English words at them.

The silent world of sign

New scientific findings support the efforts of linguists such as Bob Johnson, who are calling for an education system for deaf students based on ASL, starting in infancy. Research by Helen Neville, at the Salk Institute, shows that children *must* learn a language—any language—during their first five years or so, before the brain's neural connections are locked in place, or risk permanent linguistic impairment. "What suffers is the ability to learn grammar," she says. As children mature, their brain organization becomes increasingly rigid. By puberty, it is largely complete. This spells trouble because most deaf youngsters learn language late; their parents are hearing and do not know ASL, and the children have little or no contact with deaf people when young.

Bob Johnson notes that more than 90 percent of all deaf children have hearing parents. Unlike deaf children of deaf parents, who get ASL instruction early, they learn a language late and lag educationally. "The average deaf 12th-grader reads at the 4th-grade level," says Johnson. He believes deaf children should start learning ASL in the crib, with schools teaching in ASL. English, he argues, should be a second language, for reading and writing: "All evidence says they'll learn English better." It's been an uphill battle. Of the several hundred school programs for the deaf in this country, only six are moving toward ASL-based instruction. And the vast majority of deaf students are still in mainstream schools where there are few teachers who are fluent in ASL.

Meanwhile, researchers are finding that ASL is a living language, still evolving. Sociolinguist James Woodward from Memphis, who has a black belt in karate, had planned to study Chinese dialects but switched to sign when he came to Gallaudet in 1969. "I spent every night for two years at the Rathskeller, a student hangout, learning by observing," he says. "I began to see great variation in the way people signed."

Woodward later concentrated on regional, social and ethnic dialects of ASL. Visiting deaf homes and social clubs in the South, he found that Southerners use older forms of ASL signs than Northerners do. Southern blacks use even more of the older signs. "From them, we can learn the history of the language," he says.

Over time, signs tend to change. For instance, "home" originally was the sign for "eat" (touching the mouth) combined with the sign for "sleep" (the palm pillowing the cheek). Now it has evolved into two taps on the cheek. Also, signs formerly made at the center of the face migrate toward its perimeter. One reason is that it is easier to see both signs and changes in facial expressions in this way, since deaf people focus on a signer's face—which provides crucial linguistic information—taking in the hands with peripheral vision.

Signers use certain facial expressions as grammatical markers. These linguistic expressions range from pursed lips to the expression that results from enunciating the sound "th." Linguist Scott Liddell, at Gallaudet, has noted that certain hand movements translate as "Bill drove to John's." If the signer tilts his head forward and raises his eyebrows while signing, he makes the sentence a question: "Did Bill drive to John's?" If he also makes the "th" expression as he signs, he modifies the verb with an adverb: "Did Bill drive to John's inattentively?"

Sociolinguists have investigated why this unique language was for so long virtually a secret. Partly, Woodward thinks, it was because deaf people wanted it that way. He says that when deaf people sign to the hearing, they switch to English-like signing. "It allows hearing people to be identified as outsiders and to be treated carefully before allowing any interaction that could have a negative effect on the deaf community," he says. By keeping ASL to themselves, deaf people—whom Woodward regards as an ethnic group—maintain "social identity and group solidarity."

A key language ingredient: grammar

The "secret" nature of ASL is changing rapidly as it is being examined under the scientific microscope. At the Salk Institute, a futuristic complex of concrete labs poised on a San Diego cliff above the Pacific, pioneer ASL investigator Ursula Bellugi directs the Laboratory for Cognitive Neuroscience, where researchers use ASL to probe the brain's capacity for language. It was here that Bellugi and associates found that ASL has a key language ingredient: a grammar to regulate its flow. For example, in a conversation a signer might make the sign for "Joe" at an arbitrary spot in space. Now that spot stands for "Joe." By pointing to it, the signer creates the pronoun "he" or "him," meaning "Joe." A sign moving toward the spot means something done *to* "him." A sign moving away from the spot means an action *by* Joe, something "he" did

In the 1970s, Bellugi's team concentrated on several key questions that have been of central concern ever since MIT professor Noam Chomsky's groundbreaking work of the 1950s. Is language capability innate, as Chomsky and his followers believe? Or is it acquired from our environment? The question gets to the basics of humanity since our language capacity is part of our unique endowment as a species. And language lets us accumulate lore and pass it on to succeeding generations. Bellugi's team reasoned that if ASL is a true language, unconnected to speech, then our penchant for language must be built in at birth, whether we express it with our tongue or hands. As Bellugi (above) puts it: "I had to keep asking myself, 'What does it mean to be a language?'"

A key issue was "iconicity." Linguistics has long held that one of the properties of all natural languages is that their words are arbitrary. In English, to illustrate, there is no relation between the sound of the word "cat" and a cat itself, and onomatopoeic words like "slurp" are few and far between. Similarly, if ASL follows the same principles, its words should not be pictures or mime. But ASL does have many words with transparent meanings. In ASL, "tree" is an arm upright from the elbow, representing a trunk, with the fingers spread to show the crown. In Danish Sign, the signer's two hands outline a tree in the air. Sign languages are rife with pantomimes. But Bellugi wondered: Do deaf people *perceive* such signs as iconic as they communicate in ASL?

One day a deaf mother visited the lab with her deaf daughter, not yet 2. At that age, hearing children fumble pronouns, which is why parents say, "Mommy is getting Tammy juice." The deaf child, equally confused by pronouns, signed "you" when she meant "I." But the sign for such pronouns is purely iconic: the signer points an index finger at his or her own torso to signify "I" or at the listener to signify "you." The mother corrected the child by turning her hand so that she pointed at herself. Nothing could be clearer. Yet, as the child chattered on, she continued to point to her mother when she meant "I."

Bellugi's work revealed that deaf toddlers have no trouble pointing. But a pointing finger in ASL is linguistic, not gestural. Deaf toddlers in the "don't-understand-pronouns" stage do not see a pointing finger. They see a confusing, abstract word. ASL's roots may be mimetic, but—embedded in the flow of language—the signs lose their iconicity.

By the 1980s, most linguists had accepted sign languages as natural languages on an equal footing with English, Italian, Hindi and others of the world. Signed languages like ASL were as powerful, subtle and intricately structured as spoken ones.

The parallels become especially striking in wordplay and poetry. Signers creatively combine hand shapes and movements to create puns and other humorous alterations of words. A typical pun in sign goes like this: a fist near the forehead and a flip of the index finger upward means that one understands. But if the little finger is flipped, it's a joke meaning one understands a little. Clayton Valli at Gallaudet has made an extensive study of poetry in ASL. He finds that maintenance or repetition of hand shape provides rhyming, while meter occurs in the timing and type of movement. Research with the American Theater of the Deaf reveals a variety of individual techniques and styles. Some performers create designs in space with a freer movement of the arms than in ordinary signing. With others, rhythm and tempo are more important than spatial considerations. Hands may be alternated so that there is a balance and symmetry in the structure. Or signs may be made to flow into one another, creating a lyricism in the passage. The possibilities for this new art form in sign seem bounded only by the imagination within the community itself.

The special nature of sign language provides unprecedented opportunities to observe how the brain is organized to generate and understand language. Spoken languages are produced by largely unobservable movements of the vocal apparatus and received through the brain's auditory system. Signed languages, by contrast, are delivered through highly visible movements of the arms, hands and face, and are received through the brain's visual system. Engagement of these different brain systems in language use makes it possible to test different ideas about the biological basis of language.

The prevailing view of neurologists is that the brain's left hemisphere is the seat of language, while the right controls our perception of visual space. But since signed languages are expressed spatially, it was unclear where they might be centered.

To find out, Bellugi and her colleagues studied lifelong deaf signers who had suffered brain damage as adults. When the damage had occurred in their left hemisphere, the signers could shrug, point, shake their heads and make other gestures, but they lost the ability to sign. As happens with hearing people who suffer left-hemisphere damage, some of them lost words while others lost the ability to organize grammatical sentences, depending on precisely where the damage had occurred.

Conversely, signers with right-hemisphere damage signed as well as ever, but spatial arrangements confused them. One of Bellugi's right-hemisphere subjects could no longer perceive things to her left. Asked to describe a room, she reported all the furnishings as being on the right, leaving the room's left side a void. Yet she signed perfectly, including signs formed on the left side. She had lost her sense of *topographic* space, a right-hemisphere function, but her control of *linguistic* space, centered in the left hemisphere, was intact. All of these findings support the conclusion that language, whether visual or spoken, is under the control of the left hemisphere.

One of the Salk group's current efforts is to see if learning language in a particular modality changes the brain's ability to perform other kinds of tasks. Researchers showed children a moving light tracing a pattern in space, and then asked them to draw what they saw. "Deaf kids were way ahead of hearing kids," says Bellugi. Other tests, she adds, back up the finding that learning sign language improves the mind's ability to grasp patterns in space.

Thinking and dreaming in signs

Salk linguist Karen Emmorey says the lab also has found that deaf people are better at generating and manipulating mental images. "We found a striking difference in ability to generate mental images and to tell if one object is the same as another but rotated in space, or is a mirror image of the first," she says, noting that signers seem to be better at discriminating between faces, too. As she puts it: "The question is, does the language you know affect your other cognitive abilities?"

Freda Norman, formerly an actress with the National Theater of the Deaf and now a Salk research associate, puts it like this: "English is very linear, but ASL lets you see everything at the same time."

"The deaf *think* in signs," says Bellugi. "They *dream* in signs. And little children sign to themselves."

At McGill University in Montreal, psychologist Laura Ann Petitto recently found that deaf babies of deaf parents babble in sign. Hearing infants create nonsense sounds like "babababa," first attempts at language. So do deaf babies, but with their hands. Petitto watched deaf infants moving their hands and fingers in systematic ways that hearing children not exposed to sign never do. The movements, she says, were their way of exploring the linguistic units that will be the building blocks of language—their language

Deaf children today face a brighter future than the generation of deaf children before them. Instruction in ASL, particularly in residential schools, should accelerate. New technologies, such as the TDD (Telecommunications Device for the Deaf) for communicating over telephones, relay services and video programs for language instruction, and the recent Americans with Disabilities Act all point the way to a more supportive environment. Deaf people are moving into professional jobs, such as law and accounting, and more recently into computer-related work. But it is not surprising that outside of their work, they prefer one another's company. Life can be especially rewarding for those within the ASL community. Here they form their own literary clubs, bowling leagues and gourmet groups.

As the Salk laboratory's Freda Norman signs: "I love to read books, but ASL is my first language." She adds, smiling: "Sometimes I forget that the hearing are different."

13

SIGNS ACROSS AMERICA

Shroyer, E. H., 1984
(Signs Across America, Gallaudet College Press, Washington, D.C. 2002)

"As long as there are deaf people there will be signing." It is recognized and generally accepted that Thomas Hopkins Gallaudet, a hearing American clergyman, and Laurent Clerc, a deaf French educator of deaf children, established the first permanent school for the deaf in the United States in 1817. They brought together deaf children from a variety of places in New England to their school (now known as the American School for the Deaf) in Hartford, Connecticut. This was the children's first exposure to formal education. Clerc, who was fluent in French Sign Language, introduced his signs in this newly established school.

It would be rather naive of anyone to think that these two men are solely responsible for introducing signs in America. Clerc is reported to have frequently complained to friends that his students were not using all of the signs that he showed them. They were, according to him, changing some of his "beautiful French signs" as well as stubbornly using signs that they had brought to the school with them.

Clerc's complaints serve as one indication that signs were obviously used by deaf individuals in America prior to 1817. Further evidence can be found in Groce's research (1980) on an established sign language used on Martha's Vineyard beginning in the seventeenth century. Many of the children from Martha's Vineyard attended the school in Hartford. Current research also shows that deaf children of hearing parents make up signs to communicate with their parents and siblings. Young deaf children in schools that forbid signing are frequently seen signing to one another outside of school. There appears to be little doubt that deaf people have indeed, historically, always used signs to communicate with one another as well as with individuals who are not deaf.

If deaf people originally invented many of their own signs, then it seems logical that deaf people from New England would not be able to communicate with deaf people living in Ohio. Around the early 1800s they probably could not. Today, a deaf traveler going across America would have very little, if any, difficulty conversing with other deaf people encountered along the way. There may be an occasional sign that the traveler might not know, but context would probably clarify the sign's meaning.

The ability of deaf people from different areas of the country to communicate without any difficulty has to be attributed to Clerc and Gallaudet. The signs that they taught were carried by graduates of their school to other parts of the country. Several people trained at the American School were instrumental in establishing schools for the deaf in different parts of the country. Consequently, the signs taught at the American School were in turn taught to children and others associated with deaf people in other parts of the United States.

BIRTHDAY

When is your birthday?

1 Alabama

2 Arkansas

3 California

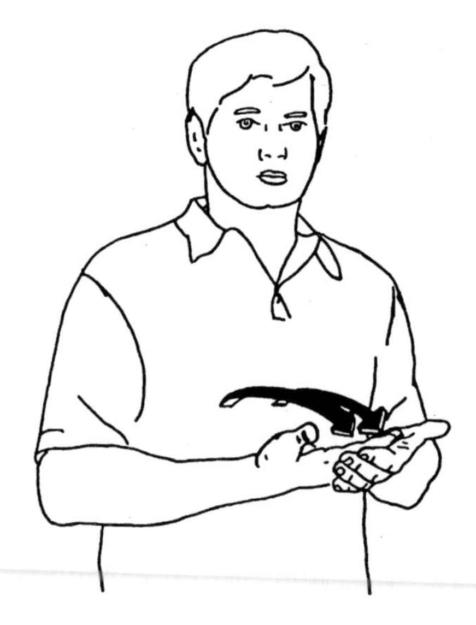

4 Colorado, Ohio

5 Florida

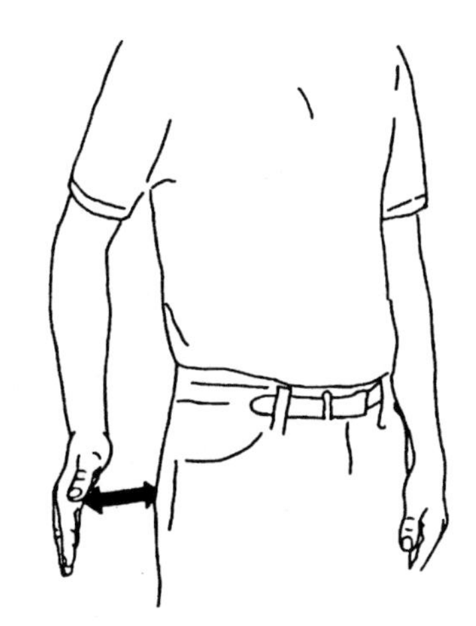

6 Hawaii

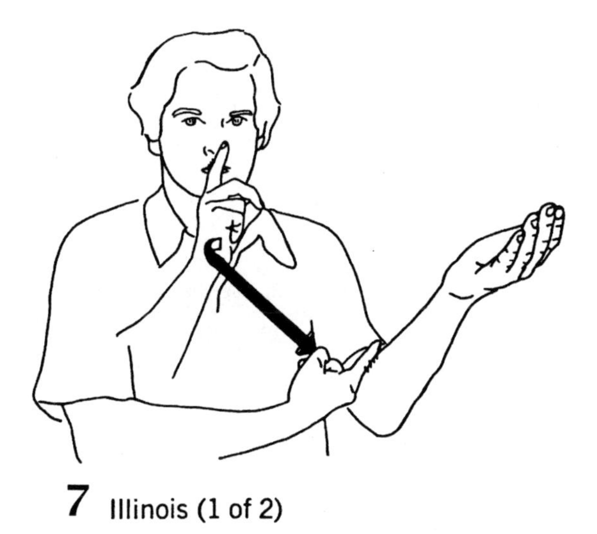

7 Illinois (1 of 2)

8 Illinois (2 of 2), Louisiana

9 Kentucky

10 Maine, Massachusetts (1 of 2), Pennsylvania (1 of 2)

11 New York

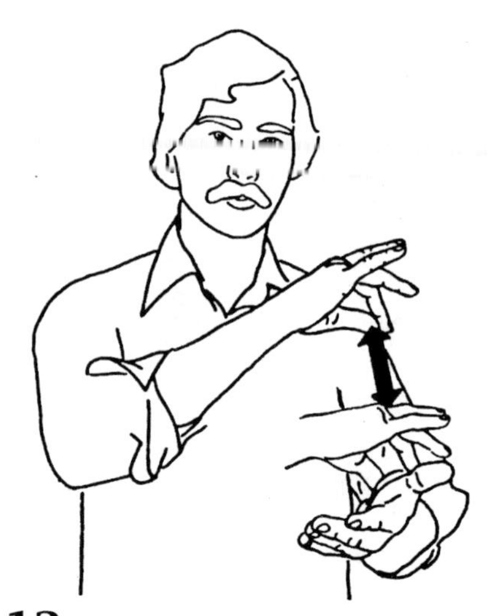

12 Pennsylvania (2 of 2)

13 South Carolina

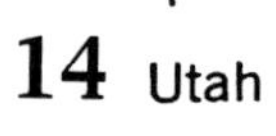

14 Utah

15 Virginia

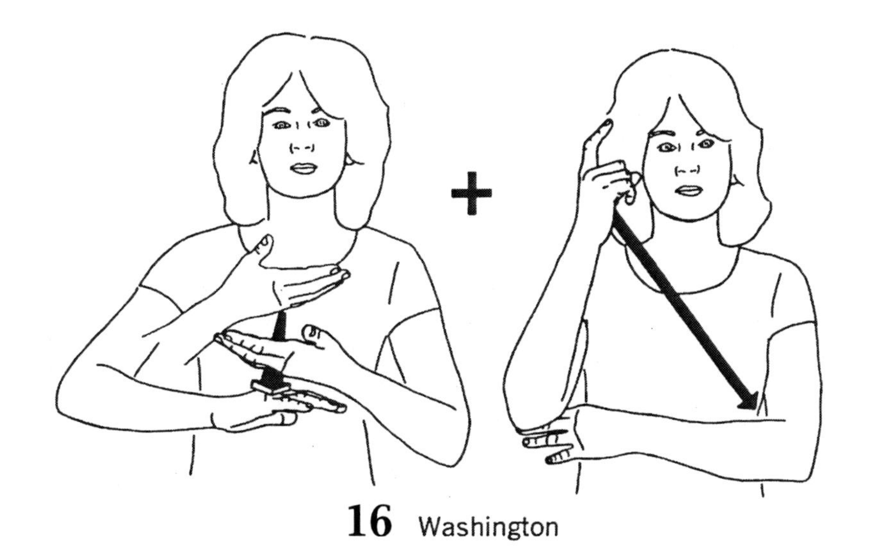

16 Washington

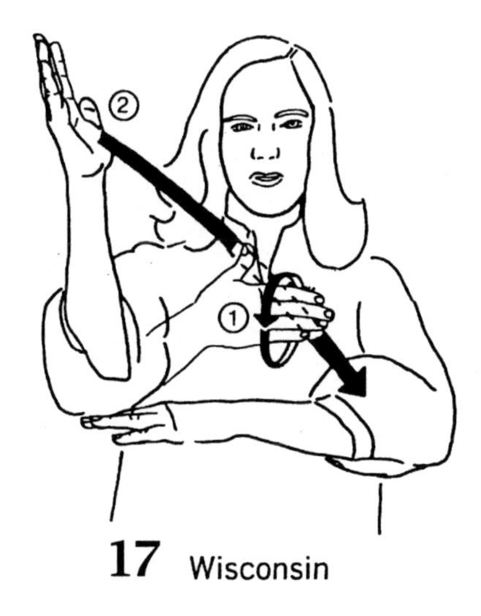

17 Wisconsin

14

THE INTERACTIONAL CONTEXT OF DEAF MOTHER-INFANT COMMUNICATION

C. J. Erting, C. Prezioso, and M. O'Grady Hynes

THE STUDY

Since 1985, as part of a larger study, we have been collecting videotapes of deaf mothers interacting with their deaf babies. All of these mothers are from the Washington, DC, area and are either students, graduates, or employees of Gallaudet University. We have been interested in the interaction that occurs between these mothers and infants in face-to-face situations. Our first questions about the earliest interactions, when the infant is younger than 6 months old, have focused on the mothers' strategies for gaining and maintaining the infants' visual attention, alerting the infant, and the mothers' linguistic communication through sign language. Our observations support previous researchers' findings that deaf mothers are in physical contact with their deaf infants throughout much of their interaction, engaging in a variety of touching behaviors such as tapping, stroking, tickling, and movement of the infant's limbs. They vary the type of movement, location on the infant's body, intensity and speed of movement, and rhythmic patterning of the tactile behaviors as they seek to get and maintain the infant's attention (Marlborough, 1986).

Preliminary analysis of videotapes collected in the face-to-face laboratory setting at 3 1/2 and 6 months of age suggests that these deaf mothers spend the major proportion of their interaction time (70%–80%) with a positive affective expression on their faces, compared with less than 50% for normally hearing mothers with their normally hearing infants (Meadow-Orlans, MacTurk, Prezioso, Erting, & Day, 1987). They also use their faces to engage in dialogues with their infants as well as for coactional duetting wherein mother and infant perform the same facial expressions simultaneously. The term "coactional duetting" usually refers to vocal matching in pitch and prosodic contours in the case of normally hearing mothers and infants (Papousek & Papousek, 1987). Finally, deaf mothers modify the sign language they use with their infants, producing signing that appears slower, formationally different, and grammatically less complex than the signing produced during adult-directed discourse. As reported in the studies reviewed above, the signing space is usually related to the infant's direction of gaze: if the infant is looking at the mother, she usually signs near her face rather than making use of the full signing space available in adult-directed discourse; if the infant is looking away or at an object, the mother will often sign near or on the object or reach into the infant's visual field to sign. As in baby-talk varieties of spoken language, the content is related to the immediate context, the baby's behavior, or the mother's interpretation of the infant's feelings.

Here we present an analysis of some baby-talk productions of eight deaf American mothers. We have focused on the American sign for MOTHER produced by these mothers during interaction with their deaf infants when the infants were between 5 and 23 weeks of age. Some of the videotapes were made in a laboratory at Gallaudet University and some were collected during visits to the homes.

Two deaf researchers viewed the videotapes and isolated those MOTHER signs that they judged to be qualitatively different from everyday adult-talk MOTHER signs. These 27 MOTHER signs were then analyzed along nine dimensions: distance of the mother from the infant, handshape, location, orientation of the palm, type of movement, number of movements, accompanying nonmanual behaviors, maternal affect, and duration of the sign. In addition, we located 27 MOTHER signs produced by these same deaf mothers during a videotaped interview with a deaf researcher and analyzed them along the same dimensions.

The citation forms for the two most frequently used variants of the sign MOTHER are shown in Fig. 1. Both variants are produced with a 5 handshape, thumb tip on the chin, and palm oriented to the right or left. They differ along the parameter of movement, however, with variant A produced by touching the chin with the thumb twice and variant B produced with a wiggling of the fingers while the thumb remains in contact with the chin. Both MOTHER sign variants, in citation form, partially block the signer's face.

When we analyzed the deaf mothers' productions of the MOTHER signs with their babies, we saw that they were not using the citation forms of these signs. Formationally, the baby-talk signs differed most noticeably on the parameter of orientation of the palm. For the purposes of our analysis, we imagined an arc, or half-circle, in front of the signer and extending from one shoulder to the other. By locating five points along the arc, from 0° to 180°, we could code five different orientations of the signer's

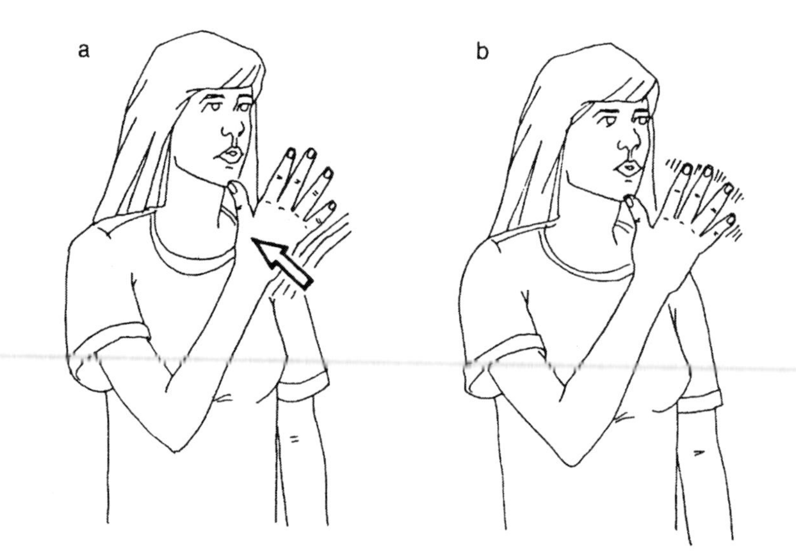

Fig. 1a,b. Citation forms for the two most frequently used variants of the American Sign Language sign MOTHER

palm as shown in Fig. 2. For example, if the MOTHER sign were produced with the thumb touching the chin and the little finger oriented toward the 0 degree point, the palm of the hand would be fully visible to the infant. If, on the other hand, the sign were made with the thumb touching the chin and the little finger oriented toward the 180° point, the back of the 5 hand would be fully visible to the infant, not the palm. At 90°, the infant would be unable to see either the palm or the back of the hand if mother were squarely in front of the infant in the face-to-face position.

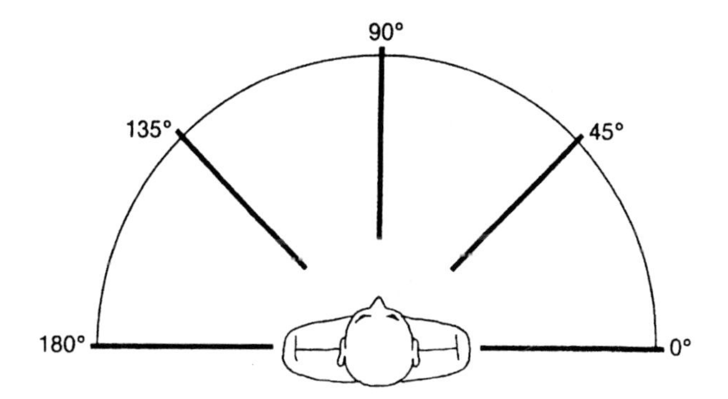

Fig. 2. Points on an arc representing five different orientations of the signer's palm

The baby-talk variants of MOTHER differed from the adult talk forms on seven of the nine dimensions analyzed as shown on Table 1. The deaf mothers produced the baby-talk MOTHER signs so that they were visible to the infants longer than the MOTHER signs that appeared during adult talk. They also showed the full palm or back of the 5 hand to the infant, making their own faces fully available for the infants to see. These mothers looked at the infant during every baby-talk MOTHER sign and expressed positive affect on their faces in every instance in which the infants were attending to them. In addition, they accompanied the manual sign with mouth movements for the English words "mother" or "mommy," with or without voice: The adult-talk MOTHER signs differed on these nonmanual dimensions: during nine of the 27 adult-talk productions the mothers' eyes were not on the conversational partner, facial expressions were neutral during most of these MOTHER signs, eight of the adult-talk MOTHER signs were not accompanied by mouth movements, and only one sign was produced simultaneously with voice.

While all of the 54 MOTHER signs were made with the same handshape and in the same location on or near the chin, the deaf mothers moved in close to the infant while they were signing the 27 baby-talk signs but maintained a constant distance from the interviewer during the adult-talk signing. In addition, even though both the "touch" and the "finger wiggle" variants were produced by these mothers during conversation with the adult, only the "touch" variant was used with the infant. More than one-third of these baby-talk signs were executed with more than two movements (touches to the chin) while the majority of the adult talk MOTHER signs were made with only one touch or the finger wiggle movement.

Table 1. Comparison of baby-talk and adult-talk MOTHER signs

	Baby-talk signs	**Adult-talk signs**
Distance from infant/adult	Close	No modification
Handshape	5	5
Orientation	25/27 show full palm or back of hand to infant	20/27—palm faces right or left or slants at angle to floor
Location	11 on chin 15 to side of chin 1 not visible	19 on chin 8 to side of chin chin
Type of movement	27—touch	17—touch 8—FW 2—touch + FW
Number of movements	27—2 or more (10/27—more than 2)	Not more than 2 (9—2 touches 8—1 touch 8—FW)
Face/head	Face fully visible 26/27—mouth movement for word "mother" or "mommy" Eye gaze on infant 12 without voice 14 with voice	9—eyes away 8—no mouth movement 26—without voice 1—with voice
Affect as expressed on the face	24/27—positive 3/27—neutral or negative (infant not attending)	23/27—neutral
Duration:		
Range	9–92 frames	4–25 frames
Mean	24.3 frames[a]	12.3 frames

Thirty frames per second. FW, fingers wiggle.
[a] $Z = 5.50$, $p < .001$.

In addition to the formational differences between baby-talk and adult-talk variants of MOTHER signs, we can see in Table 2 that the linguistic context in which the baby-talk signs occur is quite specific. All of these signs are found in nine types of sentences. In fact, if we collapse sentence numbers 5–9 into one type of sentence, one which names the signer as MOTHER, we find that 19 of the 27 baby-talk signs occur in this kind of linguistic context. The adult-talk MOTHER signs, however, appear in a variety of linguistic contexts.

Table 2. Linguistic context of baby-talk signs

	(n)	Mothers
1. MOTHER LOVE (you)	4	B,B,C,G
2. D-O (you) LOVE (your) MOTHER	2	B,G
3. MOTHER ALWAYS WITH (you)	1	G
4. PULL-MOTHER'S-HAIR (your) MOTHER + S H-A-I-R	1	G
5. (Me) (your) MOTHER	5	C,C,S,S,S
6. (Me) MOTHER HERE	4	G,W,M,Sh
7. (Me) MOTHER	4	W,M,M,M
8. MOTHER	4	Be,Be,Be,Be
9. 2-LOOK-AT-1 (me) MOTHER	2	M,Sh

CONCLUSION

We have presented some evidence that these American deaf mothers modify the sign language they use with their deaf infants under the age of 6 months at least some of the time. When producing the sign MOTHER in baby talk, they (a) place the sign closer to the infant, perhaps the optimal signing distance for visual processing; (b) orient the hand so that the full 5 handshape is visible to the infant; (c) the face, too, is fully available for the infant to see; (d) eye gaze is directed at the infant; (e) the expression on the face is positive and inviting, possibly serving to maintain the infant's interest and engagement while the sign is displayed; (f) the sign is lengthened by repeating the movement, allowing the infant more time to see the sign.

This study adds support to the claim that parents use special articulatory features in their communication with infants (Blount, 1982) including parents from a visual culture whose primary means of communication is visual-gestural rather than auditory-vocal. These deaf mothers have the cultural knowledge about how to interact with their infants in this special environment in order to get and maintain their attention, to focus their attention on signing as an activity, and to begin to relate the interaction to the environment in a meaningful way. We see, then, that during the first months of life, deaf infants who have deaf, signing parents are acquiring the necessary foundation for further language socialization through interaction which is structured according to the requirements of a visual-gestural language.

SIGN LANGUAGE SYSTEMS

15

MANUALLY CODED ENGLISH VS "NATURAL" SIGN LANGUAGES

Manually Coded English is a generic descriptive term for a variety of visual communication methods expressed through the hands which attempt to represent the English language. Unlike 'natural' Deaf Sign Languages, MCE generally follows the grammar and syntax of spoken English. Because of this, forms of MCE can successfully be used with Simultaneous Communication—this is not possible with, for example, American Sign Language, because it involves speaking two different languages at the same time. It is common for a native ASL speaker to code-switch into a form of MCE such as when conversing with someone whose first language is not ASL, or when quoting something in English.

The different forms of Manually Coded English were originally developed for use in the education of deaf children, as their literacy in written English has been typically low compared to their hearing peers. This educational method was popularised by Abbé Charles-Michel de l'Epee who in the 1750s developed a method using hand-signs to teach the French language to deaf children. The educational setting is still the most common place where Manually Coded English is found; not only with deaf students, but also children with other kinds of speech or language difficulties.

The variety of Manually Coded English include Signed Exact English (SEE), Manual Coded English and Pidgin English.

SIGNED EXACT ENGLISH (SEE)

Signed Exact English (SEE) was developed in 1972 by Gerilee Gustason. It is not a language; it is a manually coded form of English that uses ASL signs supplemented with special signs or inflections that allow English to be signed exactly as it is spoken.

The supplemental items added to SEE, which are handled differently in ASL, include things like pronouns, plurals, possession, and the verb "to be". For example, pronouns are handled via spatial reference in ASL, but would be signed as a specific sign representing (for example, the word "he" or "she") the pronoun in SEE. Also, SEE includes special signs for "is", "are", "was" and other forms of the verb "to be", which are just not used in ASL.

SEE is most often used in an educational setting, where the focus is on English as a first language.

Proponents of SEE believe that it helps with learning English, since it manually reproduces English word-for-word in the same order as English.

There is some controversy over whether someone who needs a manual language would be better off with SEE or with ASL. Proponents of ASL point to the fact that it's possible to become skilled in both English and ASL, without signing in SEE. It's very much a personal preference. People who are comfortable with ASL would never sign among themselves in SEE even though they could understand and communicate with someone who did sign in SEE. In practice, people who use SEE often sign in Pidgin Signed English (PSE) rather than "exact" English. PSE is neither ASL nor SEE, but is perhaps best described as a combination of both.

PIDGIN SIGN ENGLISH

What kind of sign language is it when you do not sign pure ASL with its own grammar, or use signed exact English? It is called pidgin sign(ed) English, or PSE. A more recent term is "contact signing."

PSE is not a true language and lacks rules. It is viewed by sign linguistics experts as a way to "bridge" the gap between native ASL speakers and native English speakers. Native speakers can be either deaf or hearing. It contains a mix of ASL rules and English grammar. The signs used in PSE come from ASL, but they are not used in an ASL-ish way, but rather in a more normal English pattern.

PSE speakers also may not utilize certain elements of the English language such as the words "the," etc., to speed up communication.

SIGNED ENGLISH

Signed English is also signed while speaking English simultaneously. English word order is generally used. This manual code was originally meant for young children, even though entire programs began using this method. Some signers are more conceptual in their signing, while others tend to be literal signers.

Most of the signs in Signed English have ASL origins. Bornstein's basic rules are: sign either a word alone or a sign word and one sign marker; fingerspell words not provided in the dictionary; and create plurals by repeating the signs for nouns.

Signed English has fourteen affix markers (e.g. ing, -s, -ed, -y etc.) Signed English has fewer markers than SEE-2 and once the child understands the use of the marker, adult users may drop the marker.

The verb "to be" is signed. Homonyms are sometimes signed the same and other times are signed based on the conceptual meaning.

16

CUED SPEECH

Amy R. Ruberi

THE MARYLAND CUED SPEECH ASSOCIATION ANSWERS FREQUENTLY ASKED QUESTIONS ABOUT CUED SPEECH

A few definitions and acronyms commonly used:

CS = Cued Speech
D/HOH = deaf and hard of hearing
phonemes = the building blocks of a spoken language, perhaps better understood as the basic sounds of a language. English has approximately 43 different phonemes. For example, the word "comb" has three phonemes—/k/ /oe/ /m/
spoken language = In this case, we are focusing on spoken American English, although CS has been adapted to over 55 languages all over the world.

Phonics? Phoneme? Phonemic? Phonetic? What's the difference between these terms and how do they relate to Cued Speech?

All of these terms are related to sound and how we use it for language. When the sounds of speech are represented by a set of distinct symbols we are using *phonetics.* The noun *phonics* refers to the study of sound or the use of phonetics in the teaching of reading. *Phonemes* are the smallest unit of speech/language that distinguish one utterance from another. Cued Speech (CS) is *phonemically* based because we cue the distinct phonemes of a traditionally spoken language.

What is Cued Speech?

Cued Speech is a phonemically based system consisting of the mouth movements utilized in speech, eight handshapes, and four placements of the handshapes. CS eliminates the ambiguity of lipreading, making spoken language recognizable through vision. This tool allows for easy communication between any cueing individuals whether they be hearing, deaf, or hard of hearing without the requirement of sound.

Why was Cued Speech developed?

Cued Speech was developed in 1966 by physicist Dr. R. Orin Cornett at Gallaudet University in order to help improve the literacy of deaf students. Dr. Cornett, who recognized the high levels of cognitive abilities of deaf students, was curious as to why the reading levels of deaf individuals was not higher. Hearing people read what they write, write what they say, and say what they hear. If you can't hear a spoken language, acquiring strong reading and writing skills is difficult. He wanted to find a way to enable deaf individuals to achieve their greatest potential in reading and writing. After examining the difficulties of lipreading the English language, he devised the Cued Speech system to take away the ambiguity of lipreading.

Who uses Cued Speech?

The list of individuals using CS continually grows. Many people are now taking advantage of the benefits of CS: D/HOH and hearing individuals of all ages: children, parents, friends, teachers, communication specialists, speech therapists, and extended family members.

Why do individuals use Cued Speech?

Hearing parents use CS to convey their native language to their children. CS provides a strong language base for deaf children by facilitating clear and fluid communication between all individuals. CS provides many individuals with access to complete communication.

When is Cued Speech used?

All the time. People cue to each other when they wish to have clear, easy communication. This happens in a myriad of environments, between a variety of individuals, at any time of day.

What are the advantages of using Cued Speech?

Utilizing CS has numerous advantages. CS facilitates the development of language, reading, and writing skills. It aids in the decoding of new words when reading and the acquisition of lipreading skills. It allows full communication between all users of CS regardless of hearing status.

Does CS help with phonics instruction for reading?

Yes! The phonemes we cue can be represented in writing using phonetics, the basis of phonics.

Does using Cued Speech prevent the learning or using of signed languages?

No. Many cuers, regardless of hearing status, know how to sign. The sign skills of these individuals range from rudimentary signed English to solid American Sign Language (ASL) skills.

How does Cued Speech work?

CS is a road map for lipreading that takes all the guess work out of any spoken message. Lipreading without cues is similar to reading a map with only the horizontal or vertical coordinates. You may know that you are going to a location in column B but have to search each grid square to find it. On the other hand you may figure out that the desired location is in row two, but are unaware of the correct column. CS allows the lipreader to know both coordinates simultaneously, removing the ambiguity of lipreading alone and providing a complete map to a traditionally spoken language. The combination of handshapes, placements, and mouth movements complete the map. No sound is required, although sound can add information to lip movements for many individuals.

How do you cue?

Remember this rule: If phonemes look the same on the lips, they must be cued differently on the hands; and if phonemes are cued the same on the hands, they must look different on the lips. This rule applies for the entire CS system, thus providing the road map to understanding a spoken language. Look at the Vowel and Consonant Code and Cuescript Chart below to see how the phonemes are grouped together.

To receive Cued Speech you must watch lip movements carefully, seeing the handshape and the hand placement at the same time. The placement of the hand shows the vowel group, and the shape of the hand shows the consonant group. The words met, pet, bet, men, and pen all look alike on the lips, but have different hand cues to show which one the speaker is saying. Conversely, many words can be cued in the same way, because they look very different on the mouth, such as meet, team, term and feet.

To cue you place a handshape at a placement to show a consonant and a vowel. The first handshape usually taught represents the sounds /m/, /f/, and /t/ represented by handshape number 5. The vowel sound /ee/ is cued at the corner of the mouth. Hence words such as /mee/, /fee/, and /tee/ are all cued with the #5 handshape at the mouth placement. The mouth will indicate the consonant in each word. We also use handshape 5 to cue a vowel phoneme that occurs with no preceding consonant. Consonants without a subsequent vowel are cued at the side placement. For example eat is cued /ee/ at the mouth and /t/ at the side. We always move to the side position for a final consonant at the end of a word.

An example of a word being cued appears on the next page.

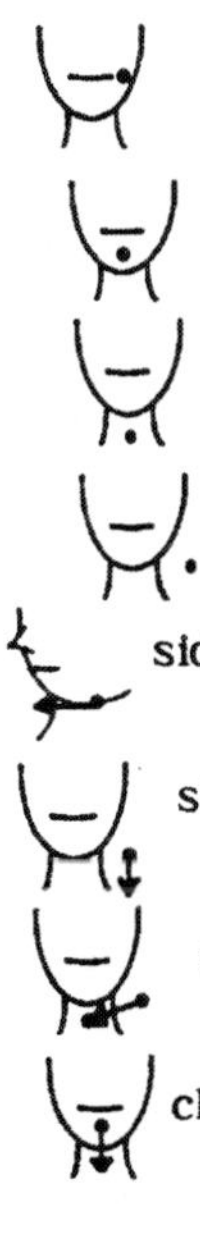

handshape & #	phonemes	phrase	placement	phonemees	phrase
1	/d, zh, p/	**déja pu**	mouth	/ee, er/	**see her**
2	/TH, k, v, z/	**the caves**	chin	/ue, aw, e/	**too tall Ted**
3	/h, s, r/	**he saw red**	throat	/i, a, oo/	**hit that wolf**
4	/b, hw, n/	**white notebook**	side	ø vowel	placement when there is no phoneme present, eg: in "tree", t has no vowel after it
5	/m, f, t/ handshape 5 is also used when no consonant phoneme is present, eg: "I"	**miffed**	side-forward	/oe, ah/	**Oh, Mom!**
6	/w, l, sh/	**Welsh**	side-down	/uh/	**Duh!**
7	/j, g, tH/	**joggeth**	side-throat	/ie, ow/	**eyebrow**
8	/y, ng, ch/	**young child**	chin-throat	/oi, ae/	**Oy vay!**

Who can I contact to get more information about CS?

Maryland Cued Speech Association(MDCSA)
An affiliate of the National Cued Speech Association, P.O. Box 9173, Silver Spring, MD 20916.

National Cued Speech Association (NCSA)
The NCSA has a rotating address which travels with the association president. The current address can be found through Cued Speech Discovery Bookstore. The address from Fall 1996–1998 is: Cathy Quenin, Speech-Language Pathology Department, Nazareth College of Rochester, 4245 East Avenue, Rochester, NY 14618-3790.

Cued Speech Discovery Bookstore
The Bookstore of the National Cued Speech Association: 23790 Hermitage Road, Cleveland, Ohio 44122-4008, 1-800-459-3529.

TECUnit (Testing, Evaluation, & Certification Unit)
P.O. Box 3116, Silver Spring, MD 20918, (301)434-1137. This organization provides assessments of professional transliteration and basic cueing as well as, certification of transliterators.

Language Matters, Inc.
P.O. Box 3326, Silver Spring, MD 20918, (301)439–5766. LMI provides resources designed in support of language learning and language use among Deaf and hearing people. They offer educational opportunities, educational materials, and interpreting / transliterating services through various divisions.

What other materials are available to learn about CS?
Contact Cued Speech Discovery and Language Matters Inc. for catalogs of available materials.

Here is an example of the phrase "I cue," being cued:

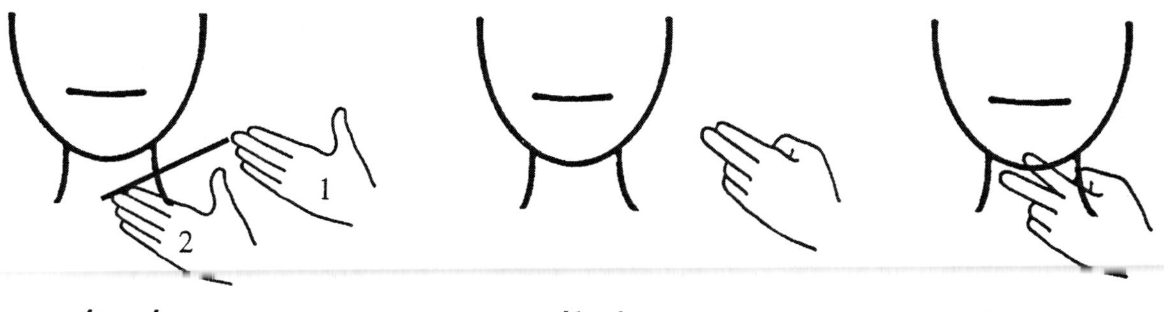

/ie/ /k/ /yue/

17

GESTUNO: INTERNATIONAL SIGN LANGUAGE

Travis Rolan Jones

"GESTUNO"

The need to communicate is universal. For those within the deaf community, the need to communicate in sign is universal. Just as there are languages in the world, there are thousands upon thousands of different signed languages, each with its own "accent" and "dialect." Every different sign language is a reflection of its past, the culture in which it expanded, and the mores of its society (Grunberg 1). So what do you do when you try to gather together people of the deaf communities from all four corners of the globe? You devise an international sign language that all are capable of learning and understanding.

As early as 1951, at a gathering of the World Congress of the World Federation of the Deaf, the idea of "unifying" the sign languages was being discussed (handspeak.com). They realized that having hundreds of interpreters at every event just wasn't feasible. So around 1973 a committee was given the task to devise and standardize a system of international gestures. The Commission on Unification of Signs of the World Federation of the deaf then issued a book of almost 1500 signs, chosen or invented by them and they called the new basic international vocabulary "Gestuno." The name is Italian and roughly translated means "oneness of sign languages" (Moody 1).

Within the World Federation of the Deaf, their official languages, English and French, are still used for documentation and correspondence. Yet in general assemblies and within the bureau, Gestuno is still used. It is still not known though, if everyone fully understands the language. Inside the bureau, Gestuno is far more defined. Members with a broad cultural understanding have been able to communicate many concrete principles as well as abstract ideas. Gestuno is still used at the World Games for the Deaf and at the DEAF WAY Conference and Festival in Washington, D.C., but other than that, its use is very limited (Grunberg 2).

Like "Esperante," the idea of unifying sign language hasn't been as prolific as the Commission first intended. There just are not that many people that have been willing to learn the new language. And with the highly developed translating devices of today and the skilled hands of international translators, who would really want to take the time to learn a language no one else knows (Moody 81)?

Within the last few years in Europe, a lingua franca has developed. A sort of "creole sign language" that some have begun calling an international sign language. Whether it will ever catch on or not is unknown but is something to watch (deaflibrary.org).

18

INTERNATIONAL HAND ALPHABET CHARTS

Simon J. Carmel

INTRODUCTION

The origin of the use of the hand alphabet, also called *dactylology,* is not known, although it had been practiced for many centuries before the Middle Ages. Very early, monks had employed the manual alphabet to communicate with each other without violating their strict vows of silence. Strangely, it was not applied for communication with the deaf.

Claiming that the Spanish people were the first to use the one-hand alphabet in teaching the deaf, several manuscripts and books document that the learned Benedictine monk named Pedro Ponce de Leon (1520–1584) was the very first instructor of the deaf around the middle of the 16th century, although there was no known manuscript or book describing a hand alphabet for the deaf (Bender 1970: 39–42; Werner 1932). A Franciscan monk, Fray Melchor de Yebra (1526–1586) was the first to write a book, *Libro llamado Refugium infirmorum . . . ,* which describes and illustrates an actual hand alphabet for the particular use of deaf-mutes. It was not published until seven years after his death (Habig 1936: 287–292; Werner 1932:244). It is a rare work written at the end of the 16th century. (See the illustrations below.) There are 22 letters which are expressed by 21 signs since Y is the same as Z. Later, in 1620, in Madrid, Juan Pablo Bonet (1579–1629?) published the first known book for the teachers of the deaf, the earliest treatise on teaching the deaf to speak and write; it contains illustrations of the Spanish hand alphabet (Bender 1970: 42–45; Farrar 1923: 9–14; Werner 1932). See Bonet's Spanish Hand Alphabet below, which closely resembles Yebra's illustrations of the hand alphabet.

Around the middle of the 18th century the Spanish manual alphabet was introduced into France by Jacob Rodriguez Pereire (1715–1780), who, it is claimed, was probably the first teacher of the deaf in France. Born at Berlanga in Spanish Estremadura, he belonged to a family of Spanish Jews who were expelled by persecution to Portugal and then to Bordeaux, in southern France, where they settled in 1741. Pereire had a deaf sister whom he had become interested in teaching. Seeking for a method of instructing the deaf, he probably received books from a friend in Spain, as early as 1734, and studied them. Possibly, one of them revealed to him the manual alphabet by Bonet. Later he started to instruct other deaf pupils. In 1749 he presented one of his outstanding deaf students before the French Academy of Sciences in Paris. Appointed by the Academy, a commission studied the value and results of Pereire's teaching method and especially commented on the important use of the manual alphabet. As a result,

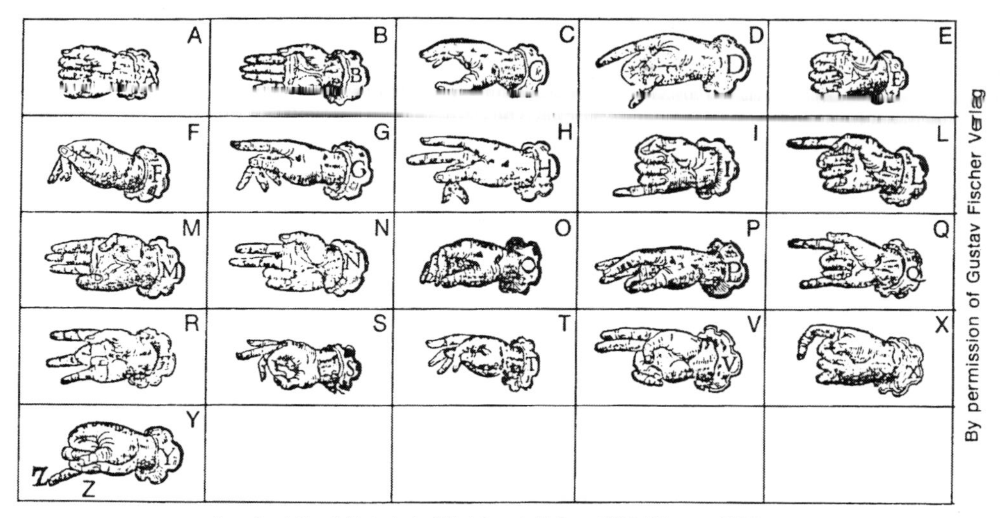

Spaniard Hand Alphabet of Melchor de Yebra, 1593 (Werner 1932)

Pereire's achievements were recognized. The most distinctive feature of Pereire's method was the use of Spanish hand alphabet which he claimed to have expanded and augmented to conform to French orthography and pronunciation (Bender 1970:73–77; Farrar 1923:32–37; Lane 1976:171–172). But we have almost no information about the earliest uses of manual alphabets in France.

In 1760 the Abbé Charles-Michel de l'Epée (1712–1789) unexpectedly met two deaf twin sisters in Paris and became interested in them. He then decided to instruct them. He had known a two-handed alphabet since his childhood (Farrar 1923:40; Green 1861:12). Subsequently, he founded the first French public school for the deaf in Paris, regardless of social conditions. Some documents state that de l'Epée was acquainted with the teaching system employed by Pereire and used the manual alphabet in instruction (Farrar 1923:44), although he had never met Pereire nor any of his pupils (Green 1861:12). However, another document states that an admirer who had witnessed a public instruction, sold to de l'Epée a Spanish book that contained a beautiful illustration of the manual alphabet of Bonet (Bender 1970:80; Farrar 1923:42–47).

After the death of the Abbé de l'Epée, Roche-Ambroise Sicard (1742–1822) became the director of the school in Paris. He continued the use of the one-handed alphabet, accompanied with methodical signs. An alphabet very similar to de l'Epée's was then brought to the United States by the young American Thomas Hopkins Gallaudet (1787–1851) who came to Paris in 1815 to acquire the art of teaching the deaf for his country. With French signs and the modified "Spanish" hand alphabet, Gallaudet returned to the United States in 1816, accompanied by Laurent Clerc (1785–1869), the gifted deaf French teacher. The following year, on April 15, 1817, the Hartford School for the Deaf was founded. Thus, the French manual alphabet with several modifications became the *American* hand alphabet.

Meanwhile, the French manual alphabet from Paris was introduced into different countries in Europe between 1779 and 1846 (von der Lieth 1967:63), with various modifications according to their respective linguistic orthographies. Other manual alphabets (for example, Austria, Denmark, Italy, Russia) have some clear similarities to the French alphabet, but they may have developed independently of the French traditions. We simply do not have enough historical information yet in this area.

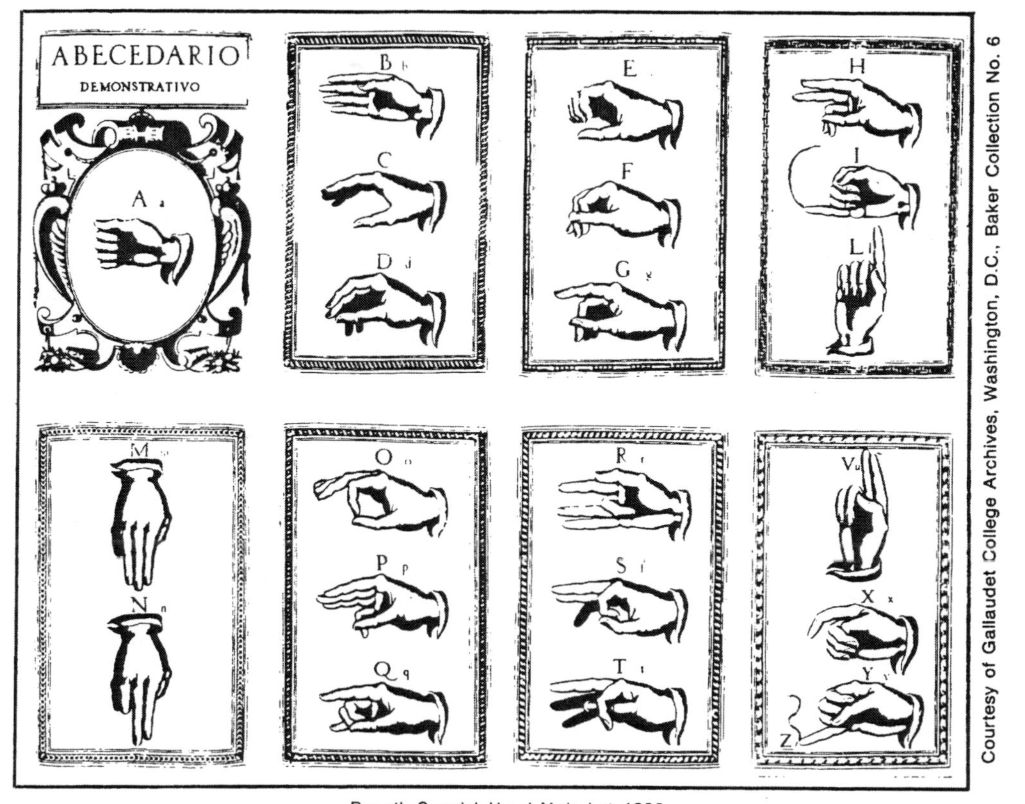

Courtesy of Gallaudet College Archives, Washington, D.C., Baker Collection No. 6

Bonet's Spanish Hand Alphabet, 1620

The two-handed manual alphabet has been widely used in Great Britain since the seventeenth century. There is no record to reveal who the inventor of this system was, but it was published in a book, *Digiti Lingua,* by an anonymous author in London in 1698 (see page 26). The handshapes for vowels are very close to those of the British two-handed alphabet today. Most of the handshapes for consonants are also very close.

Two-handed alphabets similar to the British one were or are still in use in a number of countries. But in recent years there has been a trend to adopt a one-handed alphabet as an international standard, beginning with the Fourth Congress of the World Federation of the Deaf in Stockholm, Sweden in 1963. The alphabet adopted there is shown on page 87 as the International Hand Alphabet. Its varieties, and similarities and differences between it and the manual alphabet of the U.S.A., are discussed on page 76.

I would like to point out something interesting about the letter "T" in several hand charts, which is seemingly controversial. For instance, the American "T" is not used in France, Spain or other countries, because it is considered an extremely obscene sign in these countries, but it is a "good luck" sign in some South American countries. Therefore, the "T" from the Swedish chart was adopted in the international hand alphabet in order to lessen unfortunate connotations.

Any information or comments from readers regarding these or additional hand alphabet charts would be greatly appreciated.

The International Hand Alphabet shown on the next page was adopted at the Fourth Congress of the World Federation of the Deaf (WFD) in Stockholm, Sweden, in 1963. The handshapes are similar to those of the standard hand alphabet in the United States of America, and also to several other one-handed alphabets of Europe.

Differences are most obvious in forms of the letter "T". The handshape used for "T" in the U.S.A. is regarded as an obscene gesture in France, parts of South America, Italy, Spain, Romania, and many other countries. In Europe there are two handshapes used widely for "T". The one shown here is used mainly in northern Europe. Another handshape with the weaker fingers opened (see for example France) is used mainly in southern Europe, and in parts of South America. A third handshape is used in certain nations of Asia (see for example Hong Kong). We might thus speak of "dialects" of an International Hand Alphabet, slight differences which do not make serious problems for communication among deaf people.

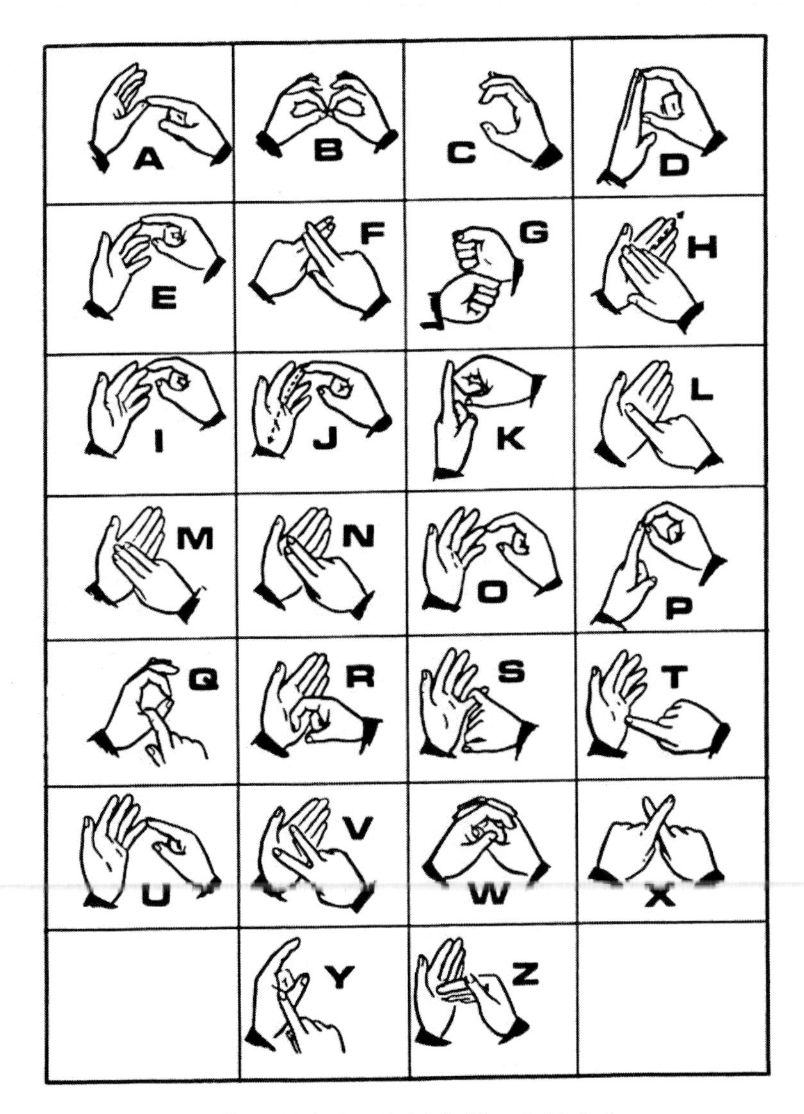

Great Britain: British Hand Alphabet

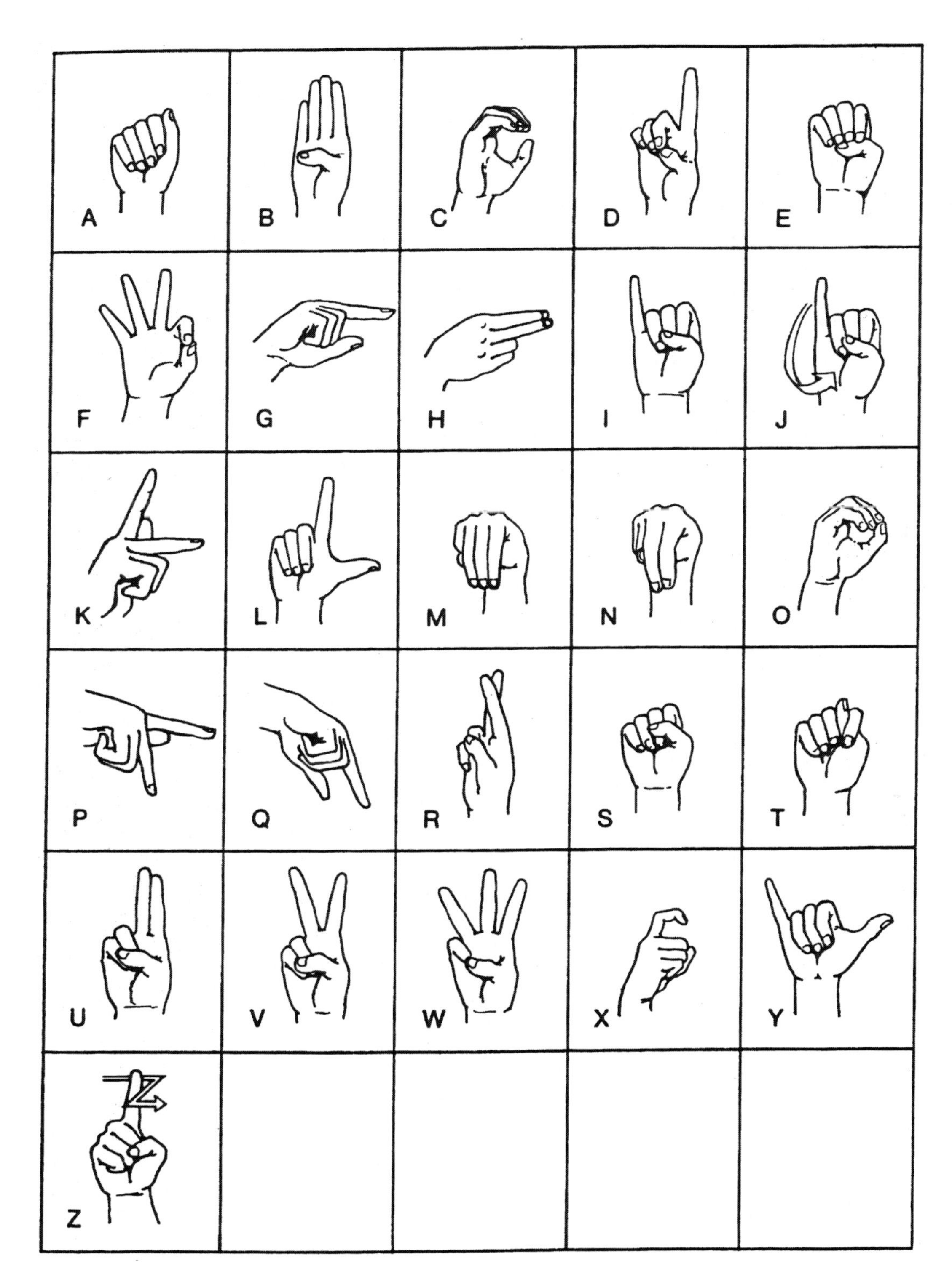

United States America: American Hand Alphabet

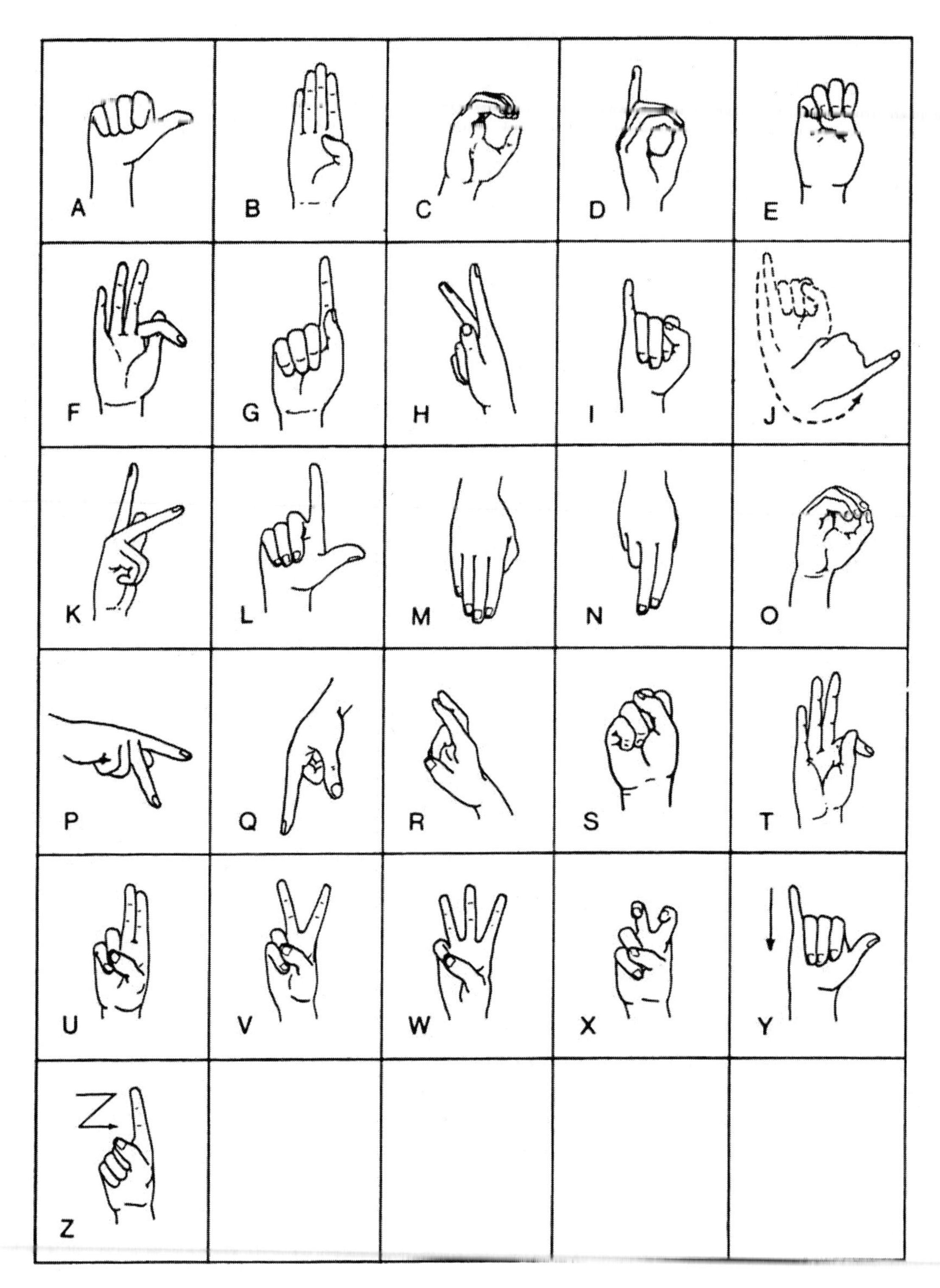

France: French Hand Alphabet

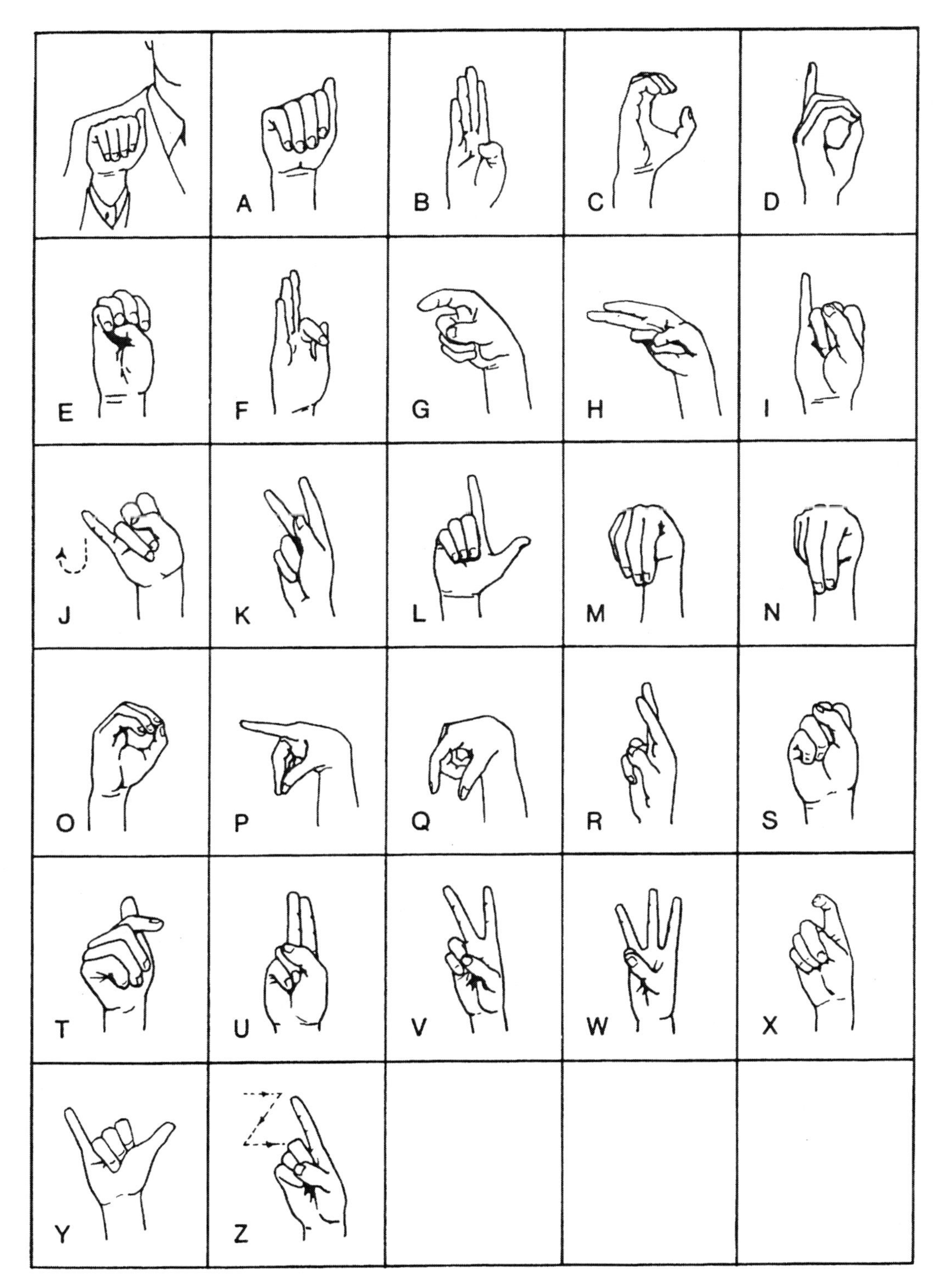

International Hand Alphabet Chart

DEAF CULTURE: CULTURAL SELF IDENTITY

19

TERMINOLOGY USED TO REFER TO DEAF PEOPLE

Michael Schwartz

A long time ago it was acceptable to refer to a deaf person as "deaf-and-dumb." Many institutions that shouldered the responsibility for caring and educating deaf children were called "Institution for the Deaf and Dumb." The term, "dumb," did not mean that the person was stupid or low in intelligence; rather it was a reference to the inability of many deaf children and adults to speak. Not being able to speak gave rise to another common term: "deaf-mute."

"Dummy" was another expression used to denote a Deaf person. William Ellsworth (1862–1961), known as "Dummy Hoy," was a deaf baseball pitcher who helped umpires develop hand signals to inform the pitcher of the count at the plate and whether a runner was safe or out at a base. Luther Haden (1875–1958), another deaf baseball player who enjoyed a 21–15 season for the 1904 New York Giants, was called "Dummy Taylor." "Dummy" was also the moniker for a deaf African American man charged with the murder of a prostitute in Chicago in the early 1960s. Because these men were deaf, the media affixed the term, "Dummy," to their names, all because these deaf men could not speak. In these days being called "Dummy," "deaf-and-dumb," or "deaf-mute" carried no stigma or shame.

Today the terms, "deaf-and-dumb" and "Dummy" have fallen out of favor. The reference to "dumbness" nowadays carries a negative connotation: the person so labeled is considered lacking in intelligence. The Deaf community takes offense at this term, and it is no longer used in books, movies, schools, the workplace and other public sites. However, the term, "deaf-mute," has proved to be more resilient. It still retains a place in many English language dictionaries. Many newspaper articles use it in referring to deaf people. It pops up in colloquial conversations around the country. Until a few years ago the leading law dictionary used by thousands of law students and professors listed the term so that when a lawyer looked up the word, "Deaf," his or her assumption that Deaf people cannot speak was reinforced.

The truth of the matter is, many Deaf people can speak or vocalize intelligibly enough to be understood by a hearing person. Speech training is available for many deaf children in the public schools as well as the residential schools for the deaf. Ninety percent of deaf children are born to hearing parents, and many of these children are raised under the oral method, which stresses speech training and lip-reading practice. Many acquire the ability to speak intelligibly. By no stretch of the imagination can these children and adults be termed, "mute."

The most appropriate term, and the simplest, is "deaf" or "Deaf." The former refers to a deaf person who regards himself as a person with a medical condition, while the latter refers to a Deaf person who identifies with a larger community of Deaf people and a Deaf culture. As many Deaf people view it, the former term retains a medical flavor, and the latter term reflects a political consciousness of their place in the larger community. Another appropriate term for some people is "hard-of-hearing," which refers to people who are not totally deaf but have residual hearing in one or both ears, enough to hear sounds, listen to music and speak over the telephone. Many hard-of-hearing people do not consider themselves part of the Deaf community.

20

AUDISM

Tom Harrington

Audism (from Latin *audire,* to hear, and *-ism,* a system of practice, behavior, belief, or attitude) has been variously defined as:

- ... the belief that life without hearing is futile and miserable, that hearing loss is a tragedy and "the scourge of mankind," and that deaf people should struggle to be as much like hearing people as possible. Deaf activists Heidi Reed and Hartmut Teuber at D.E.A.F. Inc., a community service and advocacy organization in Boston, consider audism to be "a special case of ableism." Audists, hearing or deaf, shun Deaf culture and the use of sign language, and have what Reed and Teuber describe as "an obsession with the use of residual hearing, speech, and lip-reading by deaf people." (Pelka 1997: 33)
- The notion that one is superior based on one's ability to hear or behave in the manner of one who hears. (Zak 1996)
- ... an attitude based on pathological thinking which results in a negative stigma toward anyone who does not hear; like racism or sexism, audism judges, labels, and limits individuals on the basis of whether a person hears and speaks. (Humphrey and Alcorn 1995: 85)
- ... the corporate institution for dealing with deaf people, dealing with them by making statements about them, authorizing views of them, describing them, teaching about them, governing where they go to school and, in some cases, where they live; in short, audism is the hearing way of dominating, restructuring, and exercising authority over the deaf community. It includes such professional people as administrators of schools for deaf children and of training programs for deaf adults, interpreters, and some audiologists, speech therapists, otologists, psychologists, psychiatrists, librarians, researchers, social workers, and hearing aid specialists. (Lane 1992: 43)

Persons who practice audism are called *audists.* Audists may be hearing or deaf.

The first appearance of the term *audism* in print seems to have been by Harlan Lane in 1992. However, Lane credits the invention of the term to Tom Humphries' unpublished 1977 doctoral dissertation (Humphries 1977). After Humphries coined the term *audism,* it laid dormant until Lane revived its use 15 years later. It is increasingly catching on, though not yet in regular dictionaries of the English language. Humphries originally applied *audism* to individual attitudes and practices, but Lane and others have broadened its scope to include institutional and group attitudes, practices, and oppression of deaf persons.

The first half of Lane's book *The mask of benevolence: disabling the deaf community* is the most extensive published survey and discussion of audism so far (Lane 1992).

21

REFLECTIONS OF AMERICAN DEAF CULTURE IN DEAF HUMOR

M. J. Bienvenu

Mainstream American culture teaches that "normal" people are born with five senses: hearing, sight, smell, taste, and touch. Of course, Deaf people can't hear, and this causes many people to view the Deaf as deficient and deprived. But nothing could be further from the truth—we have always had five senses: sight, smell, taste, touch, and a sense of humor.

Humor is one way that people share their perceptions of the world, express different levels of intimacy, and find comfort in knowing that others share their beliefs. I am going to focus specifically on four categories which reflect the values, norms, and belief systems of our American Deaf Culture.

VISUAL

As most of you know, Deaf people perceive most things through their eyes. We acquire language visually. It is worth noting that Sign Languages throughout the world adapt to meet the visual needs and comfort of the people who use them. We also acquire world knowledge visually. It should come as no surprise, then, that Deaf humor also has a strong visual base. To many Deaf people, the world is filled with comical sights. But the humor is not always apparent to the majority of hearing Americans.

An experience I had several years ago may illustrate this point: One night while I was coordinating an intensive ASL retreat for a group of non-Deaf people, we gathered together to watch the movie *King Kong* on TV. The volume was off, and for the first time, they realized what Deaf audiences have known all along: the actors' expressions are hysterically funny. As New Yorkers were running for their lives with the shadow of a monster ape looming over their heads, our group was laughing uncontrollably. I asked them what they found so funny. They replied, "Their faces!" The same people would have felt frightened if they had heard the actors screaming in terror or, with threatening music in the background. Instead, they got a glimpse of the movies from a Deaf perspective.

Deaf people find many visual things humorous which aurally dependent people may not. Often Deaf people are quite creative in their descriptions of people and events. This talent is fostered in residential schools where many children learn the art of storytelling, and most importantly, how to vividly re-create events and characters. When I was in school, no one was safe from our stories. Every identifying characteristic of a person would be imitated, right down to the way s/he walked. This intricate detail is a crucial part of the humor, because it reflects how acutely Deaf people perceive the world, and how adept a tool our language is for expressing our perceptions.

Often people who are not members of the culture will respond negatively to this form of humor. This is a common misunderstanding with outsiders. Deaf people are not insulting the individuals whom we describe; we are delighting in the precision of our language to accurately convey these details. Our culture is reinforced through the shared experience of how we, as a group, see the world and translate it into humor.

CAN'T HEAR

As we all know, deafness is much more than the inability to hear. It is a complete culture, where one's decibel loss is far less important than one's allegiance to the Deaf Community. Yet, a significant amount of Deaf folklore contains jokes and stories which deal with the inability to hear.

There are many stories that have been handed down for generations in Deaf folklore which illustrate the convenience of deafness. The following popular tale shows how Deaf people can solve a problem creatively and humorously: *A Deaf couple arrives at a motel for their honeymoon. After unpacking, the nervous husband goes out to get a drink. When he returns to the motel, he realizes that he has fogotten the room number. It is dark outside and all the rooms look identical. He walks to his car, and leans on the horn. He then waits for the lights to come on in the rooms of the waking angry hearing guests. All the rooms are lit up except his, where his Deaf wife is waiting for him!*

Interestingly, in Ray Holcomb's book, *Hazards of Deafness,* the humor does not follow the culturally Deaf tradition, but rather focuses on stories in which Deaf people lament their "condition." This humor is typical of an "outsider's" view of deafness. Here is an example of one of the scenes in the book: *A deaf person is having a difficult time vacuuming the carpet. He goes over the same spot of dirt repeatedly, to no avail. In a fit of frustration, he turns around and notices that the machine is unplugged.*

This is a perfect example of humor that is *not* Deaf centered. Such a situation would never happen because a Deaf person would naturally feel that the motor was not running and immediately respond appropriately. What is most disturbing is the emphasis on hearing and the dependency on sound which the book portrays. Culturally Deaf people are quite articulate in defining the world in terms other than sound, and have adapted to technology as swiftly as non-Deaf people. The fact that the author does not address Deaf people's keenly developed sense of sight and touch is rather significant.

LINGUISTIC

Another component of Deaf humor can be categorized as linguistic. Production and misproduction of signs is a common way to elicit laughs in ASL. One example, described in Bellugi and Klima's book, *The Signs of Language,* is how we can change the root sign, UNDERSTAND, to LITTLE UNDERSTAND by using the pinkie rather than the index finger.

Much of this linguistic humor is lexically based, and the punch lines to many ASL jokes are related to the production of the words. One of my favorites is the "giant" joke. It is funny both culturally and linguistically: *A huge giant is stalking through a small village of wee people, who are scattering through the streets, trying to escape the ugly creature. The Giant notices one particularly beautiful blonde woman scampering down the cobble-stoned street. He stretches out his clumsy arm and sweeps her up, then stares in won-*

der at the slight, shivering figure in his palm. "You are so beautiful," he exclaims. The young woman looks up in fear. "I would never hurt you," he signs, "I love you! We should get MARRIED." Producing the sign MARRY, he crushes her. The giant then laments, "See, oralism, is better."

There are several components which make this joke successful in American Sign Language. First, it is visually active, because the expressions of the townspeople, the beautiful girl, and the giant can be dramatized to perfection. Secondly, it is linguistically funny because of the sign production MARRY which causes the girl of his affection to splat in his palm. Thirdly, it is humorous in its irony. Culturally Deaf people detest oralism; therefore, the irony in the giant's conclusion that oralism would have saved his beloved girl is funny.

RESPONSE TO OPPRESSION

It is no secret that Deaf people are an oppressed minority, and one way that minority cultures deal with oppression is through humor. Often this category of humor, sometimes called "zap" stories, features Deaf people getting even.

Often when Deaf people are naturally conversing in public, hearing people will stare at them in disbelief. When they finally gain the courage to initiate conversation with a Deaf person, they will inevitably ask, "Can you read my lips?" Well, of course, Deaf people are keenly aware of the configuration of this one sentence, and will always answer "No!" which is pretty funny, indeed.

Another way Deaf humor fights back at oppression is to show hearing people being outsmarted by a Deaf person. One famous example, which is a true story, provides the required ending: *A group of Deaf people was at a restaurant, chatting away when a group of non-Deaf people at the next table began to rudely mimic their signs. One of the Deaf women decided she' d had enough. She walked to the public telephone, inserted a coin, and making sure she was being observed by the hearing group, signed a complete conversation into the handset, including pauses for the person on the other end to respond. When the Deaf group left the restaurant, they were amused to see the hearing people run over to inspect the phone.*

Deaf people love this one, because we finally have the last laugh. These tales are rich with justice, and always the rude offender is put in her/his place.

In the same way that American Deaf Culture, as well as European Deaf Culture, is oppressed by the majority community, so our language is oppressed. From oralism to Signed English systems and other forms of English/sound coding, Deaf people have suffered under the thumb of hearing educators for many years. From the signs that these "experts" invent, it is obvious they have little knowledge of Deaf Culture or ASL. Often the invented signs already have an established meaning. Many of them look sexual, and are really inappropriate for young children to see, which is ironic, since school systems teach them. It's even worse when they are printed in "sign language" books. Deaf children leaf through these sign-code manuals with delight, snickering at all the "dirty" signs pictured in the textbook.

As one response to these oppressive attempts at linguistic isolation, Deaf people have chosen to incorporate into their discourse some of the artificial codes created from the oral/cued speech/Signed English systems. Coded signs for IS, AM, ARE, WERE, BE, -ING, -ED, etc. have all been reclaimed by Deaf speakers, and used with sarcasm directed toward those who created them. Of course, the humor is most pronounced when a contorted face accompanies the deviant signs—an editorial on the ineffectiveness of these codes.

In closing, let me say that humor is an essential part of our lives. I'm sure you've all heard the expression, "laughter is the best medicine." Well, there is much truth to that, particularly when you analyze minority cultures, and realize that they all incorporate fighting back at oppression into their humor. It is a common response to the frustration of our everyday lives, for in humor, the storyteller determines who will "win." Someone told me this joke the other day, and it seemed like a perfect way to end my presentation:

Three people are on a train—one is Russian, one is Cuban, and one is Deaf. The Russian is drinking from a bottle of vodka. She drinks about half the bottle, then throws it out the window. The Deaf person looks at her, surprised. "Why did you throw out a bottle that was only half-empty?" The Russian replies, "Oh, in my country we have plenty of vodka." Meanwhile, the Cuban is smoking a rich, aromatic cigar. He smokes about half the cigar, then throws it out the window. The Deaf person is again surprised, and asks, "Why did you throw out the cigar?" He replies, "Oh, in Cuba we have plenty of cigars!" The Deaf person nods with interest. A little while later a hearing person walks down the aisle. The Deafie picks him up and tosses him out the window. The Russian and Cuban look up in amazement. The Deaf Person shrugs, "Oh, we have plenty of hearing people in the world."

22

CULTURAL PATTERNS OF DEAF PEOPLE

Linda A. Siple

With the onset of multicultural awareness, Americans are now viewing society as a "tossed salad" of cultural diversity versus a "melting pot" of homogenized members. Even the terms we are now using reflect a changing attitude toward those many cultures that co-exist within American culture. No longer are these various cultures referred to as subcultures, implying inferiority or secondary status. The term *co-culture* is now being used to recognize the equal status and equal importance of the culture. Increased interest in the co-cultures of the United States has encouraged researchers to take a closer look at the cultural patterns that make these groups unique. Of late, co-cultures drawing the most attention have been the cultures of African-Americans (Weber, 1991), Latinos (Albert & Triandis, 1991), Native Americans (Madrid, 1991), and the cultural differences that exist between men and women (Tannen, 1990). Awareness of the multicultural nature of the United States has led to the identification of otherwise overlooked groups that also manifest cultural characteristics. For example, the aged (Carmichael, 1991), paraplegics (Braithwaite, 1991), and gays (Majors, 1991), to name a few, have received attention.

Deaf culture, although manifesting significant differences in language, behavior, values, and beliefs, has not been fully recognized as a domestic co-culture of the United States. The main reason for this oversight is twofold. Deafness is viewed by the majority as a disabling condition that should be corrected. From this perspective, a reasonable conclusion would be that anyone who is Deaf would like to be cured of this condition. Therefore, it does not make sense to view Deaf people as voluntarily belonging to a social system based on this identity. Second, the very nature of deafness presents a major communication obstacle. Without knowledge of Sign Language, the only avenues left to communicate are writing and speech on the part of the hearing individual, and writing, speech reading, and use of any residual hearing on the part of the Deaf person. Both modes assume the Deaf person knows English and can effectively speech read. These abilities will vary greatly depending on the Deaf individual, but, regardless of ability, communication becomes a chore instead of a naturally flowing interchange.

The view that deafness is disabling and its resulting communication barrier have both prevented the hearing majority from learning about the cultural patterns of the Deaf and, as a result, has led to stereotypes

From *The Journal of Intercultural Relations,* Volume 18 (1994), 345–367. Reprinted by permission of the publisher. Linda A. Siple is affiliated with the Rochester Institute of Technology at the National Technical Institute for the Deaf Center for Sign Language and Interpreting Education.

and the use of terms such as *deaf mute* or *deaf and dumb*—labels that more accurately reflect the point of view of the labeler, not the abilities of the labeled.

Viewing deafness as a disabling condition has led to seeing behavioral differences as evidence of social immaturity, eccentricities, lack of intelligence, or even signs of mental illness. According to Lane (1988), many of the studies conducted on Deaf people "reflect not the characteristics of Deaf people but the paternalistic posture of the hearing experts making these attributions" (p. 7).

Having more than 20 years experience as a Sign Language interpreter and Professor of Interpreting at the National Technical Institute for the Deaf in Rochester, New York, I have seen how these misconceptions have led to discrimination and communication conflict. By viewing the Deaf as a group with a unique culture, behavioral differences take on new meanings. This article discusses several cultural characteristics of the Deaf community in America and presents evidence for viewing Deaf people as a co-culture. The information presented within this article comes from numerous printed sources as well as personal experience interacting with the culture.

BACKGROUND

According to the National Center for Health Statistics, there are approximately 20 million Americans who have some type of hearing loss; however, very few of these people know Sign Language or consider themselves members of Deaf culture. There are approximately 1 million Americans who use American Sign Language (ASL) and consider themselves members of Deaf culture.

Those who are deaf and do not use Sign Language tend to have enhanced visual perception; however, these individuals do not exhibit significant behavioral differences from the hearing majority. The cultural differences discussed in this article are specifically related to differences in language, behavior, values, and beliefs exhibited by the 1 million deaf individuals who make up Deaf culture.

The causes of deafness vary throughout history due to epidemics or medical advances. However, of the current population, the best estimates are that 50% of early childhood deafness is inherited. Up to 40% is recessive and 10% is dominant (Moores, 1987). "Maternal rubella was identified as the greatest cause of hearing loss in the middle 1960s and has been recognized as the major non genetic cause of deafness in school-age children in the 1980s" (Moores, 1987, p. 104). Other commonly reported causes include mother–child blood incompatibility, spinal meningitis, scarlet fever, prematurity, congenital cytomegalovirus infection (i.e., herpes virus), whooping cough, and accident or injury. Furthermore, many recent studies investigating the etiology of deafness still cite "etiology unknown" as accounting for more than 30% of the total number of reported cases (Moores, 1987; Schein & Delk, 1974; Vernon, 1968)—a surprising number given our current level of medical sophistication.

A unique aspect of Deaf culture is that most Deaf children have hearing parents, siblings, and extended family members. Less than 10% of Deaf children have Deaf parents. This is significant because if they are exposed to Deaf culture and Sign Language, it is through contact with other Deaf children and teachers at schools for the Deaf (Moores, 1987).

It is important to note that not all deaf people belong to Deaf culture. As Kannapell (1982) stated, "the degree of hearing loss is not the most important requirement for being in the Deaf community [nor is] sharing a common language . . . enough to be admitted to the Deaf community" (p. 25). Higgins (1989) stated that membership is achieved through "(1) Identification with the Deaf world, (2) shared experiences that come of being Deaf, and (3) participation in the community's activities" (p. 38).

To more fully understand Deaf culture and its communication practices, it is important to discuss the sociocultural elements that make this culture distinct. Porter and Samovar (1988) proposed a model for the analysis of intercultural communication that addresses three main elements of culture: perception, verbal processes, and nonverbal processes.

PERCEPTION

Porter and Samovar (1988) defined perception as "the internal process by which we select, evaluate and organize stimuli from the external environment" (p. 24). That is to say, a culture behaves in certain ways based on how they perceive the world. To understand how a group perceives the world, we must gain an appreciation for its perceptual frames.

Visual Orientation

How one perceives the world is influenced by the communication channel used when exchanging messages. For the Deaf individual, the very nature of deafness shifts the primary channel for information exchange from auditory to visual. The visual channel becomes the mechanism for message exchange, and its use permeates the entire conversational structure. For example, turn taking, back-channel feedback, conversational repairs, and attention getting all follow visual structural rules. The auditory channel, even for those who have some hearing in the speech range, often is not an effective or reliable channel. Of the three most commonly used channels (sight, sound, and touch) the auditory channel is the least utilized. The secondary channel of communication becomes touch. As discussed later, touch serves many important conversational functions.

When channel utilization is compared between hearing individuals and individuals belonging to the Deaf culture (see Table 1), the difference is clear. However, it is not simply that different channels are used but how this difference affects perception.

The Deaf culture's primary utilization of the visual channel influences perception in two major ways. First, the visual channel is continuous whereas the verbal channel is discrete. Speech starts when sound is produced and stops when vocalization ceases. However, the visual channel continues as long as two people are in each other's presence. This factor greatly influences how communication is perceived by Deaf individuals. Discussions with Deaf culture members appears to suggest that "communication" is perceived to occur even if signs are not being exchanged. The following personal experience is particularly illustrative of this point.

Table 1. Channel Utilization

	Hearing	**Deaf**
Visual	Secondary	Primary
Auditory	Primary	Tertiary
Tactile	Tertiary	Secondary

> While attending a lecture at a convention, I ran into a Deaf friend I had not seen for many years. We had a very brief conversation before we needed to sit down and direct our attention to the lecture. When the lecture was completed, my friend needed to leave immediately to catch a plane. I said I felt bad that we didn't have any time to talk. His response was, "We can talk on the TTY anytime, it's actually *seeing* you that is most important to me. Now I feel reconnected with you."

A second perceptual difference is that visual communication is multichanneled, whereas verbal communication is a single-channel event. Baker and Padden (1978) suggested that ASL discourse occurs in five separate visual channels: (a) the hands and arms, (b) the head, (c) the eyes, (d) the face, and (f) the total body posture. A message may be sent using all five channels simultaneously or shift from the hands, to the nose, back to the hands, and end with a change in eye gaze. This multi-channeled approach to communication is particularly evident to hearing individuals who are new to Deaf culture. One student expressed it this way: "I feel visually overwhelmed. I get tired just trying to see it all at once."

This multichanneled approach to communication is further developed in the art of storytelling. A frequent technique used by Deaf individuals when storytelling is called visual vernacular (B. Bragg, personal communication, 1974). It is a technique that makes a visually told story more dynamic through change of perspective. The effect of this technique is similar to what occurs in a movie with change of camera angle. A story may start out with a long shot of the scene, pan various characters, and then take a close-up of one particular character. The use of visual vernacular provides an interesting technique when telling a story that contains two perspectives. For example, a well-known story starts with a long shot showing a calm prairie. Then the scene is presented from the perspective of an eagle searching for food then shifts to the perspective of a rabbit, unaware of potential danger. The story continues to shift back and forth, utilizing many different camera angles, with each scene occurring faster and faster until the killing frenzy is over. The story ends with a long shot. Calm has returned to the prairie as the eagle flies farther and farther away, disappearing out of sight over a mountain (C. Baird personal communication, 1973). …

Cultural Values

Porter and Samovar (1988) identified cultural value as having a direct influence on perception. Values being the evaluative aspect of culture, inform a member what is right or wrong, which behaviors are important and which should be avoided. By analyzing the values of the Deaf culture, a deeper understanding of communication behavior can be gained.

Face-to-Face Communication

Deaf culture places much importance on face-to-face communication. Only when a Deaf person is in the presence of another Deaf person does freedom of expression exist. Given the visual nature of ASL, it is logical that this aspect of interaction has become an important value.

This value can be seen in the interaction pattern of Deaf people. For example, when two people agree to meet at a certain place and time and one is an hour late, it is not uncommon to find the first still waiting patiently. This behavior may be influenced by restricted use of the telephone; however, the advent of telecommunication devices and telephone relay services have not significantly changed this behavior.

Face-to-face communication is so powerful within the Deaf culture it, at times, may violate "hearing" social interaction rules. For example, two Deaf people may be conversing in a theater. If the lights dim to signal that conversations are to end and attention should be directed to the stage, the conversation between two Deaf people will only cease if the lighting is insufficient to see and, if not completed, will quickly resume when the stage lights come up. Only when the conversation is completed will attention be directed to the stage.

Interfering with face-to-face communication sometimes requires a type of public apology. It has been frequently observed that when a Deaf person is conducting a workshop or group meeting and a Deaf participant gets up to leave, a one- or two-sign explanation is often subtly given. The person departing never interrupts the presenter as in "taking the turn" but recognizes that standing visually disrupts the communication, thus requiring an explanation.

One way that the value of face-to-face communication has been maintained within the culture is the existence of social and recreational clubs for the Deaf. A club for the Deaf can be found in every major city in the country. It is here that Deaf people gather to socialize, problem solve, and maintain the community. The Deaf club offers a variety of activities not found in any other place (e.g., sports activities with all Deaf teams, bingo presented in sign, card tournaments where all the players are Deaf, etc.). Captioned films were also an activity that drew many Deaf individuals to the club; however, with the advent of closed captions on many television programs and videotaped movies that can be rented, Deaf families are spending more time in the home. Although closed captioning has provided Deaf people with much greater access to hearing culture, it has changed the interaction patterns of Deaf people (K. Cagle, personal communication, October 14, 1991).

Directness

Directness for Deaf culture means being straightforward and unambiguous in the messages sent. This value can be seen in several conversational behaviors. Jankowski (1991), in her discussion of Deaf culture, compared the public speaking styles of both hearing and Deaf cultures. Hearing speakers often start a speech with a joke or some other "warm-up" technique. Only after several minutes do the listeners find out the topic of the speech. Deaf public speakers, on the other hand, use a more direct approach. The topic is clearly stated at the beginning of the speech, then each point is presented with several examples. Humor is often used to reinforce the main points of a speech.

Deaf people are more attuned to the visual environment than hearing people. They tend to notice subtle and not so subtle changes in a person's posture, stature, complexion, or overall appearance. Any major change in a person's appearance will be acknowledged in a direct manner. In general American culture, thinness, youth, and the like are valued. Comments made on physical changes toward these characteristics are seen positively; whereas physical change away from these characteristics (weight gain, aging, balding, etc.) are viewed as negative and are therefore not acknowledged.

The Deaf culture, being visually based, places more emphasis on physical characteristics, particularly unique physical characteristics (e.g., tallness, fatness, large nose, curly hair, etc.). These characteristics are not seen as good/bad or positive/negative. They are simply characteristics unique to the individual. If a person's physical appearance undergoes a change, regardless of the type of change, it would be rude not to acknowledge the change.

Openness

A third value of Deaf culture is the free exchange of information or openness. In contrast to the majority's value of privacy, Deaf culture members often freely discuss topics that might otherwise be considered too intimate for public conversation. For example, discussing a hysterectomy, mastectomy, or other intimate medical details is no more a violation of personal privacy than discussing a new car or a favorite television program. The sharing of more intimate information helps to maintain close social bonds between members. In this way, the culture functions as a support group when members need assistance.

In work environments that involve the Deaf and hearing individuals who know Sign (e.g., a school for the Deaf), the issue of open communication often is a source of conflict. When meetings occur involving both groups, hearing people will often group together and engage in spoken conversations and will not use sign. Deaf people feel this behavior is isolating and represents a deliberate attempt to exclude them from conversations. Hearing people will defend their actions, saying that the Deaf person need only to walk up to the conversation to be immediately included. This inability to overhear the conversation places the Deaf person at a conversational disadvantage in two ways: Interactants may first overhear a conversation to determine the desire to participate, and possessing a sense of context allows for ease of entry.

Pride

A fourth important value in Deaf culture is pride in being Deaf. This is often a source of confusion for hearing people who view deafness as a disabling condition. This confusion was very evident in an observed meeting with a doctor and an expectant couple. The doctor questioned the Deaf couple about their genetic history. Her conclusion was, "You'll be happy to know that I am quite sure your baby will be hearing." The couple looked very disappointed and indicated that they knew but would love the baby just the same. The doctor, convinced the interpreter misunderstood her statement, repeated it several times. The Deaf couple indicated they understood but given the choice would prefer to have a Deaf baby.

Pride in being Deaf is also seen in how Deaf people have reacted to cochlear implants. A cochlear implant is a system of electrodes that electronically stimulates the acoustic nerve. The device consists of a tiny microphone (placed in the ear canal) that picks up sound waves and transmits them to an electronic language processor that transforms the sound into electrical stimulation. The stimulating signal is applied to the acoustic nerve via a receiver coil implanted in the skull (Merzenich, 1985). Deaf culture recognizes that cochlear implantation may have a value as a biotechnical assistive device for postlingually deafened adults; however, the implants are often touted as being a medical device that can "cure" deafness, especially for children, thus continuing to promote deafness as a disabling condition. "This viewpoint denies the reality of deafness and fails to acknowledge the existence of the sizable deaf minority whose members consider themselves a viable cultural group, leading satisfying, creative and productive lives without any need for *sound*" (Canadian Cultural Society of the Deaf, 1989, p. 2).

For the hearing majority, cochlear implants are viewed much the same as corneal transplants or prosthetic devices that greatly improve the overall quality of life. A major difference is that cochlear implants do not dramatically change one's ability to hear. In addition, people who are blind or who are amputees do not belong to a separate linguistic culture. Deaf people are a minority group with a separate language and cultural identity that has resulted from their inability to hear. For this reason, some deaf people view cochlear implants as a threat to their culture.

Humor is another way Deaf pride is maintained. Deaf jokes, like humor in most cultures, show variation in topic and structure. There are puns based on visual similarity of signs, one liners, long complex narratives, and "off-color" jokes. However, the overriding theme in all Deaf jokes is that the Deaf person always comes out on top. She or he is portrayed as coming up with an ingenious solution to an impossible problem or simply outwitting a hearing person.

The following two jokes are examples involving a Deaf character from the non-Deaf as compared to the Deaf culture perspective. The value of pride can be seen in the latter whereas the former presents the Deaf character in a stereotypical "deaf-and-dumb" manner.

> *Non-Deaf Perspective*: The Godfather was checking his books one day and found he was missing a large sum of money. He called in Tony, a deaf-mute, who was supposed to have collected the money. Tony shows up with his friend, Sam, who uses sign language and acts as Tony's interpreter. The Godfather says to Sam, "You tell Tony that I'm missing a half million dollars and I want to know where it is." Sam turns to Tony and signs the message. Tony signs back, "I don't know where it is" and Sam tells the Godfather, "He don't know where it is." The conversation goes back and forth several times more when in frustration the Godfather takes out a gun and places it at Tony's temple and says, "Tell him if he doesn't tell me in two seconds where my money is, I'll blow his head off." Sam turns to Tony and signs the message. Tony quickly signs to Sam, "OK, it's in my garage behind the wood pile." Sam tells the Godfather, "He still don't know where it is."

> *Deaf Culture Perspective*: A Deaf couple stops at a motel for the night. About 4 o'clock in the morning the Deaf husband decides that he's thirsty and goes out to get a soda from the machine. When he starts back to his room he realizes he doesn't know which room is his. After several minutes of thought, he goes to his car and continues to honk the horn. As he does, one by one lights turn on in each room except one, the one his Deaf wife occupies.

"Success stories" are another mechanism for teaching and maintaining pride within the culture. Padden (1989), in her analysis of the values of the Deaf culture, cited the following example. A typical story may go like this:

> A deaf person grows up in an oral environment [using speech and lipreading], never having met or talked with deaf people. Later in life, the deaf person meets a deaf person who brings him to parties, teaches him Sign Language and instructs him in the way of deaf people's lives. This person becomes more and more involved, and leaves behind his past as he joins other deaf people. (p. 11).

VERBAL PROCESSES

The previous section discussed how several aspects of the sociocultural element of perception influence the communication patterns of Deaf culture. The second major grouping of sociocultural elements, as identified by Samovar and Porter (1991), fall under the category of verbal processes. These include the language used by a particular culture and the patterns of thought that exist within a culture.

Language

Language is an organized set of learned symbol systems used to represent our experiences (Samovar & Porter, 1991). For Deaf culture, their symbols are expressed in ASL. "Their language is a fully developed language which allows for a full range of human activities, from complex problem solving and social relationships to delicate and beautiful storytelling" (Higgins & Nash, 1987, p. 4).

ASL is not related to spoken English, and it is not a modern day Native American sign language. As explained earlier, linguistically, it is most closely related to FSL. The origins of ASL point to an important feature of Sign (i.e., Sign Language is not universal). Foreign Sign Languages (e.g., British Sign Language, Japanese Sign Language, Finnish Sign Language) are similar to ASL in that they are also visual languages, but the similarity ends there. Each has its own unique phonology, vocabulary, and syntax (Sandager, 1986). That is, a Deaf person from Germany and a Deaf person from Great Britain will probably face the same communication difficulties as hearing individuals from these countries. However, Deaf people from around the world seem to strongly value face-to-face communication and many place more effort in intercultural communication than hearing individuals.

Although ASL has existed in America for quite some time, it was not recognized as a language until recently. In 1965, the publication of *A Dictionary of American Sign Language* by Stokoe, Croneberg, and Casterline first described ASL as a language separate and distinct from spoken English. For the first time, a group of linguists analyzed ASL and identified its building blocks. Cheremes, similar to phonemes, make up the three major parameters for signs. Each sign uses a particular handshape, is produced at a particular location in space, and utilizes a particular motion. In addition, signs are produced "within a highly restricted space defined by the top of the head, the waist, and the reach of the arms from side to side (with elbows bent)" (Klima & Bellugi, 1979). Figure 1 shows the space in which signs are produced.

According to Porter and Samovar (1988), "language is the primary vehicle by which a culture transmits its beliefs, values, and norms" (p. 27). ASL, being a visual-gestural language has many features that reflect these aspects of culture.

Unequivocal Communication

Directness is reflected in ASL's relatively few euphemistic phrases. Euphemisms develop when a particular term is strongly associated with being unpleasant. When this association occurs, a substitute word or euphemism develops that is free of these negative associations. In English, euphemisms are commonly developed for body parts, bodily functions, sexual acts, and death to name a few. In English, we have numerous

Figure 1. *The region in which Signs are made. From* Technical Signs: Manual One *(p. 28) by F. Caccamise et al., 1982, Rochester, NY: Rochester Institute of Technology at the National Technical Institute for the Deaf. Copyright 1982 by Rochester Institute of Technology at the National Technical Institute for the Deaf. Reprinted by permission.*

euphemisms that function as a substitute for the phrase, "I need to go to the bathroom" (e.g., "I need to powder my nose"; "I need to go to the little girls room"; "I have to go see a man about a horse"). In Sign Language, informants could only identify one direct way to express this message (a "T" handshape, shaken right to left, twice) and two euphemistic phrases: (a) "R-R" (meaning rest room) and (b) "I have to go make a TTY (teletypewriter) phone call." The only other euphemism identified was one frequently used by teenage girls for the term *menstruation.* This sign is rather unique in that it does not require the use of the hands. The sign is made by quickly puffing one cheek, thus, it can be secretly communicated to another girl by turning the head away from any boys who may be watching. With the exception of these three examples, euphemisms tend to be avoided by the Deaf culture because they are often vague and may lead to misunderstandings. A more direct approach is preferred.

Communication of Sound

The Sapir–Whorf hypothesis suggests that the structure of a language influences how the user of that language perceives the world. If your language requires that snow, colors, or dogs be classified in a particular way, then these objects will be perceived differently from someone who is not required to make these differentiations. ASL offers an opportunity to investigate how language may affect perception; that is, How might the users of a language based on vision (ASL) perceive and talk about a concept like *sound?*

To fully understand how sound is perceived by Deaf culture, it is helpful to first compare the concepts *quiet* and *noise.* The sign for *quiet* has two components. The first is an index finger placed over the lips, and the second involves both hands moving in a downward motion. In general, this sign is produced in a slow manner. This sign is also used for the concepts of calm, peaceful, silent, tranquil, and so forth. In contrast, the sign for *noise* involves first pointing to the ear and then both hands shaking as they move away from the signer (see Figure 2). The second component of *noise* is also used to mean *vibration.*

With Sign Language, various noises are communicated by converting the noise into its associated motion. For example, here is how Sign expresses the following noises:

A gun shot involves the sign for gun with the added motion depicting the kick of the gun.
A ringing phone involves the sign for phone with the added motion of the handset shaking with each ring.
A scream involves the sign for vibrations emanating from the mouth and moving out away from the signer.
Thunder (or a very loud noise) involves pointing to the ear, with the two fists producing a violent shake.
Alarm involves depicting a bell clapper hitting the side of the bell.

The culture has also modified traditions involving sound. At Deaf culture weddings, the tapping of the wineglass requesting the bride and groom to kiss is replaced with the waving of the napkin. Applause has also undergone a visual modification, particularly when the performer is Deaf. The hand clap is used for hearing performers, whereas the hand wave (both hands extended overhead and rotated back and forth) is used for Deaf performers.

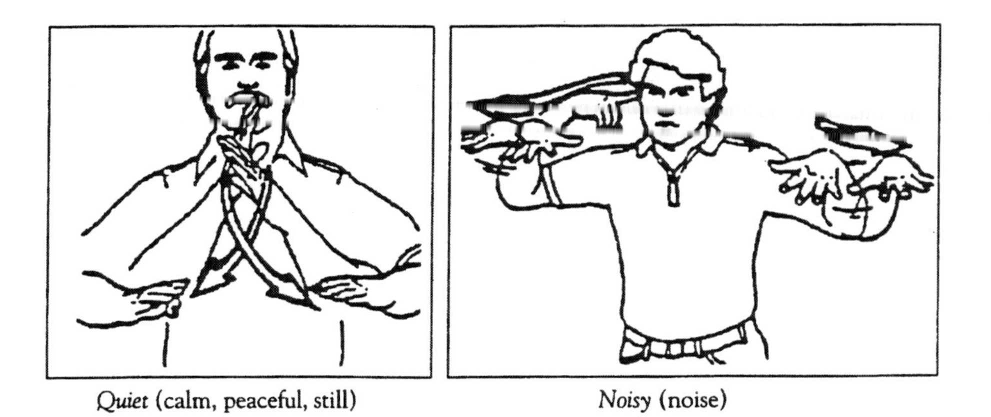

Figure 2. *Comparison of the Signs for* quiet *and* noise. *From* Basic Sign Communication: Vocabulary *(pp. 75, 86) by W. Newell, 1983, Silver Spring, MD: National Association of the Deaf. Copyright 1983 by Rochester Institute of Technology at the National Technical Institute for the Deaf. Reprinted by permission.*

Name Signs

Name signs, according to Supalla (1990), are the proper names of persons living within the Deaf community. All Americans are given a spoken and written name at birth; however, Deaf individuals and hearing members of the culture are also given a name sign. Name signs are most often given by a parent who is Deaf, a Deaf peer, or a Deaf teacher.

Supalla (1990) showed that a name sign can be descriptive or arbitrary. A descriptive name sign is based on a personal characteristic (e.g., large eyes, a birth mark on the cheek, curly hair) or an arbitrary name sign that involves the initials of the person and then is assigned a specific movement and location.

Mindess (1990) found that name signs reflect two major aspects of the culture: identity and solidarity. A name sign is unique in that it symbolizes a specific person. It is generally given to an individual by another Deaf person and not self-assigned. Most people have only one name sign that stays with them for life; however, some individuals may acquire a different name sign as time goes on. However, one cannot just arbitrarily decide to change one's name sign. There must be a very good reason; for example, when a woman marries, she may decide to add the initial of her husband's last name to her name sign. Another reason for changing one's name sign is if two people in the same community happen to have the same name sign. If such a circumstance arises, one of the two must change or modify his or her sign name. However, there are social status rules associated with the change. It is generally the newer person, or if one of the two is hearing, who is expected to change.

Name signs also provide group solidarity. As Mindess (1990) pointed out, "the strongest value, which I heard expressed in many different ways, was that name signs serve as connections to the group" (p. 7). As stated earlier, one generally does not invent his or her own name sign—it is given. Deaf individuals with hearing parents received their name signs from peers or teachers when they entered the school for the Deaf. Deaf individuals who did not identify with the culture until much later in life are not given their name signs until someone in the culture feels the individual is a member. The idea that a name sign reflects identification *and* affiliation is often overlooked by hearing individuals new to Deaf culture. Students of Sign Language, like students of any foreign language, want to be able to introduce themselves using cultural conventions. In Sign Language, one's name can be expressed through finger spelling, but the student soon becomes aware that culture members have name signs. Thus, students may ask an inappropriate person for a name sign or invent one themselves. It is interesting to note that often these name signs subtly violate the structure rules of name signs. For example, a former hearing student was also an accomplished dancer. Her self-assigned name sign involved her initial plus the sign for dance. This name sign violated a structure rule in that descriptive name signs must have contact with the body. The sign for *dance* is produced in front of the signer and does not come in contact with the body. These subtle violations communicate to Deaf culture members that the owner of the name sign is probably hearing and/or may not be a bona fide member.

NONVERBAL PROCESSES

The nonverbal systems of a culture, like the verbal systems, are learned as part of the socialization process. As Porter and Samovar (1988) suggested, they may include eye gaze, touch, silence, space, time, and para-language. An analysis of some of the nonverbal processes of Deaf culture provides a deeper understanding into the culture's structure.

Time

The value of face-to-face interactions can also be analyzed from the perspective of the length of time involved in communication interactions. As Jankowski (1991) pointed out, socializing is an important Deaf culture event that extends the time required for any group meeting, in that Deaf participants must first share the latest news and renew cultural relationships. At major conventions, involving Deaf people who have not seen each other for a long period of time, conversations often continue into the wee hours of the morning. Hopper and Mowl (1987), in their description of Deaf congregations and religious services, showed how this value is incorporated throughout the service.

> The service usually begins with Deaf church members socializing for up to ten minutes. The pastor mingles as well and after about five minutes leaves to put on the vestments. . . . The worship service is participatory, often referred to as a dialogue homily, as there is interaction between the pastor conducting the service and the congregation. (p. 3)

This value is further exemplified in extended leave-taking behavior. Interactants delay the termination of a conversation by prolonging closure. "Good-bye" may be said only to be followed by the introduction of a new topic requiring several more minutes of conversation. This process may be repeated several times before the person actually departs.

This extension of time is also evident when one attempts to enter an already established conversation. When two people are engaged in conversation and a third party approaches, the third member is often left to wait on the outside of the conversational boundaries much longer than in conversations involving hearing individuals. The conversation might continue until the current topic is completed or there is a convenient place to pause and acknowledge the third party. This waiting period appears to serve two functions: It maintains the uninterrupted flow of conversation, and it permits the third party to "tune in" to the conversation before actually participating.

Eye Contact

Eye contact serves an important function for face-to-face communication. Conversations cannot start until the interactants have established eye contact. During a signed conversation, the speaker will frequently break eye contact; however, the listener cannot. This rule applies even if the listener is hearing and the speaker is a Deaf person who has good voice quality. The following quotation from a Deaf man serves as an example of this type of situation.

> Oftentimes, people tell me I speak all right and that they can understand my speech; and because of that, they often do something else while listening to me, like writing notes or reading. That really bothers me, because when they are doing that, I feel that they are not paying attention to me. I need to have eye contact with them, so that I can get some feedback about their attitudes and thoughts in response to what I am saying. (Lang & DeCaro, 1988, p. 40)

Touching

Touching serves three very important functions within the Deaf culture. First, touching is frequently used to gain attention or eye contact before a conversation can begin; second, it functions to physically connect the culture, and third, it maintains safety.

As stated earlier, a conversation cannot begin until eye contact is made. Thus, touching often precedes eye contact. For a Deaf person, a touch communicates a great deal of information. It communicates which direction to look and the urgency of communication. For example, a light, double touch on the shoulder or arm (the most frequently touched regions) simply says, "Hey, Mary." A touch that involves resting the hand on the arm communicates, "I can see you are in the middle of something, look up when you can." A hard jab or a rapidly repeating tap means, "This is very important, look immediately."

If a conversation is already in progress, a third party can gain immediate entrance to a conversation by touching the signer on the arm or gaining attention with a wave. However, this privileged entrance is only used when the interruption is absolutely necessary and what is to be communicated is important. Hearing individuals frequently violate this rule when attempting to pass through a conversation. Often, Deaf individuals will rest against the opposite sides of a hallway when conversing. This position offers the optimal distance for receiving a signed message because the face, hands, and body can all be clearly seen. Most hearing individuals assume that it is rude to walk through the conversation without first acknowledging the violation by saying "excuse me." The hearing individual believes that he or she must first get the Deaf persons' attention (i.e., a tap or wave to gain eye contact) and then sign "excuse me" or the hearing person will wait until one or both conversants stop talking and look at him or her. Once the Deaf person realizes why the conversation was interrupted, the hearing person might receive a very annoyed look accompanied with a gesture signaling to walk through quickly. From the perspective of Deaf culture, the appropriate behavior is to respect the face-to-face communication by simply passing through without interruption.

Touching also serves to physically connect culture members. Hugging is a very common part of greetings and leave taking. Rarely is a handshake used among members who know each other. Touching also occurs frequently during conversations to communicate empathy, support, or connectedness. One interesting example of this can be seen when conversations are interrupted.

A Deaf supervisor was explaining a project to her Deaf assistant when a secretary interrupted to ask a question that needed an immediate answer. Before looking away to respond to the secretary, the supervisor placed her hand on the assistant's arm, maintaining physical contact with him, responded to the secretary using her other hand, then turning back to her assistant, removed her hand and continued the conversation.

From the perspective of the interactants, this behavior functions as a means to preserve the connectedness between conversants. When the interruption occurred, it required that eye contact be broken; thus, the physical contact served to maintain a conversational bond until eye contact could be resumed.

Touch is also used to protect interactants from harm. One of the additional duties of interactants in a signed conversation is to alert the other of any danger that may be approaching from the blind side (i.e., the region behind the respective interactants). When a potential danger approaches from the blind side, it is the other's duty to move the conversation out of the path of danger. This is often accomplished by placing the hand on the arm and gently guiding to a safe location. This activity is particularly evident when two conversants are walking and talking. It is not uncommon to see one member take the elbow of the other and guide away from a fence, chuckhole, or other potential danger. It is interesting to note that this guiding behavior is so common that conversations often continue uninterrupted.

CONCLUSION

Historically, Deaf individuals have been viewed as a disabled group. This view has led to many preconceptions and stereotypes that frequently result in negative interactions between Deaf and non-Deaf individuals. The basis for the communication conflict can be traced to two major assumptions made by non-Deaf individuals: an assumption of a deficit condition and an assumption of similarity.

The assumption that Deaf individuals are in a deficit condition because they cannot hear leads to the conclusion that they are incomplete or lacking. Underlying this assumption is the belief that given the choice Deaf individuals would prefer to hear. This assumption often creates communication that is patronizing or pitying to the Deaf individual.

The assumption of similarity is that Deaf individuals share the same cultural knowledge, experiences, and meanings as all Americans. That is, they are fluent in English, follow the same interaction rules, and hold the same cultural values. It is common for those who have undergone sensitivity training for disabled groups to believe that the only difference between Deaf and non-Deaf people is that Deaf people cannot hear. Thus, behavioral differences are often attributed to eccentric behavior, inadequate social training, or mental illness.

When Deaf individuals are viewed as a co-culture of American society, these preconceptions and stereotypes are replaced with greater tolerance for difference and respect. One is not as quick to evaluate and label behaviors that are perceived as different. Communication may not always be fully understood, but there will be a greater tendency to withhold judgments and more fully evaluate prejudices.

This article has discussed the cultural patterns of Deaf people. Evidence has been presented that Deaf culture possesses a unique set of knowledge, experience, values, and meanings. As a co-culture of American culture, Deaf culture provides a rich source for further intercultural communication research. Of great value would be a further investigation of interactional pattern differences when Deaf culture is viewed from a cultural perspective versus a disabled perspective. This line of research would provide much needed information to the non-Deaf majority, thus opening up more successful lines of communication.

REFERENCES

Albert, R., & Triandis, H. (1991). Intercultural education for multicultural societies: Critical issues. In L. Samovar & R. Porter (Eds.), *Intercultural communication: A reader* (pp. 411–426). Belmont, CA: Wadsworth.

Baker, C., & Padden, C. (1978). Focusing on the non-manual components of American Sign Language. In P. Siple (Ed.), *Understanding language through Sign Language research* (pp. 27–57). New York: Academic.

Braithwaite, D. (1991). Viewing persons with disabilities as a culture. In L. Samovar & R. Porter (Eds.), *Intercultural communication: A reader* (pp. 136–142). Belmont, CA: Wadsworth.

Canadian Cultural Society of the Deaf. (1989). *The use of cochlear implants: A position paper.* Unpublished manuscript.

Carmichael, C. (1991). Intercultural perspectives of aging. In L. Samovar & R. Porter (Eds.), *Intercultural communication: A reader* (pp. 128–134). Belmont, CA: Wadsworth.

Cokely, D., & Baker, C. (1980). *American Sign Language: A teacher's resource text on grammar and culture.* Silver Spring, MD: T. J. Publishers.

Gallaudet, E. (1887). The value of the sign-language to the deaf. *American Annals of the Deaf,* **32,** 141–147.

Gannon, J. (1981). *Deaf heritage.* Silver Spring, MD: National Association of the Deaf.

Gannon, J. (1989). *The week the world heard Gallaudet.* Washington, DC: Gallaudet University Press.

Groce, N. (1988). *Everyone here spoke Sign Language.* Cambridge, MA: Harvard University Press.

Higgins, P. (1989). *Outsiders in a hearing world.* Newbury Park, CA: Sage.

Higgins, P., & Nash, J. (1987). *Understanding deafness socially.* Springfield, IL: Charles Thomas.

Hopper, M., & Mowl, G. (1987, August). *United States of America Deaf culture.* Paper presented at the meeting of the Registry of Interpreters for the Deaf, St. Paul, MN.

Jankowski, K. (1991). Communicating with the deaf. In L. Samovar & R. Porter (Eds.), *Intercultural communication: A reader* (pp. 116–119). Belmont, CA: Wadsworth.

Kannapell, B. (1982). Inside the Deaf community. *The Deaf American,* **34**(4), 23–26.

Klima, E., & Bellugi, U. (1979). *The signs of language.* Cambridge, MA: Harvard University Press.

Lane, H. (1984). *When the mind hears.* New York: Random House.

Lane, H. (1988). Is there a "psychology of the Deaf"? *Exceptional Children,* **55**(1), 7–19.

Lang, H., & DeCaro, J. (Eds.), (1988). *Proceedings of the second convocation of faculty and staff.* Rochester, NY: National Technical Institute for the Deaf.

Madrid, A. (1991). Diversity and its discontents. In L. Samovar & R. Porter (Eds.), *Intercultural communication: A reader* (pp. 116–119). Belmont, CA: Wadsworth.

Majors, R. (1991). America's emerging gay culture. In L. Samovar & R. Porter (Eds.), *Intercultural communication: A reader* (pp. 160–166). Belmont, CA: Wadsworth.

Merzenich, M. (1985). *Cochlear implants.* New York: Raven.

Mindess, A. (1990). What name signs can tell us about Deaf culture. *Sign Language Studies,* **66,** 1–21.

Moores, D. (1987). *Educating the deaf: Psychology, principles, and practices* (3rd ed.). Boston: Houghton Mifflin.

Padden, C. (1989). The Deaf community and the culture of Deaf people. In S. Wilcox (Ed.), *American Deaf culture* (pp. 1–16). Burtonsville, MD: Linstok.

Porter, R., & Samovar, L. (1988). Approaching intercultural communication. In L. Samovar & R. Porter (Eds.), *Intercultural communication: A reader* (pp. 15–30). Belmont, CA: Wadsworth.

Samovar, L., & Porter, R. (1991). *Communication between cultures.* Belmont, CA: Wadsworth.

Sandager, O. (1986). *Sign languages around the world.* North Hollywood, CA: OK Publishing.

Schein, J., & Delk, M. (1974). *The deaf population of the United States.* Silver Spring, MD: National Association of the Deaf.

Stokoe, W., Croneberg, C., & Casterline, D. (1965). *A dictionary of American Sign Language.* Washington, DC: Gallaudet College Press.

Supalla, S. (1990). The arbitrary name sign system in American Sign Language: *Sign Language Studies,* **67,** 99–126.

Tannen, D. (1990). *You just don't understand.* New York: Ballantine.

Vernon, M. (1968). Current etiological factors in deafness. *American Annals of the Deaf,* **113,** 106–115.

Weber, S. (1991). The need to be: The socio-cultural significance of Black language. In L. Samovar & R. Porter (Eds.), *Intercultural communication: A reader* (pp. 277–282). Belmont, CA: Wadsworth.

Woodward, J. (1973). Some characteristics of Pidgin Sign English. *Sign Language Studies,* **3,** 39–46.

Woodward, J. (1978). Historical bases of American Si Language. In P. Siple (Ed.), *Understanding language through sign language research.* New York: Academic.

CONCEPTS AND QUESTIONS

1. Why does Siple suggest that the term *co-culture* is being used instead of the term *sub-culture?* Do you agree with the shift in terminology? Why?
2. According to Siple, why has the deaf co-culture not been recognized as a domestic co-culture?
3. What characteristics of the deaf co-culture seem to make it a co-culture?
4. What are some of the "perceptual frames" discussed by Siple?
5. What are some of the differences in perceptual frames between the hearing and deaf cultures?
6. What are the major cultural values existing in the deaf co-culture? How would you compare these values with the ones held by the hearing culture?
7. Why is directness valued by the deaf?
8. Why are there very few euphemistic phrases in American Sign Language?
9. What are "name signs," and why are they important in the deaf co-culture?
10. What aspects of nonverbal communication are somewhat different when applied to the deaf co-culture?

DEAF CULTURE: DEAF COMMUNITY

23

INSIDE THE DEAF COMMUNITY

Barbara Kannapell

"When I think of communication," the first thing that comes to my mind is the free flow of communication in the Deaf Community. Deaf people feel so comfortable in communicating with each other at deaf clubs, church services for the deaf, or any event for deaf people given by deaf people, as opposed to the discomfort that they feel outside of the Deaf Community.

Then what is communication? Eileen Paul wrote an article, "Some Notes On Communication ...," in which she defines the meaning of communication which is most relevant to that in the Deaf Community.

This last statement is the theme throughout this paper. I will show how it is relevant to the communication in the Deaf Community.

Now, let's look inside the Deaf Community. The question I'd like to ask is: "What makes deaf people feel at ease in communicating with each other?" I will offer three explanations.

THE FIRST EXPLANATION

Deaf people can understand each other 100 percent of the time, whereas outside of the Deaf Community they get *fragmentary information* or *one-way communication.* Fragmentary information means that the deaf person may get 50, 60, or 70 percent of the information communicated through a not-so-skilled interpreter, or through a hearing person who uses speech or who has just learned Sign Language.

One-way communication can mean an interpreter who can express from voice to sign, but can't interpret from sign to voice. It can also mean a hearing person who can express him/herself in Sign Language, but cannot read the signs of a deaf person. Deaf people experience this kind of one-way communication very often when they are with hearing people.

THE SECOND EXPLANATION

Deaf people share a common language—American Sign Language (ASL). ASL seems to be the primary communication mode we use among ourselves. Everything else—English in different forms—is the secondary communication mode for some deaf people. It does not necessarily mean that all deaf people are fluent in ASL. It can mean that those who are not fluent in ASL are skilled in English, or it can mean that they have no skills in English. It is possible that there are deaf people who are bilingual in varying degrees. I'd like to show some variations in communication styles in the Deaf Community:

ASL monolinguals—Deaf people who are comfortable expressing themselves only in ASL, and in understanding only ASL. They have no skills in English.

ASL dominant bilinguals—Deaf people who are more comfortable expressing themselves in ASL than English, and are able to understand ASL better than English (either printed or signed English).

Balanced bilinguals—Deaf people who are comfortable expressing themselves in both ASL and English, and who are able to understand both equally well.

English dominant bilinguals—Deaf people who are more comfortable expressing themselves in English, and who are able to understand English (in printed English or signed English) better than ASL.

English monolinguals—Deaf people who are comfortable expressing themselves only in English (oral or signed English) and in understanding English (in printed or oral or signed English). They have no skills in ASL.

Semi-linguals—Deaf people who do have some skills in both English and ASL, but are not able to master either language fully.

Based on these variations, I would like to raise several questions: 1) Who is really in the core of the Deaf Community, and who is on the fringe of the Deaf Community? 2) Are English-dominant bilinguals and English monolinguals in the core of the Deaf Community, or are they on the fringe? 3) Are there deaf people who use only ASL and understand only ASL (ASL monolinguals)? In other words, are there deaf people who know absolutely no English?

Within the Deaf Community, deaf people have a complex system of evaluating who should be in the core or on the fringe of the Deaf Community. It is important to mention here that the degree of hearing loss is not the most important requirement for being in the core of the Deaf Community. Deaf people just identify themselves as deaf or hard of hearing, no matter what their degree of loss is. They do not need to show their audiogram to enter the Deaf Community. Sharing a common language seems, however, not to be enough to be admitted to the Deaf Community.

THE THIRD EXPLANATION

"Communication is the process of sharing what things mean to us with ourselves and with other people." I think this is the most important explanation of all. Deaf people share what things mean to each other, i.e., the word "deaf" means different things to deaf and to hearing people. Also, the word "hearing" has a different meaning for deaf people. Deaf people communicate those meanings through ASL. Such meanings extend to the following:

The bond of communication and strong relationships—Deaf people experience a strong bond of communication because they have common topics to share which are based on common experiences, such as the history of deaf people, school experiences, family experiences, sports, movies, stories and jokes. They develop strong relations based on these common experiences with other deaf people. Many deaf people develop strong relationships during school years and maintain these relationships throughout their lives. This feeling may be carried over from residential schools, where they developed a strong bond of communication for the purpose of survival skills.

Cultural beliefs and values—Carol Padden offers a good explanation of cultural beliefs and values in her essay in *Sign Language in the Deaf Community.* These beliefs and values are also related to the complex system of evaluating who should be in the core of the Deaf Community and who should be on the fringe. For example, deaf people have a way of evaluating who behaves like a deaf person and who behaves like a hearing person.

If a deaf person behaves like a hearing person, other deaf people will sign "hearing" on the forehead to show "he thinks like a hearing person." Thus, he is on the fringe of the Deaf Community, depending on his/her attitudes. Conversely, if a deaf person behaves like a deaf person, other deaf people may sign "strong deaf" or "fluent ASL," which means that the person is culturally deaf. Thus, he or she is admitted to the core of the Deaf Community.

If a hearing person wants to meet a deaf person, the rules of the Deaf Community dictate that he/she must be introduced as a "hearing" person in the Deaf Community. Then, the deaf person being introduced will ask questions such as "you from Gallaudet?" or "from deaf family?" or "teach deaf children?" If the hearing person has something to do with working with deaf people, or comes from a deaf family, a deaf person would be satisfied, since this would meet his/her expectations of a hearing person. But, if the hearing person is just interested in learning ASL as a foreign language and has nothing to do with deafness, deaf people will become suspicious and on guard. It is true that a few hearing people who have nothing to do with the education of deaf children or who do not come from a deaf family may eventually be admitted to this Community. These are just two examples relating to cultural beliefs and values in the Deaf Community.

Feeling equal—The bond of communication and strong relationships and similar cultural beliefs and values are equated with feelings of equality among deaf people. Within the Deaf Community is the only place that deaf people experience equality with others. Usually, deaf people do not feel equal with hearing people outside of the Deaf Community.

Thus, ASL is a powerful tool for identity in the Deaf Community, along with the cultural beliefs and values that are expressed through ASL. This suggests that ASL is the cultural language of the Deaf Community.

However, I want to emphasize that the knowledge of ASL alone seems not to be enough to qualify a person to be in the core of the Deaf Community. Everything else—shared common experiences, and cultural beliefs and values which are attached to ASL also seem to be important requirements for admittance to the core of the Deaf Community. A deaf person who is in the core of the Deaf Community is considered to be "culturally deaf."

The more culturally deaf a person becomes, the further he or she moves into the core of the Deaf Community. I suggest that the Deaf Community can be compared to the majority community of hearing people in terms of language supremacy. Deaf people experience ASL supremacy in the Deaf Community similar to hearing people's English supremacy in the majority community.

In relation to deaf people's experience of ASL supremacy, we also need to look into the functions of ASL in the Deaf Community. Language can serve many functions, i.e., Pidgin Sign English functions as a way for deaf people to communicate with hearing people. ASL serves as a way for deaf people to communicate with each other, but there is much more to it than just a function of language. There is a symbolic function in relation to identity and power, and we often keep our use of ASL limited to ourselves to preserve these factors of identity and power.

As a protection of our own identities, deaf people keep thinking that hearing people cannot learn ASL, but really deaf people exert their power in using ASL. For example, we can talk about anything we want—right in the middle of a crowd of hearing people. They are not supposed to understand us. In a classroom, for example, deaf students often talk about the hearing teacher right in front of him or her. They may say "understand zero" or "it went over my head" in ASL. The hearing teacher is not supposed to understand ASL.

If hearing people understand ASL, then deaf people are no longer in power using ASL. Here is what happened to me several years ago: I realized that a deaf friend of mine and I were no longer in power using ASL in front of two hearing friends. One of them knew no Sign Language, but the other one knew ASL fairly well. As my deaf friend and I began a deep personal discussion, the hearing person who knew ASL was able to understand us and felt awkward intepreting to the other hearing person what we were talking about.

I did not expect her to understand our discussion in ASL or to interpret to the hearing person because hearing people are not supposed to understand the conversation of deaf people in ASL. That's how deaf people experience ASL supremacy. ASL is the only creation which grows out of the Deaf Community. It is our language in every sense of the word. We create it, we keep it alive and it keeps us and our traditions alive.

I suggest another reason why deaf people do not use ASL with hearing people: *Language choice reflects identity choice.* Somehow, deaf people learn not to use ASL with hearing people in their school years. Deaf persons choose ASL or English depending on the identity the system wants for them. When they are with hearing people, they try to communicate in English—trying to use voice or sign in English—or both at the same time. When they are with other deaf people, they feel more like themselves and use ASL, and experience a strong sense of group identity.

I also suggest that in relation to the theme of this paper again, these words, "hearing person," "speech," and "English," are equivalent. When a deaf person meets a hearing person, the word "English" is strongly attached to that hearing person, so a deaf person tries to communicate on a hearing person's terms—using voice or signing in English order or both.

All those explanations of why deaf people do not share ASL with hearing people support this statement: "Communication is a process of sharing what things mean to us with ourselves and with other persons." This statement can be rephrased as follows: *Deaf people share what things mean to them with themselves and with other deaf people.* They do not usually share their own special meanings with hearing people probably because 1) Hearing people will never understand what it is like to be deaf; 2) Deaf people do not have a chance to share what things mean to them with hearing people; and/or 3) Deaf people think hearing people are not interested in hearing what we would like to share with them.

I can tell you from my experiences of sharing what the deaf experience or world means to me with deaf and hearing people. I needed to develop trust in myself before I could share my world with deaf and hearing people. The more I share with them, the more they share with me. In other words, we need to respect ourselves as deaf persons and respect our language first before we can share what the deaf world means to us with other deaf and hearing people.

In conclusion, I see this paper as only a beginning in the understanding of the meaning of communication in the Deaf Community.

24

EDUCATING CHILDREN WHO ARE DEAF OR HARD OF HEARING: RESIDENTIAL LIFE, ASL, AND DEAF CULTURE

Judith Gilliam and Susan Easterbrooks

A residential school for students who are deaf has a comprehensive academic, health, and socialization program including dormitory living equipped for students who are deaf. Most programs serve preschool ages through grade 12, although some schools also have parent-infant, vocational, and outreach services. Dormitories are divided according to age groups. All staff and personnel are expected to communicate with students fluently in all areas: academic, recreation, sports, leisure, field trips, and residential settings. Next to coming from a deaf family or a family with some fluent sign communication skills, many view residential life as the ideal opportunity for students who are deaf to become familiar with and enculturated into the Deaf community. In the dining room, for example, students get direct and firsthand experience of true dinner conversation, because the language of the Deaf community, American Sign Language (ASL), is used. In after-school activities students are on equal footing with their peers, and communication is not a barrier to social life because students do not have to depend on an interpreter, enabling them to express themselves freely to their peers. The residential school provides a great opportunity for socialization and is a great environment for developing self-worth.

If a culture is defined as heritage, language, and a set of customs and values shared by its members and transmitted from one generation to the next, then the Deaf community truly is a culture. Members of the Deaf culture are a group of individuals who have a common heritage (historical events, famous figures, art, literature, and scholarly organizations), a common language (American Sign Language), and a set of customs and values (cherishing Deaf children, expecting participation in cultural events, valuing the visual world, protecting one another) (Padden & Humphries, 1988). This heritage is passed on from one generation to the next via the residential school, where they learn such things as Deaf folklore and folklife (jokes, legends, games, riddles, etc.) from other children, Deaf teachers, and Deaf houseparents. Most schools for the deaf use some form of sign language (Padden & Humphries, 1988).

WHO CAN ATTEND A RESIDENTIAL SCHOOL?

According to the April 1996 issue of the American Annals of the Deaf, there were 78 residential schools for the deaf and blind in the United States with only four states not reporting a residential school. Most schools accept students based on degree of hearing loss, academic needs, parental choice, and other factors. Usually these schools have an established relationship with the child's local education agency. This issue of the *Annals* also reported that 21% of the population that was studied attended residential schools. Many schools accept children at about the age of three. For younger children, participation in a Parent/Infant program administered by the school provides much needed services until the child is ready to attend. Residential schools are an alternative to placements in local schools. Parents who are Deaf themselves often choose a school for the Deaf over local schools because of the opportunity for their child(ren) to participate in the life of the Deaf community and culture. Hearing parents of children who are deaf seem to have greater reluctance about sending their children because they do not want to be separated from them (Scheetz, 1993). Separation may cause feelings of guilt in the parents, confusion and homesickness in the child, and depression in both, but once the child has adjusted, he usually embraces the experience wholeheartedly. Houseparents and classroom teachers are often Deaf themselves, and a unique bond may develop between the Deaf child and other Deaf members of the school and community, where the child has access to role models who are Deaf.

HOW DOES ONE BECOME A MEMBER OF THE DEAF CULTURE?

The primary avenue by which a child with a hearing loss becomes a member of the Deaf culture is through the residential schools, but any child who has a hearing loss and uses sign language can become a member of the Deaf community. Students who are deaf and who attended mainstream schools must continue to prove their allegiance to the Deaf culture if they have chosen participation in adulthood (Reese, 1996).

WHAT ARE THE BENEFITS OF RESIDENTIAL SCHOOL PLACEMENT?

Deaf students who are mainstream miss out on the feeling of belonging that individuals from the Deaf culture associate with their residential schools, and their experience is very different from those who attend residential school. Mainstreamed students often are singled out in many respects. Although they have access to interpreters, notetakers, and other special assistive devices, they still may be loners, especially in mainstream environments where there are few other students with hearing losses.

The residential school acts as a melting pot for the majority of the students. They are able to become personally involved with those of the same educational or interests levels. In school, with an abundant number of students, they are able to be grouped homogeneously, thus facilitating learning. Residential schools also enhance competition among one another. The students are exposed to deaf adults with various types of careers. The residential school is the point of contact for the Deaf culture where deaf students can pass on the stories or history to be shared from one generation to another. Residential students are immersed in the genre of deafness and exchange the mannerisms, the differences, the values, the folklore of the Deaf culture.

The majority of graduates from a residential school develop a strong bond with their alma mater. Going to homecoming games, for example, is a thrilling experience. It is like a home away from home. The alumnae also have a sentimental attachment to and value the well being of the school.

WHAT ARE THE LIMITATIONS OF PLACEMENTS AT A RESIDENTIAL SCHOOL OR MEMBERSHIP IN THE DEAF CULTURE?

This question is difficult to answer because the answer depends on the perspective of the person answering. Many students who have attended residential schools and who are members of the Deaf culture will admit to some regret over missing out on a closely knit family life but quickly add that the freedom of communication, sense of belonging, sports and other group events, and opportunities to experience success far outweigh the disadvantages. From the perspective of people who hear, there are concerns that the child who is deaf will have greater difficulty adjusting to adult life due to learned dependency and limited contact with the larger community. Further, the curriculum of the typical residential school tends to be less rigorous than that of other schools (Lane, Hoffmeister, & Bahan, 1996). Deaf culture members are almost unanimous in their response that the Deaf culture more than makes up the difference. In addition, because many families live at some distance from the school, parents tend not to participate in their child's education to a sufficient degree. The choice of residential placement must be made with the child's educational and emotional needs in mind, weighing the pros and cons carefully and with the best interests of the child as a guide.

25

MORE MARRIAGES AMONG THE DEAF MAY HAVE LED TO DOUBLING OF COMMON FORM OF GENETIC DEAFNESS IN THE U.S.

VCU RESEARCHERS ALSO LINK SELECTIVE MATING TO EVOLUTION OF SPEECH

RICHMOND, VA—A high rate of marriage among deaf individuals can explain the increased frequency of connexin deafness in the United States and may have led to a doubling of its occurrence during the past 200 years, according to a study by hereditary deafness experts at Virginia Commonwealth University.

The VCU researchers used an innovative computer simulation to show that intermarriage among the deaf can dramatically accelerate the frequency of mutations in the gene encoding the protein connexin 26 that are responsible for most of the inherited hearing loss in the United States. That occurs because parents who both have connexin deafness pass the gene mutation to their child, usually causing deafness at birth and making a disproportionate contribution to the pool of deaf individuals in the next generation, according to the study (which will be published in the June issue of the American Journal of Human Genetics. The study was published early online.)

"In the United States, at least 85 percent of individuals with profound deafness marry another deaf person," says Dr. Walter Nance, professor of human genetics and lead author on the article. "Because we now know that more than 100 different genes are responsible for deafness, most deaf parents have children with normal hearing because they pass different genes to their offspring. "But in the case of marriages among couples who both have the same form of recessive deafness, all their children will be deaf and capable themselves of also passing on the altered gene to their offspring. In addition, as many as 3.5 percent of the hearing population in the United States may carry single mutations involving the connexin 26 complex, making this one of the most commonly recognized single gene defects."

About one in 800 infants has profound hearing impairment, and about half of these cases are thought to be genetic in origin. Investigators are interested in learning more about deafness genes because deafness sometimes is accompanied by other conditions, such as blindness, and they are seeking ways to avoid or prevent these serious side effects.

Nance notes that intermarriages among the deaf started to increase about 1800 after the first schools to teach sign language were opened, improving the social and economic circumstances of the deaf and allowing them to communicate among themselves and with non-deaf individuals who learned sign language. Before that time, marriages among the deaf were rare.

"In regions where national or statewide schools for the deaf have been established and marriages among students have occurred, we've seen an amplification of the commonest form of recessive deafness in the overall population," he said.

These findings about how sign language contributed to intermarriages among the deaf and led to an increase in the frequency of connexin deafness in the Untied States and other developed countries have led Nance and his colleagues to speculate about how this genetic mechanism also may have been involved in the evolution of speech. This acquisition of syntactic speech generally is viewed as the most significant event in human evolution of the human because it set man apart from other primates and led to an explosive evolution of the human brain by facilitating the transfer of abstract knowledge, experience and culture.

There is general agreement that there has been an explosive acceleration in human evolution in the last 100,000–200,000 years, but the precise way in which the fixation of favorable genes in our species was accelerated has been one of the most important unresolved problems about human evolution.

"When you think about how the onset of selective marriages among deaf populations led to an increase in specific mutations for deafness, you easily can see how these same forces might have contributed to the spread of genes for speech among Homo sapiens 160,000 years ago, " Nance said. "If you were one of the first primates with an ability to communicate by speaking, wouldn't you want to select a partner who could whisper sweet nothings in your ear?"

EDITORS' NOTE: A copy of Dr. Nance's article is available via e-mail in PDF format or by fax. For information, please call VCU News Services at (804) 828-1231.

About VCU and the VCU Medical Center: *Located on two downtown campuses in Richmond, Va., Virginia Commonwealth University is ranked nationally by the Carnegie Foundation as a top research institution and enrolls 26,000 students in more than 170 certificate, undergraduate, graduate, professional and doctoral programs in the arts, sciences and humanities in 11 schools and one college. Forty of the university's programs are unique in Virginia, and 20 graduate and professional programs have been ranked by* U.S. News & World Report *as among the best of their kind. MCV Hospitals, clinics and the health sciences schools of Virginia Commonwealth University compose the VCU Medical Center, one of the leading academic medical centers in the country. For more, see www.vcu.edu.*

26

BERNARD BRAGG

Actor, Mime, Educator
Founder of National Theatre of the Deaf

Bernard Bragg began his life in Brooklyn, New York on September 27, 1928. Born deaf like his parents, Bragg enrolled in the Fanwood School for the Deaf (now New York School for the Deaf). One of his memorable teachers was Robert Panara, who was noted for his theater experience, advised Bragg in his theatrical ventures. Bragg's father, Wolf Bragg, ran a local theater company in New York—coupled with two distinguished mentors, Bragg's love for the stage was inevitable when he began studying at Gallaudet in 1952. He juggled English and Education while working as editor of the Buff and Blue and garnered Best of the Actor of the Year awards twice for his lead roles at Gallaudet. 1956 was the beginning of a pinnacle; Bragg met Marcel Marceau, the great French mime, who brought him to Paris to study mime. Upon returning to the United States, Bragg performed traditional mime, hitting San Francisco's nightclubs and other clubs across the nation. On February 3, 1958, Life magazine commended him as one of the best small nightclub performers in America. Bragg taught at the Califormia School for the Deaf in Berkeley while he appeared regularly on the San Francisco television show, **"The Quiet Man"**, where he performed in accordance to phoned-in requests. Bernard also appeared in the made-for-TV movie, ***"And Your Name Is Jonah"*** as well as performing throughout Europe, appearing both on television and on stage.

Bragg helped found the National Theatre of the Deaf and the *Little Theatre of the Deaf*; he appeared on NBC to introduce the prestigious NTD performing company. Bernard continued his involvement with NTD as a leading actor, adaptor of works, administrator and sign master for over ten years. Among his students at NTD was a young Marlee Matlin.

He served as artist-in-residence in Russia, New York and Washington D.C. In 1979 he wrote and directed, **"That Makes Two of Us,"** a romantic comedy and co-authored, **"Tales from a Clubroom."** Gallaudet University awarded him exceptional actor-author-mime with an honorary doctorate in Humane Letters for his venerable service to the deaf.

Stage and Television Credits with the National Theatre of the Deaf

1967–68	EXPERIMENT IN TELEVISION (NBC TV special)
1967–68	TYGER! TYGER! AND OTHER BURNINGS
1967–68	GIANNI SCHICCHI
1968–69	BLUEPRINTS
1968–69	THE CRITIC
1969–70	SGANARELLE
1969–70	SONGS FROM MILK WOOD
1970–71	WOYZECK
1970–71	JOURNEYS
1971–72	*MY THIRD EYE*
1973–74	A CHILD'S CHRISTMAS IN WALES (CBS-TV narrator)
1973–74	OPTIMISM: THE MISADVENTURES OF CANDIDE
1974–75	THE DYBBUK
1974–75	PRISCILLA, PRINCESS OF POWER
1975–76	PARADE
1977–78	WHO KNOWS ONE (CBS TV special)

27

DANCE TECHNIQUES FOR DEAF AND HARD OF HEARING DANCERS

Many people have the misconception that deaf people "hear" by feeling vibrations through the floor. How is this possible, especially if a person is moving and jumping so that they do not keep in continuous contact with the floor? What if the floor is not wood, but solid concrete?

The Gallaudet Dancers need many hours of practice in order to develop an inner sense of timing for a specific dance. Some dancers who have some residual hearing may pick up cues from the music to assist them in knowing where they are supposed to be in a dance, but this does not happen the first time they learn a new dance, but rather after countless hours of practice and counting all the movements in a dance step. Whether the dancer can use his or her residual hearing will also depend on his or her type of hearing loss (high or low frequency loss) and the music (bass or treble tones). Many deaf dancers can discriminate bass tones better than treble.

When a dance instructor is teaching a new dance routine to deaf performers, counting visually helps establish the basic rhythm pattern and facilitates the development of inner rhythm and timing for a particular dance. In addition, when teaching a new dance step, it helps if the instructor gives a sign count for each step, similar to giving a verbal count with hearing dancers. Occasionally, we use a drum to demonstrate the precise rhythm of a piece of music. Often a deaf dancer will use his or her eyes to watch and follow the movement of a fellow dancer who may be able to hear and follow the music.

It is important to note that the Gallaudet Dance Company remains "in time" with or without music. This is a parallel experience to that of an experienced musician, especially a drummer, who has a highly developed sense of timing.

In summary, when teaching dance to deaf students, the most effective technique is to count visually, use a high quality sound system, and communicate through signs.

28

DEAFLYMPICS HISTORY

The athletes of the Deaflympics set records and break barriers every time they participate in the Summer and Winter Games.

The first games, known as the International Silent Games were held in 1924 in Paris. They were the brainchild of Eugène Rubens-Alcais, himself deaf and President of the French Deaf Sports Federation.

At a time when societies everywhere viewed deaf people as intellectually inferior, linguistically impoverished and often treated us as outcasts, Monsieur Rubens-Alcais envisioned the international sports event as the best answer. Antoine Dresse, a young deaf Belgian, was instrumental in helping him accomplish his dream.

The competition at the games immediately became the social context for countries to deliberate about similarities and differences in the welfare of their deaf people. Over the years, games have been awarded with the aim of spreading these deliberations into new areas.

Misconceptions about deaf people persist to this day in many parts of society and around the world. But inroads are being made in the battle against prejudice, as more nations and individuals join in the Deaflympic movement and more games are held.

The Silent Games were the first ever for any group of people with disabilities. After the initial Paris Games, deaf sporting leaders assembled at a café and established Le Comité International des Sports Silencieux (the Committee of Silent Sports), CISS, which was later renamed Le Comité International des Sports des Sourds (The International Committee of Sports for the Deaf).

The Deaflympics are distinguished from all other IOC sanctioned games by the fact that they are organized and run exclusively by members of the community they serve. Only deaf people are eligible to serve on the CISS/Deaflympics board and executive bodies.

Participants in the first games arrived from nine European countries. Today, the number of national federations in the CISS membership has reached 94. Among relative newcomers enjoying the benefits of this worldwide network of sports and social inclusion are such geographically disparate countries as Mongolia, Bangladesh, Cyprus, Estonia, Uruguay, Iceland and Swazliand.

Twenty Summer Games have been held since the initial Paris games with 145 athletes. No games were held between 1939 and 1949 because of World War II.

The first Winter Games were held in Seefeld, Austria, 1949 with 33 athletes from five countries.

The first games outside of Europe were the Summer Games held in Washington DC in the United States, in 1965.

29

DEAFLYMPICS LOGO

The Deaflympics logo, designed in 2003 by graphic design artist Ralph Fernandez, is a positive and powerful symbol of the international deaf sports community. It ties together strong elements: Sign language, deaf and international cultures, unity and continuity.

The hand shapes, "ok", "good", and "great" that overlap each other in a circle, represent the original sign for "deaf Olympics". Together, the hand shapes represent the sign for "united".

The center of the logo represents the iris of the eye, which defines deaf people as visual people; they must use their eyes to communicate.

The logo incorporates the four colors of the national flags of the world. The red, blue, yellow and green represent the four regional confederations – the Asia Pacific Deaf Sports Federation, the European Deaf Sports Organization, the Pan American Deaf Sports Federation and the Confederation of African Deaf Sports.

DEAF CULTURE: EUGENICS

30

ALEXANDER GRAHAM BELL

BIOGRAPHY

Born **Alexander Bell** in Edinburgh on March 3, 1847, he later adopted the middle name *Graham* out of admiration for Alexander Graham, a family friend. Many called Bell "the father of the Deaf." This title may be regarded as somewhat ironic due to his belief in the practice of eugenics. He hoped to one day eliminate hereditary deafness from the population.

His family was associated with the teaching of elocution: his grandfather in London, his uncle in Dublin, and his father, Alexander Melville Bell, in Edinburgh, were all professed elocutionists. The latter has published a variety of works on the subject, several of which are well known, especially his treatise on Visible Speech, which appeared in Edinburgh in 1868. In this he explains his method of instructing deaf mutes, by means of their eyesight, how to articulate words, and also how to read what other persons are saying by the motions of their lips.

Alexander Graham Bell was educated at the Royal High School of Edinburgh, from which he graduated at the age of 13. At the age of 16 he secured a position as a pupil-teacher of elocution and music in Weston House Academy, at Elgin, Moray, Scotland. The next year he spent at the University of Edinburgh. He was graduated from University College London.

From 1867 to 1868, he was an instructor at Somersetshire College at Bath, Somerset, England.

While still in Scotland he is said to have turned his attention to the science of acoustics, with a view to ameliorate the deafness of his mother.

In 1870, at the age of 23, he emigrated with his family to Canada where they settled at Brantford. Before he left Scotland, Bell had turned his attention to telephony, and in Canada he continued an interest in communication machines. He designed a piano which could transmit its music to a distance by means of electricity. In 1873, he accompanied his father to Montreal, Canada, where he was employed in teaching the system of visible speech. The elder Bell was invited to introduce the system into a large day-school for mutes at Boston, but he declined the post in favor of his son, who became Professor of Vocal Physiology and Elocution at Boston University's School of Oratory.

At Boston University he continued his research in the same field, and endeavored to produce a telephone which would not only send musical notes, but articulate speech. With financing from his American father-in-law, on March 7, 1876, the U.S. Patent Office granted him Patent Number 174,465 covering "the method of, and apparatus for, transmitting vocal or other sounds telegraphically . . . by causing electrical undulations, similar in form to the vibrations of the air accompanying the said vocal or other sound", the telephone.

After obtaining the patent for the telephone, Bell continued his many experiments in communication, which culminated in the invention of the photophone-transmission of sound on a beam of light—a precursor of today's optical fiber systems. He also worked in medical research and invented techniques for teaching speech to the deaf. The range of Bell's inventive genius is represented only in part by the eighteen patents granted in his name alone and the twelve he shared with his collaborators. These included fourteen for the telephone and telegraph, four for the photophone, one for the phonograph, five for aerial vehicles, four for hydroairplanes, and two for a selenium cell.

In 1882, he became a naturalized citizen of the United States. In 1888, he was one of the founding members of the National Geographic Society and became its second president.

Bell married Mabel Hubbard, who was one of his pupils at Boston University and also a deaf-mute, on July 11, 1877. His invention of the telephone resulted from his attempts to create a device that would allow him to communicate with his wife and his deaf mother. He died at Beinn Bhreagh, located on Nova Scotia's Cape Breton Island near the village of Baddeck, in 1922 was buried atop Beinn Bhreagh mountain overlooking Bras d'Or Lake. He was survived by his wife and two of their four children.

Bell and decibel

The *bel* (B) is a unit of measurement originally proposed by 1929 W. H. Martin of Bell Labs (*Bell System Techn. Jrnl. VIII. 2*) and named after Bell. The bel was too large for everyday use, so the decibel (dB), equal to 0.1 B, became more commonly used.

The dB is commonly used as a unit for expressing sound pressure level and sound power. Since the decibel is a ratio it must be related to a reference value, commonly 20 μPa for sound pressure level and 10^{-12} watts for sound power level. Decibels are also used to express electrical ratios such as power.

EUGENICS

Along with many very prominent thinkers and scientists of the time, Bell was connected with the eugenics movement in the United States. From 1912 until 1918 he was the chairman of the board of scientific advisors to the Eugenics Record Office associated with Cold Spring Harbor Laboratory in New York, and regularly attended meetings. In 1921 he was the honorary president of the Second International Congress of Eugenics held under the auspices of the American Museum of Natural History in New York. Organizations such as these advocated passing laws (with success in some states) that established the compulsory sterilization of people deemed to be, as Bell called them, a "defective variety of the human race." By the late 1930s about half the states in the US had eugenics laws, the California laws being used as a model for eugenics laws in Nazi Germany.

His ideas about people he considered defective centered on the deaf because of his long contact with them in his work with deaf education. In addition to advocating sterilization of the deaf, Bell wished to prohibit deaf teachers from being allowed to teach in schools for the deaf, he worked to outlaw the marriage of deaf individuals to one another, and he was an ardent supporter of oralism over manualism. His avowed goal was to eradicate the language and culture of the deaf so as to force them to integrate into the hearing culture for their own long-term benefit and for the benefit of society at large. Although this attitude is widely seen as paternalistic and arrogant today, it was mainstream in that era.

Although he supported what many would consider harsh and inhumane policies today, he was not unkind to deaf individuals who proved his theories of oralism. He was a personal and longtime friend of Helen Keller, and his wife Mabel was deaf, though none of their children were. Bell was known as a kindly father and loving family man who took great pleasure in playing with his many grandchildren.

31

BEFORE MILAN 1880

Milan 1880 History

In the Beginning

Firstly, a little Deaf history leading up to Milan 1880 . . .

At the beginning of the time when records started, the situation of Deaf people was usually negative.

Deaf people were perceived as being uneducable by Aristotle ("it is impossible to reason without the ability to hear") and St. Augustine ("faith comes only through hearing"). In the Mediterranean countries Roman law forbade the inheritance of family fortunes by those who could not speak.

Development of Methods

The first known teacher of the Deaf was Pedro Ponce de Leon, a Spanish monk (early 1500s). He taught an 18-year-old Deaf son of a Mayor to say a few words. Deaf sons of rich people were able to 'perform' speech to gain inheritance, and also were able to overcome the stigma of producing abnormal children that existed within their social circles. These wealthy parents were willing to pay anyone who could make their Deaf children "normal".

Pedro Ponce de Leon's success encouraged further education techniques for the Deaf. He was followed by Manuel Ramirez de Carrion (late 1500s), the man who is seen as the inventor of speech training for Deaf people.

Carrion taught speech using a phonetic method, which involved pronouncing individual letters of the alphabet correctly. By associating individual letters with specific sounds, Carrion claimed that he could teach the Deaf to speak. The training in speech involved learning to make vowel sounds using a model tongue!

Another important figure around that time was Juan Pablo Martin Bonet. Bonet was the first to publish a method for educating the Deaf. According to this method, the Deaf were taught to read, write, and use the one-handed manual alphabet system.

The impact of the work of these great Spanish pioneers was felt throughout Europe, including the UK.

The De l'Epée Era

Around the 1750s, certain important developments took place in France.

A French priest, Charles Michel de l'Epée, was very concerned that Deaf people were not receiving the sacraments. According to the beliefs of the Church, failure to receive the sacraments would send them to Hell. Yet he did not know how to help them.

One day, he noticed two Deaf girls communicating with each other in their own sign language. He observed them carefully, and could soon exchange simple ideas with them. After a short time, he had learned their language and found that he could communicate complicated religious ideas to them.

In 1760, he opened at first a shelter for the poor Deaf, and by 1762/3 he had created a school for the education of the Deaf in Paris. Before de l'Epée opened the school, education was only available to rich deaf children. He gave educational opportunities to poor deaf children. Almost immediately, he was overwhelmed with the number of poor deaf children coming to his school.

He very soon came to the conclusion that teaching through sign language was proving to be effective and efficient. He developed a very high and well-structured educational system for deaf children. He also invented new signs to show grammatical features of the French language. His system for teaching the Deaf became known as the French Method which became the foundatioin of the world's sign languages to this day.

One of de l'Epée's students, the Abbé Sicard, continued his work. He opened a school of his own, and in 1818 he published an important study called "Theory of Signs", which included a grammar and dictionary of sign language.

From the 1780s onwards, Deaf people had no problems with education, and they were even writing books (e.g. Ferdinand Berthier and others). It should be noted that most of the important Deaf writers during the next century were French, where education via sign language was the norm.

Ferdinand Berthier was a gifted Deaf student. He became a teacher's assistant at 21, a professor at 26, and then became the Dean of Professors. During his time he was a well-known writer, his works including biographies of de l'Epée and Sicard. He was also a political man who fought for the rights of signing deaf people.

Another leading Deaf professor was Pierre Pelissier. In 1844 he published a collection of poems that were very well received. Pelissier was fluent in French and French Sign Language, a skilful poet in both languages. Pelissier hated oralism and loved to sign. He disagreed with the oral method and went around saying so. He also published the first sign dictionary.

There is also evidence that Deaf people were successful lawyers, artists, politicians and so on.

Sign Vs Oral

Parallel to these positive developments, in 1770 a Swiss doctor called Johann Conrad Amman wrote a famous book called "The Speaking Deaf", in which he strongly stated that the oral method was the best for deaf people.

Amman's ideas about the importance of speech and speech reading were followed in Germany by Samuel Heinicke. Around the same time as the Abbé de l'Epée founded his school in Paris, Samuel Heinicke was developing in Germany his own oral approach to teaching the Deaf. Heinicke's oral approach became so popular it became known as the German Method.

De l'Epée also had a strong French rival, Jacob Rodrigues Pereire, a leading Oralist who had often challenged de l'Epée's work and his legacy. He was developing "secret" methods on how to instruct deaf pupils orally. De l'Epée, at one time, invited Pereire to his school to prove that the deaf could be educated through signs, and de l'Epée seemed to have made his point—or so he thought. How was he, or anyone else, to know that Jacob Pereire would have the last laugh almost a century later!

Thomas Braidwood opened the first school for the education of deaf children in Britain in the first quarter of 1760 in Edinburgh. This, and other early schools, used the idea of what we call the combined system, which is the forerunner of "total communication"—the use of sign language and speech at the same time. Under this system, Deaf Braidwoodian pupils excelled and went on to achieve great things—two became members of the Royal Society, one went on to become an Auditor of Excise (Scotland), seven went on to become noted artists, and so on.

In the USA, Thomas Hopkins Gallaudet founded the American School for the Deaf in Hartford, Connecticut, and used sign language (based on de l'Epée's methods). But at the Clarke School for the Deaf in Massachusetts, the oral methods developed by Heinicke were strongly advocated by Alexander Graham Bell!

An important point to make here is that Abbé de l'Epée and Heinicke were rivals. De l'Epée was a strong supporter of education through sign language and Heinicke an advocate of the oral method. There were similar tensions between oral and sign methods in the UK and USA.

It is interesting that the argument on the topic of Sign Language vs Oralism happened then, and it's still happening now.

Dawning of Hear And Speak

The climax of the controversy regarding oral versus sign language in the schools for the deaf came in 1880, at the Second International Congress on the Education of the Deaf in Milan.

Milan 1880. No other event in the history of deaf education had a greater impact on the lives and education of deaf people. This single event almost destroyed sign language and created a turbulent legacy.

MILAN 1880 CONGRESS

Overview

Event
The Second International Congress of Teachers of Deaf Mutes.

Date
6th 11th September 1880.

Venue(s)
Regid Istitutio Tecnico di Santa Marta, Milan, Italy (for the Congress); Royal Institution for the Deaf and Dumb Poor of the Province and Royal School for the Poor, both of Milan (for the demonstrations).

Number of Delegates
Although the attendance numbers may have varied each day, 164 was generally the average.

Countries Represented
87 Italians, 53 French, 8 British, 5 Americans, 3 Swedish, 1 Belgian and 1 German. The rest remains unknown.

Number of Deaf Delegates
Only 2 James Denison, Principal of the Columbian Institute in Washington DC, USA and Claudius Forestier Director of Lyon School for the Deaf, France

Aim of Congress

1. To push and vote for the Pure Oral Method to be used in the instruction of the deaf and to discourage sign language in the education of the deaf.
2. To monopolise deaf education and remove deaf teachers.

No of Resolutions Passed
8, especially the two topmost Resolutions 1 & 2.

The Eight Resolutions

The following eight resolutions were submitted during the Congress and were declared / recommended which had created a legacy to this day, most evidently by the two topmost resolutions.

Resolution 1
Considering the incontestable superiority of speech over signs in restoring the deaf-mute to society, and in giving him a more perfect knowledge of language,

Declares
That the Oral method ought to be preferred to that of signs for the education and instruction of the deaf and dumb.

Voted 160 to 4 in favour on 7/9/1880.

Resolution 2
Considering that the simultaneous use of speech and signs has the disadvantage of injuring speech, lip-reading and precision of ideas,

Declares
That the Pure Oral method ought to be preferred.

Voted 150 to 16 in favour on 9/9/1880.

Resolution 3

Considering that a great number of the deaf and dumb are not receiving the benefit of instruction, and that this condition is owing to the "impotence" (impotenza) of families and of institutions,

Recommends
That Governments should take the necessary steps that all the deaf and dumb may be educated.
Carried unanimously on 10/9/1880.

Resolution 4

Considering that the teaching of the speaking deaf by the Pure Oral method should resemble as much as possible that of those who hear and speak,

Declares

a) That the most natural and effectual means by which the speaking deaf may acquire the knowledge of language is the "intuitive" method, viz., that which consists in setting forth, first by speech, and then by writing the objects and the facts which are placed before the eyes of the pupils.

b) That in the first, or maternal, period the deaf-mute ought to be led to the observation of grammatical forms by means of examples and of practical exercises, and that in the second period he ought to be assisted to deduce from these examples the grammatical rules, expressed with the utmost simplicity and clearness.

c) That books, written with words and in forms of language known to the pupil, can be put into his hands at any time.

Carried on 11/09/1880.

Resolution 5

Considering the want of books sufficiently elementary to help the gradual and progressive development of language,

Recommends

That the teachers of the Oral system should apply themselves to the publication of special works on the subject.

Carried on 11/09/1880.

Resolution 6

Considering the results obtained by the numerous inquiries made concerning the deaf and dumb of every age and every condition long after they had quitted school, who, when interrogated upon various subjects, have answered correctly, with sufficient clearness of articulation, and read the lips of their questioners with the greatest facility,

Declares

a) That the deaf and dumb taught by the Pure Oral method do not forget after leaving school the knowledge which they have acquired there, but develop it still further by conversation and reading, when have been made so easy for them.

b) That in their conversation with speaking persons they make use exclusively of speech.

c) That speech and lip-reading so far from being lost, are developed by practice.

Carried on 11/09/1880.

Resolution 7

Considering that the education of the deaf and dumb by speech has peculiar requirements; considering also that the experience of teachers of deaf-mutes is almost unanimous,

Declares

a) That the most favourable age for admitting a deaf child into school is from eight to ten years.
b) That the school term ought to be seven years at least; but eight years would be preferable.
3) That no teacher can effectually teach a class of more than ten children on the Pure Oral method.

Carried on 11/09/1880.

Resolution 8

Considering that the application of the Pure Oral method in institutions where it is not yet in active operation, should be to avoid the certainty of failure prudent, gradual, progressive,

Recommends

a) That the pupils newly received into the schools should form a class by themselves, where instruction could be given by speech.
b) That these pupils should be absolutely separated from others too far advanced to be instructed by speech, and whose education will be completed by signs.
c) That each year a new speaking class be established, with all the old pupils taught by signs have completed their education.

Carried on 11/09/1880.

DEAF FAMILY EXPERIENCE

32

NOTHING IS IMPOSSIBLE— THE HUGHES FAMILY

Patty Hughes

As the second child of deaf parents who have four deaf children, I would not want to replace our communication method with any other. We have a very good communication line among each member of the family. All of us are profoundly deaf, and we all use American Sign Language. Each of us children acquired language when we were about nine months old.

My two sisters, my brother and I were all born in Missouri. My oldest sister, Bonnie, and I received most of our education from the Missouri School for the Deaf in Fulton, and some from the Virginia School for the Deaf and the Blind in Staunton. My younger sister, Mary, and my brother, Billy, attended both schools too, but stayed at the Virginia School longer. My parents both graduated from the Missouri School for the Deaf.

I don't recall if I ever felt that I was "deaf" when I was a child. My parents taught us to rely upon ourselves first, and being in a deaf family made it hard for me to realize that there was anything different about being deaf.

We shared a lot of things in growing up together. For example, we'd watch TV programs and guess together what was happening. We'd exchange our guesses with each other and usually agree on some conclusion. It didn't matter if our conclusion was right or wrong, since we had no way to find out what was actually occurring on the TV screen.

Before we owned a TDD, we used to ask one of our neighbors to make occasional phone calls. If our neighbors were not available, we'd have to ask a stranger to make it. That could be embarrassing at times. However, my parents always made the point to us that we could not help but to swallow some of our pride and approach strangers for help if a phone call was urgent.

Our family would go out to eat once or twice a week. During these dinners out, my parents set an example for us in writing down their orders and encouraging us to do the same. They emphasized to us that it made things much easier to write the order down, than trying to talk, as talking could lead to unnecessary misunderstandings and frustrations. We were also encouraged by my parents to write down a note for our doctor, before the actual appointment, to save time and to make sure the doctor got an accurate description of what the problem was.

The only time in my childhood years that I actually wished my parents were hearing was when I was introduced to some "bad" signs for the first time by friends at school. I knew I could not use them in front of my parents, because I'd be punished, whereas my deaf friends who had hearing parents could sign all the "bad" signs they wanted at home without their parents understanding a word!

In my family, it almost seemed as if my parents had two separate families to raise. Bonnie and I are less than two years apart, but Mary and I are five years apart. Thus, there were different things about Bonnie's and my upbringing, and Mary's and Billy's.

Bonnie and I grew up in Missouri whereas Mary and Billy grew up in Virginia. When we lived in Kansas City, Missouri, there were clubs for the deaf, a kindergarten for deaf children, and oral programs in the schools. My parents usually took Bonnie and me to the clubs for the deaf so we could play with the other kids there. They also sent us to a kindergarten with a program for deaf children, and Bonnie and I also attended the Troost School, which had an oral program.

The main reason we attended the Troost School was so that we could associate with the hearing kids. My parents thought this was very important for us. About the time that Billy and Mary would have entered school, we moved to a town up north in Missouri, and all of us attended the Missouri School for the Deaf.

We moved up north so that my Dad and his deaf partner could establish themselves in a dry-cleaning business in Moberly, Missouri. Then he and the partner decided to open up two more dry-cleaning businesses in Kirksville, Missouri. Bonnie and I spent our summers helping Dad by working at the counters (with customers coming in). We communicated by writing, and memorized most of our frequent customers' names. By watching Dad, we learned how to be comfortable with different communication modes, such as writing, with the customers.

When I was younger, I did not fully realize how frustrating it must have been for Dad when he opened up the businesses, as many of his deaf friends discouraged him from doing this just because he was deaf. Some people even stopped by the store and told Dad he was crazy. But these frustrations only made him more determined to prove to both deaf and hearing people that deaf people *can* do it!

Dad and his partner operated the businesses for eight years. Then Dad got a job offer to teach dry-cleaning at the Virginia School for the Deaf and the Blind. He grabbed the opportunity because he felt that he needed a change in his life and because he wanted to be able to spend more time with the family. He also felt we could get a better education at the Virginia School, and he wanted to go into the field of missionary work with deaf young people. Thus we moved to Virginia, and all of us girls have graduated from the Virginia school. Billy is still a student there.

In spite of the differences in ages the communication link in my family is very strong and powerful. We usually spend hours and hours talking together during and after supper. My parents believe strongly in encouraging us to share our thoughts and feelings with each other.

When my parents quarrel, all of us know what they are quarreling about, as they believe in open communication between them and us. There is a funny incident I remember well. When Billy was about four years old, my parents were quarreling one evening and Billy was trying hard to figure out what was going on. Finally, in the middle of a hot moment, he politely interrupted and asked them to slow down so he could understand better!

We rarely visit our relatives, because we don't enjoy feeling "left out of it" as we do when we visit them. All of our relatives except an uncle and a cousin are hearing, and most of them don't know Sign Language. I do wish sometimes that we had better communication because it would be nice to get to know them better.

When I was about 20 years old, it was the first time I really worked with hearing people, and my first experience in realizing that I am deaf and will experience some frustrations as a deaf person. The building where I worked was nearly full of people who had never met a deaf person before. When my boss and I were introduced to each other, he looked awed, and I was tempted to say, "Hey, I look normal, don't I?"

But we shook hands, and his first question to me was if I could lip read. I told him yes, but I'd rather write. Thus, all afternoon on that first day we spent hours writing back and forth to get acquainted.

The first week at work was very frustrating, since it was the first time I'd really had to deal with a communication barrier. As time passed, things became much better at work. I felt great working there for the summer as I felt I had won a battle in learning how to cope with communication barriers, and when I was asked to work there again, I felt good about it.

Sometimes I imagine that my family was hearing, and wonder if I would encounter this kind of frustration. But most of the time I am glad I have encountered it, and consider myself very lucky to be born into a family where my parents succeeded in teaching me to let nothing stop me just because I am deaf. That is the greatest lesson I have learned from them.

33

THE DEAF CHILD IN FOSTER CARE

M. Teresa Arcari and Beth Gwinn Betman

Although considerable emphasis has been placed on the issue of permanency planning for children in foster care, significant barriers must often be overcome in order to attain this goal. This is especially true when children who have special needs—in this instance, deaf children—are placed in homes ill prepared to meet their needs, and when workers responsible for planning for them do not have sufficient information about the disability or available resources. Although reference is made to foster care throughout this article, all points made are equally valid in the identification of appropriate adoptive homes.

Advocates for Hearing Impaired Youth, Inc., which was formed in 1982 for the specific purpose of assessing the needs of the estimated 4,000 to 5,000 children with hearing impairments placed under the care of social service agencies, is committed to providing child placement professionals with some awareness of and sensitivity to these special needs. The effort has grown out of the perception that in most cases, deaf children are inappropriately placed in substitute care. Increased knowledge of the issues specific to hearing impairment will help to ensure progress toward the goal of permanency planning for deaf children and avoid needless multiple moves.

A central area of concern involves the identification of foster families with communication skills that match the needs of individual deaf children. Those children with severe to profound hearing loss will most often use manual communication—sign language—in place of, or in addition to, speech. In seeking parents with sign language proficiency, the value of working with the child to attain as much speech as possible should not be overlooked. However, the use of total communication (both signing and speech) in order for deaf children to achieve early exposure to language is also important.[1] Whatever the final decision regarding the most appropriate communication style, it must be based on adequate knowledge about these issues.

PLACEMENT CONCERNS

Typically, social workers have had little, if any, exposure to deafness and have only a limited idea of what the "individual needs" of a deaf child are. Because of family crises, placements frequently occur without much time for planning. The deaf child is often placed with foster families who have boundless good will but no knowledge of the disability and no sign language skills.

[1] E. Mindel and M. Vernon, "Oralism Only or Total Communication." in *They grow in silence,* Silver Spring. Md., NAD Press, 1971.

In those rare cases where the social worker has some beginning knowledge of sign language, his or her skills most often fall short of the ability to explain to a child the events that are taking place. Frustration and disappointment for family and child usually result. The child faces two alternatives: quiet "adjustment" to a setting that affords very limited communication and often results in a sense of isolation that is extremely damaging, or acting out behavior that precipitates one move after another.

Angie's case illustrates the difficulties that may be encountered by the child, the foster family and the social worker.

Angie, an 11-year-old girl living in a large institution for dependent children, was one of the first children assigned to the social worker—who had had no previous contact with deaf individuals—for placement in a foster home. Prior to that, Angie had been placed in a residential center for severely disturbed children with the diagnosis—later to be found inaccurate—of "selective mutism" thought to result from Angie's experiences with her schizophrenic mother, whose bizarre behavior left her without any clear idea of normal, day-to-day life. (The children in this family often needed to beg meals from the neighbors or look for food in the trash. The mother performed strange religious rituals in the home and was often found wandering naked in the streets.) Based on this history, the original diagnosis was, in fact, a good guess, but wrong. The correct diagnosis of profound hearing loss was finally made when Angie was 10 years old and she was moved to the institution.

Although neither the worker nor the prospective foster parents had any sign language ability, they tried to prepare Angie for placement through drawings, gestures and carefully planned day trips. Despite their efforts, the final placement was quite traumatic. When she saw her suitcase, Angie knew that this was to be a big step and she was terrified. She threw a temper tantrum and attempted to get out of the car while it was moving on the highway.

After arriving at the new foster home, Angie sat on her suitcase for several hours. Through drawings and the kind, patient behavior of the new foster parents—and perhaps because she was too tired to fight anymore—Angie agreed to stay overnight. This began a long, uphill battle toward successful adjustment and growth.

Unlike Angie's foster family, most do not follow through to learn sign language—a process that takes a significant investment of time and energy—even after expressing an initial interest. While they are trying to help the child fit in with the new family, foster parents of a deaf child are simultaneously working cooperatively with special school placements, learning about the care and use of a hearing aid and taking the child for further audiological tests and perhaps additional speech therapy. Only the very committed succeed with so many demands.

In order to be fair to both the deaf child and foster family, foster parents must be identified who already possess basic communication skills and a knowledge of the disability.

RECRUITMENT

Where would a child placement agency begin to recruit foster parents with the necessary knowledge and skills? If the agency has the good fortune to be located near a school for the deaf, this facility may have staff with sign language ability who would be interested in accepting a child into their home. Parents with a deaf child who have developed self-confidence from dealing successfully with their own child's disability may possess the needed communication skills and be willing to extend themselves to other children.

Individuals who grew up with a deaf sibling or whose parents were deaf often have fluent sign language skills and the needed sensitivity. Because these individuals frequently have regular contacts with hearing impaired adults in the deaf community, they can provide their deaf children with successful role models. The well-developed network of deaf clubs and deaf church congregations provides additional major meeting places for those with the skills necessary to raise deaf children, and these sources should not be overlooked in any serious effort to recruit appropriate foster homes.

This, of course, raises the question of active recruitment of deaf adults as foster parents. Why not tap this ready-made resource? The practical problem that must be confronted is the communication barrier between worker and prospective foster parents—a barrier that is not insurmountable.

A fundamental question that may need to be addressed first is whether agency administrators and workers view deaf indivduals as "handicapped." When deaf adults are seen in this light, they are perceived as those who *receive* services rather than as possible service *providers.* Often, child placement professionals do not see the deaf community as having capable adults who can impart valuable coping skills to deaf youngsters. Agencies do not seem to be aware of a responsibility to hire qualified sign language interpreters to facilitate the process of identification and matching of deaf children with deaf foster parents. These service gaps tend to be pervasive in spite of the provisions of Section 504 of the Rehabilitation Act of 1973 (P.L. 93–112). This Act states that any agency may not deny a handicapped person the opportunity to receive benefits or services that are equal to those offered non-handicapped persons, and may not provide them with benefits or services that are not as effective as the benefits or services provided to others.

ISSUES DURING PLACEMENT

With the arrival of a deaf child in the foster family, new demands are inevitable. Accommodation always requires a shift in attention and efforts to help the newcomer gain an equal footing with existing family members. Obviously, this does not happen overnight. Considerable adjustment is required for each person in the home. For example, any discussion in the presence of the hearing impaired child, whether directly related to the child or not, should be signed. Allowing conversations to be "overheard" enables the child to become privy to the thousands of incidental exchanges that normally occur in any household. A considerable amount of information about relationships and day-to-day living is learned in this way.

If the family does not already have strong ties in the deaf community, special efforts may be required to find appropriate church congregations and social clubs. Visits with deaf peers from school, who often live some distance away, will need to be arranged. Such requirements must be identified and discussed with prospective foster parents ahead of time. They should also be encouraged to ask themselves two basic questions: Will I become tired of the extra effort? Will I wish these special needs would go away?

Frequently there is the subconscious hope, by both natural and foster parents, that if enough energy is invested, the deaf child will eventually become like a hearing person. Helping the child to maximize residual hearing through the use of hearing aids and fostering development of verbal skills through speech therapy are desirable steps to be taken. However, when the disability does not magically disappear, many parents become discouraged. The reality is that the deaf child does not become like them, a part of their hearing world. At this point parents often feel that they have failed and greatly curtail efforts on behalf of their child. Realistic recognition of the child's limitations from the beginning and encouragement of his or her strengths, interests and abilities can guard against their fantasy of "rescuing" the child from deafness.

Natural parents raising a deaf child need to know something about how hearing loss affects the stages of development.[2] Foster parents must consider this information, as well as additional factors related to the more complicated life experiences of children who come into foster care.

It may also be that the child's natural parents—overwhelmed with personal problems and unable to communicate effectively—abandoned any effort at consistent discipline. In addition, the child probably harbors deep anxieties about the meaning of the placement. Without clear and consistently available communication to ease these anxieties and set up behavioral guidelines, the child's activity level may be well beyond what is acceptable.

At the opposite extreme is the youngster who has deep-seated feelings of worthlessness related to the handicap. This child is convinced that the disability, which may have represented additional stress for the family, ultimately resulted in his or her rejection. In the new foster home the child pushes aside needs and worries in an effort to be found acceptable. If the child learns that it is desirable to express feelings and that people are sensitive to concerns, such groundwork will build a foundation for healthy interpersonal relationships.

The young deaf child who "adjusts" to a foster home and to the measure of security it provides in spite of very limited communication initially presents few difficulties for foster parents or the agency. This is not to say that the situation is problem-free for the child. Rather, issues tend to lie dormant, only to appear with the onset of adolescence.

For example, the concern has often been voiced that deaf individuals are slow to develop an appreciation for the feelings of others.[3] This should not be a surprise if the deaf child has not had continual help in sorting out the reactions of others to specific behaviors or in the comparison of feelings. Again, professionals working with deaf teenagers in foster care say that these youngsters seem to have missed out on internalizing the foster family's rules and values. The question to be answered is the same: Can one internalize values without continued exposure to them through family communication?

Yet another problem to be considered is that many children come into placement as the result of physical and sexual abuse. Deaf children are particularly susceptible to both. Physical abuse may have occurred because of the added frustration the disability posed for the family. The incidence of sexual abuse is believed to be high because of the perception that deaf children cannot "tell" about these experiences. Because most deaf children do not receive help in sorting out these events, they are ill prepared to deal with such normal adolescent issues as developing self-esteem and sexual development.

ADOLESCENT CONCERNS

Parents and workers who do not have a means of coping with significant issues early in placement face almost certain failure during adolescent years. This point is illustrated by Dana, a teenager who grew up in foster care.

---

2 For a discussion of this issue, see H. Schlesinger and K. Meadows, *Sound and Sign, Childhood Deafness and Mental Health,* Berkeley, University of California Press, 1972.

3 Ibid.

During the early years Dana exhibited few difficulties and, in fact, was exceptionally compliant and not very outgoing, even among deaf peers. She had been sexually abused as a child but no one had helped her to work through these incidents. In an effort to protect her, her foster parents set up strict limits regarding her socialization outside the home, while communication at home remained on a superficial level.

Adolescent conflicts brought extreme rebellion from Dana, sexual acting out and an inability to discuss her feelings or to be helpful in making decisions regarding her future. She was finally admitted to an inpatient psychiatric unit, a placement which helped her to stabilize and then move on with her life. It seems clear that a crisis of this proportion could have been avoided 10 years earlier by more sensitive planning that included help with building on the understanding, self-esteem and communication necessary to cope with adolescent pressure.

While identity is an issue faced by all teenagers, it is further complicated for those in foster care by the need to resolve conflicted feelings related to both birth and foster families. The issue of security vs. independence can also trigger heightened anxieties. Because the deaf adolescent in foster care deals with these issues and with identity as they relate to the disability, problems of wanting acceptance and not wanting to appear different become intensified. Often, there is a time of rejecting either the deaf or the hearing world in an effort to find a "fit" that is comfortable. The deaf adolescent is seeking answers to the questions of Who am I? and Can I negotiate both worlds?

Preparation for independence from the foster home presents a final area of concem. Do the foster parents have a sufficient grasp of career possibilities for their deaf youngster to encourage creativity in setting up employment goals? Or do they—through a lack of knowledge of these possibilities—demonstrate overprotectiveness and the expectation that deaf individuals will always have to depend on others? Deaf teenagers must possess the confidence that comes from knowing that they have been prepared for independence. Without this, the future is bleak, and serious depression can develop.

WORKER-AGENCY RESPONSIBILITIES

Helping foster parents to cope with so many issues on a daily basis underlines the role of the social worker and agency. The worker must be attuned to many factors that affect success in planning, including the implications of the degree of hearing loss; the pros and cons of various communication methods and educational placements; and the validity of psychological/I.Q. testing methods. In addition, the worker must be knowledgeable about the use of TDD'S, T.V. decoders, interpreters and signaling devices; Social Security benefits and other aspects of federal law as it relates to education and access to other public services; and career planning and vocational rehabilitation services.

Open communication with the deaf child is as important for the social worker as it is for foster parents. A social worker who can use sign language effectively is able to communicate directly with the child and can broach the many ongoing problems needing clarification. When social workers do not have this skill, they need to know how to identify qualified interpreters and how to use them appropriately. Workers demonstrate an understanding of the importance of maintaining confidentiality and impartiality by following these procedures and avoiding the use of family and friends as informal "interpreters."

It is important that agency policy backs these efforts fully. For example, agencies need to spell out clearly how a social worker is to obtain an interpreter for court appearances or for an individual interview with a deaf client. Who pays? Is there a special contract for hiring interpreters? Is the procedure clear and reasonably quick?

Traditionally, social service agencies have not made an effort to hire deaf social workers or workers with any specialized knowledge of deafness. As a result, cases involving deaf children are often randomly distributed among workers, a procedure that precludes the identification of special needs and the development of adequate services. Resources remain scattered. The recruitment of foster parents who already possess an awareness of deafness-related issues and communication skills is not generally recognized as necessary. Moreover, recruitment of deaf foster parents—ready-made role models for deaf children—has rarely been pursued as a solution.

It is imperative that child placement agencies begin to develop increased sensitivity to these issues. Until tangible changes occur, permanency planning for deaf children simply will not exist.

SIGN LANGUAGE INTERPRETATION

34

BEING IGNORED CAN BE BLISS: HOW TO USE A SIGN LANGUAGE INTERPRETER

Barbara Fink

Much can be learned about an individual from the family, friends, and colleagues who are close to that person. Some understanding of deaf people and what it is like to be deaf and to live independently can be acquired from learning how Sign Language interpreters perform their work.

While an interpreter is a communication aid, he or she has a more extensive working relationship with a deaf person than a reader has with a blind person.

Nevertheless, this relationship is not as intimate as between a personal care attendant and a person with a severe mobility impairment. Most interpreters work with a deaf person for only three or four hours at a time. Rarely do they work repeatedly with the same individual, and when that does happen, it happens sporadically.

Deaf persons do not select interpreters from a group of interviewed candidates. Almost never does a hearing impaired person train an interpreter to the work. In fact, in many instances, interpreters, unlike attendants, are not working for a deaf person, but for the agency, school, or meeting in which deaf persons participate.

Finally, an attendant is involved with many aspects of a disabled person's life, from bathing to transportation. A sign interpreter is there for one specific purpose: Communication between the hearing world and deaf persons.

There is a poster at the bookstore at Gallaudet University, a post-secondary school for deaf persons in Washington, DC. A little elf smiles down saying, "I'm not deaf, I just ignore you." How well that describes my own situation!

Ironically, as a Sign Language interpreter, I am constantly in situations where I have to ignore people. I am most successful when I can get others to ignore me, too.

What's the big secret? Because I am certified by the Registry of Interpreters for the Deaf, I must follow the code of ethics they have established. Confidentiality is first and foremost. *Nothing* can be revealed about an interpreting assignment, including the fact that it even occurred.

So if you arrive late at a meeting or duck out for a cigarette, don't ask me what happened; I won't tell you. But all is not lost. Simply ask me to interpret while you ask one of the deaf people. That's why I am there.

Basically, it comes down to the fact that I wouldn't be there if it weren't for a communications problem between two parties. Deaf people have the same right to privacy as anyone else. It's not my right to take that away from them.

Suppressing just names and places doesn't work. The deaf community is so small, it is very easy to figure things out with a minimum of information. Suppose I tell you I'm going to traffic court on Wednesday morning, and later you meet a deaf person who has "some legal problems to take care of on Wednesday, but nothing serious." If that person also has a dented fender on his or her car, it's not hard for you to realize who else is going to court.

Other situations that can jeopardize confidentiality are more obvious. For instance, teachers ask me how deaf students are doing in school. Or employees want to know if their hearing impaired boss made the phone calls as promised. Also, many hearing people expect interpreters to be thoroughly familiar with the deaf individuals for whom we interpret.

Frequently, when I arrive at a new job, the teacher or the lawyer will question me about the deaf person's residence, employment, and other personal matters. It's hard for them to believe that, nine times out of ten, I have never met the deaf person before either. In all cases, my answer to questions about deaf individuals is the same: I will be happy to interpret when you ask the deaf person directly.

Another part of the code of ethics requires me to refrain from influencing in any way the communication I am facilitating. This means more than simple impartiality. Interpreters must in a real sense fade into the background. Sometimes, however, I can't help intruding.

Once while interpreting before a packed auditorium, I made the sign for "dream" and swung my arms wide. (Signs are made as large as possible on stage so that they are easily seen from a distance.) Somehow I knocked an entire pitcher of ice water off the podium and into the face of the speaker.

Another interpreter, also before an audience, once locked arms with a wildly gesticulating speaker. Needless to say, on such occasions, the interpreter unavoidably influences what happens next.

Actually, the code prohibits deliberately altering what someone says. I cannot add my own opinions, change that angry "damn" to a modest "heck," or leave anything out. Anything. If you say, "Ask her if she took any science in high school," I sign exactly that, including the "Ask her."

If the deaf person replies "Tell him just a year of biology," I vocally communicate every word to the hearing person. Usually, people soon realize how stiff they sound to each other and begin to speak more directly.

Sometimes, however, people are determined to involve me in the conversation. This is something I must resist. If you ask me a question or speak to me directly while I am interpreting, I will sign what you say, but I will avoid making any eye contact. Occasionally, people become aggressive, grabbing my arms in frustration and yelling, "You. You. I'm talking to you!"

Ideally, all parties will arrive early and give me a chance to explain my work. Sometimes this actually occurs, but most often people don't show up until the time for the class or the appointment, leaving me no opportunity to clarify my role.

This clarification is important for the hearing person unused to depending on a third party for communication. How unnatural this arrangement is became clear to me while learning Sign Language.

Every night my classmates and I would come back from our practicum assignments and moan, "When, oh when, will people stop this 'tell him' and 'ask her' and talk directly to each other?"

Then one day we had a lecture on interpreting for deaf-blind people given by a person both visually and aurally impaired. This was the first time that many of us found ourselves having to communicate through an interpreter. The first question someone in the class asked began, "Ask him if . . ."

We all looked around in shock. If we, who supposedly knew better, found ourselves talking to the interpreter instead of to the lecturer, was it any wonder that the rest of the world was having the same problem?

American Sign Language (ASL) provides a means for deaf people to express themselves and to comprehend others as naturally as speech does for persons who hear and speak. But ASL does not simply *translate* spoken English. It *interprets* English into a different language with its own grammar, rules, and forms of expression. Like written characters in the Chinese language, many signs in ASL express concepts, not simply individual words.

Because eyes strain and get tired after even brief periods of concentration, ASL is very economical. What might take ten words to say in English is communicated in ASL by two signs and some facial expression. Even the position of the hands in relation to the body (and both the obvious and subtle movements of the hands) communicate meaning.

Still, as precisely as it has been developed, ASL has some limitations. It is very difficult to learn thoroughly and perfectly. Also, it sometimes requires more time to interpret spoken English into ASL than the interpreter has available. Consequently, we interpreters often mix interpreting in ASL along with "translating" into elemental signs some of what is spoken.

Sometimes signs and words just do not match. Nothing stops an interpreter faster than a joke like "What's black and white and red all over?" A newspaper, right? But when I sign the punch line for this type of joke, the deaf person usually wonders why everybody else is laughing. On the other hand, puns are possible in Sign Language that, when interpreted into English, mean nothing.

Fortunately, people need not worry themselves about the technical end of interpreting. That is my job. Nevertheless, if people understand the common sense limitations of interpreting, they can help me greatly. This goes for deaf people as well as hearing people. I've heard deaf people complain unjustly that their interpreter is lazy for failing to interpret conversations on the other side of a room.

While I am obligated to interpret everything I hear (including the dog barking outside or the airplane overhead), I can't hear what goes on outside in the hall or in a noisy crowd. Unfortunately, some people who always have been deaf just don't fully understand the limits on the sense of hearing.

Similarly, many hearing people do not understand the interpreter's basic need to be readily visible while working. On occasion, I have been positioned in out of the way spots, such as behind a post, or so far over to the side that deaf people couldn't possibly watch both the interpreter and the person actually speaking.

Another problem is fatigue. For a two- or three-hour class, a break after each hour gives my arms (and the deaf person's eyes) a needed rest. For a longer meeting, two interpreters should be hired to relieve each other periodically, usually every 30 minutes.

Interpreting is hard physical work. If you don't think so, try waving your arms constantly for 45 minutes. And I have the added stress of analyzing sentences to choose the correct signs and the dry throat from mouthing all the words while I interpret to aid deaf people who read lips. After fatigue sets in, it becomes harder to concentrate and I find myself thinking more about how tired I am than what is being said.

From experience, I have learned to dash for the door whenever a meeting calls a break. If I don't, invariably someone will decide they have to ask a deaf person some questions, and I spend my precious rest time interpreting. I'm only human, let me have my ten minutes.

Another thing. If you are running a meeting, look around and make sure I'm back before you resume business. I've returned to meetings before the end of the break time only to find business in full swing. The deaf people in attendance had no way of knowing the chairman, who appeared to be talking to someone across the room, had already called the meeting to order.

Another predicament can occur when a deaf person reads something while someone else gives verbal instructions, such as in many test situations. In one class I interpreted, the teacher would give out an exam, then talk constantly. For most students this was no problem, but the deaf student could not easily watch me and read at the same time. During one exam, the teacher started changing the questions verbally. To quickly get the deaf student's attention, I began flicking the light switch off and on.

The same teacher's love for slide shows also caused problems. At a moment's notice, the classroom would be plunged into darkness. My request for a little light during slide presentations was countered with the teacher's suggestion to wear day-glo gloves. But eventually he agreed to leave one light on during slide shows.

It is extremely difficult to interpret when more than one person speaks. (No, I can't sign one person on each hand.) Usually this happens when people are arguing, so it's even more difficult for me to follow along. Interpreters are divided on how to handle this. Some say it is alright to request people to slow down and stop interrupting each other.

Other interpreters feel you should just sign as much as possible, since the hearing people probably aren't getting it all either. Another difficulty: I usually point to whoever is speaking; and if people are cutting each other off, I spend more time pointing than signing.

A blind woman told me about a similar problem she had, but in reverse. At one meeting, the same interpreter vocalized what two different deaf people were signing. Since there was only one voice, the blind woman assumed only one deaf person had the floor and kept contradicting himself. When she finally realized the true situation, the blind woman asked the deaf participants to identify themselves each time one of them spoke. Some meetings avoid this problem altogether by hiring more than one interpreter.

This brings me to a sore topic. People hate to pay interpreters. Apparently, it is thought that this takes advantage of the deaf person's handicap. But then so do doctors, hearing aid dealers, and hospitals. No one denies that they should be paid for their services.

Look at the truth of the situation. First, we interpreters are professionals who have trained long and hard to perfect our skills. Secondly, if you are not willing to pay me, I have to take another job and not be available for the 10:00 a.m. conference or the 2:00 p.m. doctor's appointment.

Still, interpreters who volunteer do not necessarily act unethically. Occasionally, we donate services to worthy causes or to help out friends. Certainly, I am not going to send a bill for every joke I sign at a party. But generally, I have found that the people who are *always* willing to volunteer get into interpreting situations beyond their skills.

They also tend not to follow ethics because "after all, I wasn't really interpreting, I just went along to help out." That might be alright for a meeting or a chat at the water cooler. But it is a bad bargain for anything else. The money you pay an interpreter is well worth it.

Certification of interpreters is done by the Registry of Interpreters for the Deaf. Like other applicants, I was tested by a panel of both hearing and deaf interpreters. (Yes, there is such a thing as deaf interpreters. They work in special situations, usually with deaf people who have minimal English or minimal language skills.)

The panel questioned me about my background, my interest in Sign Language, and my reasons for wanting to be certified. Then came a series of ethical questions, mostly in the form of "What would you do if . . ."

A test of my expression skills involved my listening to two tapes and signing what I heard. The first was a story which lent itself very well to ASL: It was very descriptive with different characters and lots of action. The second tape was a lecture full of technical terms read by someone who spoke faster and faster as the tape progressed.

To demonstrate my receptive skills, I had to voice (in proper English and with appropriate word choices) what I saw being signed on a videotape. For the benefit of the deaf panelists, one of the hearing panelists sat behind me and signed to them everything I said. When he put his hands in his lap, they knew I was stumped.

Of course, certification is no guarantee of quality. It is only a guide. I know some excellent interpreters who, for various reasons, decline to take the test. On the other hand, some certified interpreters seem to memorize the code of ethics before the test and then immediately forget it. Still, unless you know the interpreter's skills personally, it is safer to hire a certified person.

When calling an interpreter to arrange a job, be specific about your needs. Realize that we are people and have different combinations of skills and expertise. Also, there are various types of certification. Interpreters are supposed to refuse any job for which they are not qualified, but we need to be able to make an informed decision.

Once, I arrived at a job which the referral center assured me was fine for my skill level. It turned out to be an interview between a person charged with a crime and an attorney. I turn down all legal assignments because I don't feel I have the proper skills. Also, I do not want the responsibility of a mistake that might cost someone their freedom or a great deal of money. I suggested to the persons involved that they hire someone certified for legal work.

Other situations are not as potentially dangerous, but the right interpreter can make an important difference. At a workshop or meeting where input from deaf people is needed, request someone with good skills in communicating vocally what deaf participants say in sign. Nothing inhibits a deaf person more than an interpreter who cannot communicate the deaf person's thoughts. In these situations, the interpreter's mistakes appear to be the deaf person's, and so the deaf person will tend to refrain from speaking.

A different, but related, problem once occurred at a medical school. A deaf student missed an entire lecture that accompanied an autopsy because the interpreter fainted at the sight of the corpse. Better advance information might have secured an interpreter who was a biology major, or, like one of my classmates at Gallaudet University, worked in a funeral home.

Another type of interpreter that is very new is the oral interpreter. Technically, they do not interpret, they mouth spoken English in a form that is more visible on the lips. This is more complicated than it seems. Skilled oral interpreters are familiar with how certain words and letter combinations appear on the lips and how to accentuate them. They will also use substitute words if they are more visible on the lips and have the same meaning.

Deaf people who hire oral interpreters choose not to use Sign Language and even find signing a distraction rather than a help. Most of the time, they prefer to rely on their own lipreading and speaking abilities and not on another person for communication. The oral versus Sign Language controversy in deaf education has been going on for hundreds of years and is still not settled.

The ideal interpreting experience happened to me about six months ago. I was interpreting at a meeting at which angry people were arguing with one another. My arms got progressively tired and my eyes more and more droopy. Then one of the deaf participants declared, "The interpreter needs a break."

That someone was so thoughtful was amazing. But what happened next was even more so. The hearing person who chaired the meeting turned to the deaf person who had spoken up and said, "Okay, tell the interpreter she can have a break."

I was shocked to the core. After all those months of having people talk at each other through me, these two were talking to me through each other! I had succeeded! I was being completely ignored while direct communication took place between these two people.

That may be the ideal interpreting experience. But in my mind it would be best if people took the time to communicate directly with each other through a medium they both understand. Deaf people and hearing persons have a lot to offer each other. If we all really took the time to find out what other people have to say, I wouldn't have to work so hard to be ignored. Then I'd become obsolete. And that would be terrific.

35

YOU'RE A WHAT? INTERPRETER FOR THE DEAF

Gallaudet University Public Service Programs

Imagine, for a moment, what it would be like to be deaf. You cannot hear what people say. Nor can you hear your own voice, and so you can learn to form words only with great difficulty. How would you make your ideas known? And how would you learn what others have to say?

This challenge confronts 14 million deaf and hearing-impaired Americans every day. Despite these obstacles, however, they do communicate effectively. Through methods such as sign language and finger spelling, they participate in schools, the workplace, and society generally. Some situations, however, call for a person equally skilled in speaking and signing to serve as a bridge between the world of silence and the world of sound. These people are known as sign language interpreters.

Bob Chandler is an interpreter who was introduced to sign language as a child. Both his parents are deaf, and he believes that he probably learned to sign before he learned to speak. After graduating from college with a degree in history, he did volunteer work with several organizations, including Alcoholics Anonymous. Work like this led to a position teaching sign language to mentally retarded deaf children. Eventually, Bob returned to school and earned a master's degree in rehabilitation/counseling of the hearing-impaired. Soon thereafter, he was recruited by Deafpride, Inc., an agency that provides interpreting services.

In the recent past, most sign interpreters were friends of deaf persons or members of a deaf person's family. But more and more people like Bob are earning their living as interpreters. Many, like Bob, graduated from training programs. Such programs are offered by colleges and universities in more than 30 States.

The trained interpreter is qualified in various manual communication systems, including American Sign Language and manually coded English.

Interpreters often differentiate between types of interpreting. Platform interpreting is performed near the speaker—on a platform or a stage—and in front of an audience. Such interpreters must use large, clear signs. In contrast, one-on-one interpreting is done face-to-face with the client. Janet Bailey, president of Sign Language Associates, Inc., an interpreting services firm, has experience with both types.

Janet became acquainted with sign language at an early age. Her mother, an instructor in a school for deaf children, taught her finger spelling. As an adult, her interest in signing was renewed when she helped a neighbor's child enroll in a sign language course at Gallaudet University in Washington, D.C.

Janet decided to enroll, too. She completed several more courses and began to undertake some interpreting assignments. When *Good Vibrations,* a theatrical production, was staged at the college, she became part of the show, combining her interpreting skills and her acting talents. She has gone on to interpret for the Folger Shakespeare Theater, Arena Stage, Ford's Theater, and the John F. Kennedy Center for the Performing Arts, all in Washington.

Sign language interpretation places some unusual demands on its practitioners. Michael Jay Hartmann can attest to that. He's been interpreting for 12 years and has worked in a variety of situations, including owning and running his own interpreting services firm. He, too, began his career with voluntary work, interpreting for fellow students at the University of California and at religious services at the local temple. He now works as a program specialist for the handicapped for the U.S. Department of Health and Human Services, where his duties include being the official interpreter for the Secretary.

Bob, Michael, and Janet are among the 2,600 certified sign language interpreters in the United States. Certification is awarded by the Registry of Interpreters for the Deaf (RID), a nonprofit organization of professional interpreters. RID offers three different kinds of certification: comprehensive, performing arts, and legal.

Some of the principal customers of interpreters are schools, courts, and medical institutions. Most clients hire interpreters for one assignment at a time, so interpreters are usually freelancers. As a rule, they are paid by the hour, with rates starting at $10 and going up depending on the expertise of the interpreter and the complexity of the assignment.

Freelancing can be difficult. For Maureen Baglio, a freelancer affiliated with Sign Language Associates, the nature of the work is both a drawback and an advantage. "The uncertainty can be unnerving," she says, but adds that freelancing provides a freedom not found in salaried employment. Bob Chandler agrees. "You must be able to deal with an uncertain schedule and do without the fringe benefits that most people take for granted," he states. "But," he continues, "the thing I like is being in a different situation every day."

Bob's statement points toward one advantage of being a sign language interpreter. It's easy to move from job to job and place to place. Interpreters can find work all over the country. Michael Jay Hartmann says he was working 2 days after he arrived in Washington. "This is a good profession to be in if you've been properly trained," he says.

To be a good interpreter, you must possess certain talents. Sign language interpreters have excellent listening skills, clear mouth movements, and a good imagination. The best interpreters are excellent mimics. A shrug of the shoulders or a tilt of an eyebrow might be essential to impart not only the message but the nuances as well.

Sign language interpretation also demands fortitude. The energy and concentration necessary to listen to a speaker and provide a simultaneous translation to the client are considerable. For this reason, interpreters often work in teams when doing a particularly long session, alternating about every half hour.

According to Richard Dirst, former executive director of the Registry of Interpreters for the Deaf, there is a growing need for interpreters. He states, "Opportunities in interpreting for the deaf are increasing rapidly throughout the United States. The increased demand for interpreters in all facets of the deaf individual's life has created a shortage of qualified interpreters in almost every part of the country."

A career as an interpreter for the deaf can be challenging and rewarding. The ability to communicate in another language opens up a wide variety of opportunities and offers the chance to see the world from a wholly new perspective. To be an interpreter also provides the chance to be of service to those who can use your help.

36

ON GUARD!

Elaine Gardner

An interpreter who does not recognize the possible legal ramifications of interpreting is not a true professional. The interpreter who is familiar with the laws relating to interpreting not only does a great service to the deaf community and the profession, but also avoids many legal pitfalls.

Since the implementation of Title V of the Rehabilitation Act of 1973,[1] sign language and oral interpreters have been utilized to a greater extent and by a wider range of professionals and agencies than ever before. Hospitals, health clinics, mental health programs, courts, legal aid attorneys, public defenders and law enforcement agencies are now required to ensure effective communication for hearing impaired people by providing professional interpreters.

Like other professionals, interpreters must be aware of the legal implications of their behavior to avoid inappropriate, prejudicial or unethical conduct. Inadequate interpreter skills or lack of professionalism can have grave consequences for the deaf person and serious legal implications for the interpreter. Therefore, it is important for both the interpreting profession and the deaf community to understand interpreters' legal rights and obligations.

THE PRIVILEGED COMMUNICATION

Introduction to privilege

An issue of great concern to the deaf community and professional interpreters is whether an interpreter can be forced to testify about information obtained while interpreting. The fear that such information will be revealed by interpreters voluntarily, or involuntarily pursuant to court order, causes some deaf persons to withhold important information from professionals with whom they are meeting. It is important for all parties to such communication to understand which communications are protected by law and which communications the interpreter can be forced to reveal.

For public policy reasons, the law has chosen to protect certain communications from the court's power to compel disclosure. These communications, designated as "privileged," must meet the following criteria: 1) they must be confidential in nature; 2) this privacy must be essential to promote a successful and honest relationship between the parties; 3) the relationship must be one which society

[1] 29 USC § 794, as amended.

wishes to foster; and 4) the injury the disclosure of this type of communication would cause to the protected relationship must be greater than the benefit to the court of thereby gaining information.

Simply put, there are certain important relationships in which the parties need to be sure that what they say is private and cannot be disclosed by force of court order. Examples of some of these protected relationships are wife/husband, attorney/client, doctor/patient and clergy/parishioner. Additional privileges are sometimes also available, depending on the statutory law of the individual state. These can include psychologist/patient, therapist/patient and reporter/source.

Protection of interpreters from compelled disclosure of priveleged information

Not just any communication is protected as privileged communication. Even communication between two persons who share one of the relationships listed above must be made specifically in connection with this relationship, and without the presence of third parties.

Generally, the element of confidentiality essential to the establisliment of the privilege is missing when a third party is present during the communication. Therefore, the presence of most third parties destroys the privilege.

However, exceptions have been established to this third party rule. In an otherwise privileged situation, a third party's presence will not destroy the privilege if that third party is acting as the agent for the professional, the client, or both, and the presence of that agent is necessary for the conduct of the professional counseling. For deaf persons who rely on sign language to communicate, interpreters fit squarely into this third party exception. As agents of one or both of the individuals involved, they are unquestionably essential to furthering the relationship. As a result, an interpreter's indispensability in this area has been recognized by virtually every court reviewing this issue.[2]

When there is a need for a sign language interpreter, the presence of the interpreter should not dissolve the confidentiality of an otherwise privileged communication. However, circumstances do occur when deaf persons may desire the presence of family members, in addition to the interpreter, in situations which would otherwise be privileged. Especially when a deaf person is facing serious legal or medical problems, the presence of relatives can help provide background information and support to enhance free and accurate communication.

In a case before a Maryland court, an interpreter and close relatives were present during a jailhouse interview between an attorney and his deaf defendant charged with murder. An interpreter certified by the Registry of Interpreters for the Deaf (RID) was subpoenaed to testify before a grand jury as to the communication which took place at that time. The interpreter refused to testify, saying that she preferred to face jail than betray a confidence. In a major victory, the Maryland Circuit Court judge threw out the subpoena on the grounds that even in this situation a sign language interpreter is covered by the attorney/client privilege. The court stated: "When both attorney and client depend on the presence of an interpreter for communicating to one another, the interpreter serves the vital link in the bond of the attorney/client relationship."[3]

---

[2] *Hawes v. State,* 7 So. 302 (Sup. Ct. Ala., 1890); *Mileski v. Locker,* 178 NYS 2d 911 (1958); *DuBarre v. Linette,* Peake 108, 170 Eng. Rep. 96 (1791); *Parker v. Carter,* 18 Va. 273 (1814); *Foster v. Hall,* 29 Mass. 89 (1833); *State v. Laponia,* 85 NJL 357, 83A 1045 (1913); *Jackson ex dem Haverly v. French,* 3 Wend (N.Y.) 337 (Sup. Ct. 1829); *Hatton v. Robinson,* 31 Mass. (14 Pick) 416 (Sup. Jud. Ct. 1833); *Sibley v. Waffle,* 16 N.U. 180 (Ct. App. 1857); *Sample v. Frost,* 10 Iowa 266, 267 (Sup. Ct. Iowa 1859); *Tyler v. Hall,* 17 SW 319, 321 (Sup. Ct. Mo. 1891).

[3] *Touhey v. Duckett,* 19 Crim. Law Rep. 2483, No. 23,331 Equity (Cir. Ct. Anne Arundel Co., November 30, 1976, slip op. at 3.)

Moreover, the judge went a step further and found that the presence of close relatives during a deaf person's interview by an attorney does not necessarily destroy the attorney/client privilege. The judge, sensitized to the varying communication needs of the deaf individuals, stated:

> It is readily apparent that the success of communicating through the use of Sign Language varies with the expertise of the deaf mute (sic). It would be to the advantage of any attorney who seeks to diligently represent his client, as in this case, to have members of the immediate family present to aid in the interpretation process.[4]

While an attorney, physician or member of the clergy must be duly licensed before a privileged communication with that professional can occur, there is no similar license or certification requirement for the interpreters they use. Because these interpreters are not professionals whose relationships are encouraged by law, it need merely be shown that the interpreter was an agent of either of the parties and was necessary to the communication.

The use of an interpreter should never destroy an otherwise privileged communication. Some states have taken the precaution of amending their interpreter statutes to ensure this privilege.[5] Such provisions, although often mistakenly called "interpreter privilege" legislation, do not create any new privilege; they simply ensure that existing privileges are not destroyed by an interpreter's presence.

Waiver of the privilege

Interpreters must understand that the privileges discussed above may be waived by a deaf person. In a privileged situation, the law clearly prohibits compelled disclosure of information. However, if the deaf client or patient consents to the disclosure of otherwise privileged information, a court may compel testimony by licensed professionals, or even by the interpreter who made communication possible between the professional and the deaf person. In some situations, deaf persons themselves may subpoena interpreters to testify to otherwise privileged information. Interpreters have no legal basis for refusing to testify in these situations. The privilege belongs to the deaf person, not to the professional or the interpreter.

A waiver situation usually arises when the deaf person perceives that disclosure of the privileged communication will not prejudice—and may in fact enhance—his or her case. One example would be disclosure of an interpreted medical conference in a malpractice suit. Although an interpreter may have strong opinions about whether disclosure will help or harm the deaf person, it is not the interpreter's role to advise.

When the situation is not privileged

The majority of situations involving interpretation for deaf persons are not privileged. Employment and business situations, government benefit interviews, appointments with an accountant and public meetings are all examples of situations in which privilege does not apply. An interpreter can legally be compelled to testify about information obtained through such assignments.

---

[4] This case was reversed on other grounds on appeal. 36 Maryland Appeals 238 (1977). *Touhey, supra,* slip op. at 4.

[5] See the interpreter laws of Kentucky, 22 KRS 70 (1976), Tennessee, 123 TCA 24–108(j) (1977), New Hampshire § 521-A NHSA 11 (1977), Montana, 245 MCA 11 (1979), Florida, 19 FSA 6063 (7) (1980), Iowa, 622B ICA 6 (1980), North Carolina, 8A NCGS 5 (1981), Arkansas, 5 ASA 715.1(g) (1979), Texas, TCA Evidence Code, 3712a(c) (1979), Virginia, 37 VCA 8.01-400.1 (1979), and New Mexico, NMAS 38-9-1-1.

Two common areas of confusion about the lack of privilege are police interrogations and private conversations between a deaf person and an interpreter. In either of these situations a privilege does not exist. However, in these circumstances, some deaf persons and interpreters mistakenly think that their communication can remain confidential.

The police interrogation situation clearly does not meet even the first criterion for privileged communications, as responses to the police are not confidential in nature. Indeed, the police are required to ensure that an arrested person understands the nonconfidential aspects of the communication by stating, prior to interrogation, that anything the arrested person says can and will be used against him or her in court.[6]

Many interpreters are surprised when called upon to testify regarding police interrogations which they interpreted. There is a general misconception that this critical communication is covered by a privilege of its own. But both professional interpreters and deaf persons should understand that interpreters may be legally required to repeat what is said at police interrogations.

Interpreters and deaf persons should also know that there is no legal protections for any conversation an interpreter and deaf person might have by themselves. Although they may assume that their communication is confidential, the relationship between an interpreter and a deaf person is not among those protected by privilege. Therefore, nothing communicated between an interpreter and a deaf person, in the absence of a professional carrying a privilege, can be assumed to be free from the threat of compelled disclosure.

To avoid confusion about when a privileged communication is occurring, an interpreter being used in an otherwise privileged situation may choose to step outside the room any time the professional does. This will ensure that no non-privileged communication regarding confidential issues will occur.

Responding to a proper subpoena

There may be times when an interpreter will be subpoenaed to testify about nonprivileged communications. Many courts call upon interpreters to testify, instead of the hearing individual who used the interpreter. For example, a court may ask an interpreter to testify about a police interrogation, instead of calling the police officer who was there. This is because of the court's interpretations of the rule of evidence designated as the "hearsay rule." Under this evidentiary rule, testimony cannot generally be taken regarding communications which were not received first-hand by a testifying witness. Additionally, there may be times when the interpreter is called to testify as to information other than that communicated by the deaf person, such as which sign language mode the interpreter used.

In order to avoid subpoenas, some professional interpreters insist that nonprivileged, adversarial communications such as police interrogations be videotaped. This appears to be an excellent course, especially in serious felony cases. The videotaped communication can be played directly to another interpreter in court, thus assuring the court that accurate communication occurred, and it allows an interpreter's work to be reviewed by experts. Moreover, it relieves the original interpreter from a subpoena which may conflict with professional ethics or with that interpreter's standing in the deaf community. Many police stations are equipped with videotape equipment for recording drunk driving suspects. Therefore, it is a simple matter for them to videotape an interpreted interrogation.

---

6 *See* discussion of Miranda Warning.

The RID Code of Ethics, although compelling to many interpreters, is not legally binding in the face of a subpoena to testify. This code requires that "the interpreter/transliterator shall keep all assignment-related information strictly confidential." However, there may be circumstances in which an interpreter has no choice but to testify or risk a jail sentence for contempt of court. This is not to say, however, that the interpreter should not otherwise respect this canon to the highest degree possible. It may be advisable for the RID membership to consider the possibility of relaxing this canon to reflect the legal realities.

There are several means of alerting judges to the interpreter's quandary when subpoenaed. Prior to testifying, or in open court, one can advise the judge of the conflict between the RID code and the compelled disclosure. The interpreter may also reduce the weight given this testimony by explaining that, as a simple conveyor of information, he or she experiences difficulties in recalling the processed information.

LIABILITIES OF PROFESSIONAL INTERPRETING

The deaf person's recourses

Like all other professionals, interpreters are subject to complaints from those they serve, including, ultimately, malpractice lawsuits for money damages. It is critically important that deaf consumers and professional interpreters understand that there are recourses available to deaf people for the damages inflicted by poor interpreting.

Because of the need to protect deaf consumers from unscrupulous or unqualified interpreters, the RID has established a complaint procedure for the processing of complaints against member interpreters, with the ultimate penalty of decertification. Unfortunately, no professional complaint mechanism exists for interpreters who are not RID members.

Another recourse for the deaf individual is the malpractice lawsuit for money damages. Interpreters are not immune to this type of lawsuit. Realistically, they will most probably be included in a lawsuit against a professional, where both the interpreter and professional were guilty of negligence. It is important to note that even volunteer interpreters may be sued for malpractice.

Due to the growing national trend of suing professionals and the possibility of future malpractice suits against interpreters, the RID offers malpractice insurance to its members. However, the Chicago Insurance Company, which underwrites this plan, stated that it has never had a claim against an RID interpreter.

Due to the expense of a malpractice suit, a more practical means of removing a noncertified interpreter from practice may be to file an administrative complaint against the program using the interpreter, pursuant to Section 504. This is a lengthy procedure that will not recoup any losses for the deaf consumer, but its informality and low cost sometimes makes it the most viable solution.

There will be situations in which the agency or program that uses an unqualified interpreter is not covered by Section 504. In these circumstances, and prior to initiation of any Section 504 complaint, the program employing the interpreter should be contacted directly. If the reasonable concerns of the deaf person are made known, the program may voluntarily remove that individual's name from its list of available interpreters. In these situations qualified interpreters can greatly assist the deaf community in its protest over unqualified interpreters.

Avoiding malpractice claims

The best way to avoid complaints about one's interpreting skills or conduct are: self-evaluation of one's skills with respect to the individual deaf person in a given situation; complete understanding of one's role and responsibilities; and vigilant protection of oneself against attempts to misuse the interpreter's role.

The first step, self-evaluation, is perhaps the most important. Interpreters must understand that they are vouching for their own qualifications the instant they begin to participate in an assignment. It is crucial, therefore, that an interpreter honestly appraise his or her abilities to understand and be understood by the deaf person prior to initiation of the assignment. An expression of satisfaction by the deaf person should not alleviate this responsibility.

Similarly, interpreters must evaluate their qualifications to interpret in a given situation. Even if amply qualified to communicate with a deaf individual in some situations, an interpreter may not be able to communicate the terms and concepts of a specialized profession.

A second step in avoiding complaints about interpreting skills or conduct is the complete understanding by all participants of the interpreter's role. This role may vary with the needs of the deaf person involved. A well-educated deaf person may need only a translation into Signed English. However, the role of simple translator would not be sufficient for an interpreter involved in the investigation of a criminal defendant with low English-language skills. Although opinions, advice and editing are improper, in some situations it is necessary for interpreters to stress certain information to ensure the communication of important concepts. In a criminal situation, the police certainly understand the concepts and consequences of the situation; it is up to the interpreter to ensure that there is a mutual understanding of the full import of the situation.

The interpreter should be prepared in advance to educate all parties about his or her role—and to insist on doing so when necessary. For example, everyone involved should understand the neutrality of the interpreter. An agency that summons an interpreter might expect allegiance from the interpreter. Likewise, the deaf person may expect the same allegiance. Prior to initiation of an assignment, it must be made clear that the interpreter is no one's ally or advocate in an adversarial situation.

Interpreters should also discuss the best communication mode for the assignment with the parties involved. It may be necessary to explain an individual deaf consumer's need for more than simultaneous interpretation. To fulfill this responsibility, interpreters must have a knowledge of linguistics and the ability to communicate this in an understandable manner to persons who are not experts in this area.

Finally, interpreters must protect themselves at all times against the tendency of involved parties to misuse them. When an interpreter's services are not required, it is appropriate to remove oneself from the situation. Careful explanation of the interpreters role beforehand should dispel tendencies to ask an interpreter for an opinion. However, interpreters will encounter more subtle attempts to misuse them, and they must be on guard to protect themselves and their clients.

Emergency situations

The law of malpractice liability is eased somewhat in emergency situations. However, an interpreter who doubts his or her qualifications should express them so that a more qualified interpreter can be summoned. Moreover, the interpreter should question the summoning agency's designation of an "emergency." A criminal interrogation of a deaf defendant is usually not an emergency, nor is a medical procedure, short of emergency room treatment. Interpreters should not risk the serious consequences of inadequate interpreting and possible consumer complaints except in true emergencies.

INTERPRETING IN A LEGAL SITUATION

The arrest situation

Interpreters and members of the deaf community must be familiar with deaf persons' rights in an arrest situation. The Department of Justice (DOJ) requires that law enforcement agencies receiving DOJ funding provide interpreters (certified, if possible) upon a deaf person's arrest.[7] The law enforcement agency is required to determine whether a deaf person uses American Sign Language (ASL) or Signed English, and to obtain an interpreter proficient in the preferred language.[8]

U.S. constitutional law requires that arrested persons understand certain rights and consequences at the time they are arrested. This requirement was affirmed by the Supreme Court in the case of *Miranda vs. Arizona*,[9] in which that Court set forth the Advice of Rights (the Miranda Warning) that law enforcement officials must present to arrested persons before interrogation.

The Miranda Warning is usually presented as follows:

1. You have the right to remain silent;
2. Anthing you say can and will be used against you in court;
3. You have a right to have an attorney present and consult with him before and while answering any questions; and
4. If you cannot afford an attorney, one will be provided for you without cost.

Most interpreters recognize that these warnings pose serious problems for many deaf persons. There are no commonly understood ASL signs that adequately convey terms and concepts in the Miranda Warning.[10] Because the warning is written at a sixth- to eighth-grade reading level,[11] it is meaningless to fingerspell these terms to deaf persons who read below that level.

Often, the only satisfactory means of interpreting these warnings is by rephrasing each one several different ways, and then asking the deaf person to explain what each warning means. If the police are unwilling to spend this amount of time with the Miranda Warning, the interpreter should resign from the assignment.

The exclusionary rule of evidence forbids the use of evidence procured in violation of one's constitutional rights. If an arrested person is not properly informed of these rights, statements made by that person may not be used in court. The exclusionary rule is often raised in trials involving deaf defendants.

---

[7] 28 CFR Part 42, at 42.503(f).

[8] 45 Fed. Reg. 37630, Analysis of DOJ Regulation, (June 3, 1980).

[9] *Miranda v. Arizona*, 384 US 436 (1966)

[10] For example, there is no single ASL sign which is a satisfactory interpretation of the term "right." The signs commonly used are those for the concepts "all right," "can," or "correct." None of these adequately convey the total concept of a legal right. See McCay Vernon's excellent discussion of this issue for a more detailed analysis. Vernon, McCay, *Violation of Constitutional Rights: The Language Impaired Person and the Miranda Warnings*, Journ. Rehab. of the Deaf, Vol. 11, No. 4, pp. 1–8 (April, 1978).

[11] Vernon, at 7.

Interpreters who accept pretrial criminal assignments must be aware that interpretation of the Miranda Warning should be given a great deal of prior thought because their interpretation may be subject to scrutiny at the trial.

As noted above, interpreters can protect themselves by insisting that the procedure be videotaped. Interpreters who do not wish to subject themselves to the intensive critique that a videotape allows should not be interpreting in arrest situations.

Interpreting for deaf individuals can be a very rewarding and challenging profession. Interpreters who follow the guidelines here will avoid professional and ethical dilemmas while providing the best possible services to the deaf community.

COURTROOM HINTS

Prior to any court proceeding to which an interpreter is assigned, certain steps should be taken to ensure competent and professional interpreting. First, the interpreter should find out to whom he or she should report in the courtroom, and then do so. Second, the interpreter should meet with the deaf person involved to ascertain what the communication needs will be, whether simultaneous interpretation will be possible, and if a second interpreter, with a Reverse Skills Certificate (RSC), will be needed to ensure that the court will understand the deaf person.

Next, an interpreter should attempt to meet with the judge, or with both attorneys involved. Qualifications and information regarding an interpreter's professional role should be presented. The interpreter should also explain his or her physical needs, and the deaf person's communication needs. This is a good opportunity to ask the judge the proper means to make the interpreter's needs and limitations known during the proceeding.

The interpreter should be sworn in at the very outset of the trial. Interpretation should begin immediately and, in most cases, continue through the proceedings. An interpreter should interpret everything the deaf person says and not edit any testimony.

Physical positioning in a courtroom is important to competent interpreting. Exhibits should not block a deaf person's vision. The interpreter should be positioned within ten feet of, and in full view of, the deaf person.[12]

There is no impropriety in utilizing one interpreter to serve the needs of all deaf persons involved in a trial. Interpreters in this situation are expected to remain totally neutral and must be very careful to protect themselves against future allegations of bias. One good solution is not to talk to any of the parties during breaks in the proceedings.

[12] See the interpreter laws of Louisiana, 15 LRS 270B(1) (1968), Rhode Island, GLRI § 8-5-8 (1968), and Texas, TCA, Evidence Code § 3712a(b) (1979), for state statutes which mandate this positioning.

DEAF CULTURE:
FUTURE FOR THE DEAF

37

AS TOWN FOR DEAF TAKES SHAPE, DEBATE ON ISOLATION RE-EMERGE

MONICA DAVEY

Standing in an empty field along a wind-swept highway, Marvin T. Miller, who is deaf, envisions the town he wants to create here: a place built around American Sign Language, where teachers in the new school will sign, the town council will hold its debates in sign language and restaurant workers will be required to know how to sign orders.

Nearly 100 families—with people who are deaf, hard of hearing or who can hear but just want to communicate in sign language—have already publicly declared their intention to live in Mr. Miller's village, to be called Laurent, after Laurent Clerc, a French educator of the deaf from the 1800s.

Planners, architects and future residents from various states and other countries are gathering at a camp center in South Dakota on Monday and through the week to draw detailed blueprints for the town, which could accommodate at least 2,500 people. Mr. Miller, who has been imagining this for years, intends to break ground by fall.

"Society isn't doing that great a job of, quote-unquote, integrating us," Mr. Miller, 33, said through an interpreter. "My children don't see role models in their lives: mayors, factory managers, postal workers, business owners. So we're setting up a place to show our unique culture, our unique society."

While deaf enclaves, like the one that existed in Martha's Vineyard decades ago, have cropped up throughout the nation, this would be the first town expressly created for people who sign, its developers say. Even the location, in sparsely populated South Dakota, was selected with the intent of rapidly building political strength for the nation's millions of deaf and hard-of-hearing people, a group that has won few elected offices around the country.

But in the complicated political world of deaf culture, Laurent is an increasingly contentious idea. For some, like Mr. Miller; his wife, Jennifer, who is also deaf; and their four deaf children, it seems the simplest of wishes: to live in a place where they are fully engaged in day-to-day life. Others, however, particularly advocates of technologies that help deaf people use spoken language, wonder whether such a town would merely isolate and exclude the deaf more than ever.

"We think there is a greater benefit for people to be part of the whole world," said Todd Houston, executive director of the Alexander Graham Bell Association for the Deaf and Hard of Hearing in Washington. "I understand the desire to be around people like ourselves, and I don't have a problem with that, but I don't think it's very wise. This is a little bit of circling-the-wagons mentality, if you ask me."

Over the past 15 years, he said, it has become easier for the deaf and hard of hearing to grow up using spoken language, because of a steady rise in the use of cochlear implants, more early diagnoses and therapies for deaf children and efforts to place some deaf children in mainstream schools. That fact has set off intense political debate over what it means to be deaf and what mode of communication signing or talking—the deaf should focus on.

Those who want to live in Laurent, though, say their intent is not exclusivity at all, but the inclusion of diverse people, especially those who do not have the luxury of communicating with speech. "We are not building a town for deaf people," said M.E. Barwacz, Mr. Miller's mother-in-law and his business partner in creating Laurent. "We are building a town for sign language users. And one of the biggest groups we expect to have here is hearing parents with deaf children."

Ms. Barwacz, who intends to live in Laurent, is not deaf. She has two daughters, one deaf and one not, and eight grandchildren, four of them deaf. Nationally, experts report that some 90 percent of deaf children are born to hearing parents, setting up a quandary, in some cases, about what language to use in a single household.

As early as the 1800s, deaf leaders debated the possibility of a "deaf state," said Gerard Buckley, an official at the National Technical Institute for the Deaf in Rochester. But the notion came and went. Elsewhere, because of proximity to schools and businesses tied to the deaf, large concentrations of deaf people have gathered in cities like Rochester; Washington; Olathe, Kan.; Frederick, Md.; and Sioux Falls, S.D.

The difference in Laurent, say some among the 92 families who have reserved spaces in the town from as far as London and Australia, is that every element of it would be designed with them in mind. The homes and businesses, they said, would incorporate glass and open space for easy visibility across wide distances. Fire and police services would be designed with more lights and fewer sirens. High-speed Internet connections would be available all over town, since the Internet and Video Relay Service have become vital modes of communication for deaf people. And any shops, businesses or restaurants would be required to be sign-language friendly.

Here in Salem, a dusty 125-year-old farming town of 1,300 three miles from the proposed site of Laurent, people seem unsure of what to make of the idea. "No one has ever come along and tried to start a town," said Joseph Kolbeck, the local barber.

Along the quiet main drag through town, Mr. Miller and Ms. Barwacz, who are originally from Michigan, recently opened a storefront in the old King Koin Laundromat to create and promote Laurent. They moved to Salem not long ago, choosing the area after surveying nearly the entire country looking at factors like population, climate and cost of land.

Some people here wonder how the proposed town of 2,500 would mesh with McCook County's 6,000 residents and its economy of corn, cows and pigs. Others say they doubt Laurent will ever become reality.

Mr. Miller and Ms. Barwacz have revealed little about the costs and their plans for financing Laurent. They say they are using family money, as well as some from a group of "angel investors," led by a man with a deaf daughter who wishes to remain anonymous. First Dakota National Bank is helping to secure financing, and the two have optioned 275 acres so far. They say they are spending about $300,000 for the planning work during the meetings that will end on Saturday. Those who have reserved spaces in Laurent will be expected to put down $1,000 deposits for condominiums and home lots within the next few months.

For many of those people – from states like California, Florida and New York – a move to prairie land in South Dakota (population 760,000) would seem to be an enormous culture shock. But they plan to start businesses like shops and restaurants, gas stations and hotels, and the benefits, many of them say, outweigh any concerns they have about the location.

Lawrence J. Brick, a retired school administrator from Philadelphia, said Laurent held attractions that most hearing people would struggle even to grasp: no longer having to shy away from the neighbors, fearing he could not communicate; no longer having to guess what a store clerk is saying about a price; no longer having to apologize for being deaf.

Although some people argue that Laurent might isolate deaf people, H-Dirksen L. Bauman, who directs the master's program in deaf studies at Gallaudet University, said the plans actually marked an important collaboration between the deaf and the hearing, one of a sort not always encouraged by the deaf community. This is especially significant, he said, as more hearing people are learning American Sign Language, now the fifth most-studied language on college campuses.

"Hearing people are not welcomed in deaf residential schools, in deaf clubs," Mr. Bauman said. "But there is no audiogram you will need to buy land in Laurent, South Dakota. There's simply a commitment to live in a visually centered environment that supports manual as opposed to spoken language."

But Dr. Michael Novak of Urbana, III., who has been performing cochlear implants since 1984, said he was convinced that the trend among the deaf was actually shifting toward therapies that could help the next generation of deaf people use spoken language.

"Communities like this have a real place for people who cannot or choose not to use the hearing technology," Dr. Novak said of Laurent. "But over time, that number will be reducing." He wonders then, he said, if the future of a notion like Laurent might fade away.

For his part, though, Mr. Miller said reports of the "death of sign language and deaf culture continue to be greatly exaggerated." Not everyone, he said, is eligible for or would even want to receive technologies like cochlear implants. "I do not want one for myself," he said. "I am very happy being deaf. To me, this is like asking a black or Asian person if he/she would take a pill to turn into a white person."

Correction: April 1, 2005, Friday A map on March 21 with an article about plans for a town for deaf people in South Dakota, to be called Laurent, mislabeled the highway running north and south through Sioux Falls. It is 1–29, not 1–95.

38

HEALTH: GENE THERAPY RESTORES HEARING TO DEAF GUINEA PIGS

Steven Reinberg
HealthDay Reporter

MONDAY, Feb. 14 (HealthDayNews) – For the first time, researchers have used gene therapy to grow new auditory hair cells that enabled deaf animals to hear.

Many types of permanent hearing loss are due to damage to sensory hair cells in the inner ear. If this gene therapy is successful in additional studies, it may one day help restore significant hearing loss in humans, the researchers suggest.

"New hair cells can be regenerated in animals that are deaf and have no hair cells," said lead researcher Yehoash Raphael, an associate professor of otolaryngology at the University of Michigan, whose research involved guinea pigs. "After treatment, the animal's hearing is significantly restored."

In their study, the researchers implanted a gene called Atoh1, also called Math1, into the animals' ears. "This gene, during embryonic development, signals for the development of hair cells," Raphael said. "The hope was that if we expressed this gene in the ear, they would become hair cells."

The researchers implanted a modified virus containing the gene directly into the inner ear of the animals in the spot where hair cells should normally be. This gene induced new hair cells to grow where none were present before.

Once the gene was implanted, it took about eight weeks for the guinea pigs to be able to hear. After about four weeks, the hair cells started to appear, Raphael said. "After about two months, they [the cells] look happy and contribute to the functional recovery of hearing," he added.

Raphael hopes that, in the not-too-distant future, the researchers can develop a way to implant this gene into humans. "At this stage, there is a lot more that needs to be done in animals," he said.

The finding appears in the March issue of *Nature Medicine.*

David P. Corey, a professor of neurobiology at Harvard Medical School, said he was "impressed" by the new research. "People had shown that Math1 could force cells to become hair cells, but this is the first time it has been shown that it can actually restore hearing in an animal. And that is quite significant."

Age-related hearing loss is a huge problem and is mostly caused by the death of hair cells, Corey said. "If we can replace even some hair cells, that could have a really big public health benefit," he added.

Hearing loss is one of the most common conditions affecting older adults. One in three people older than 60, and half of those older than 85, have hearing loss. Causes of hearing loss can include exposure to loud or harmful sounds, as well as a virus or bacteria, heart conditions or stroke, head injuries, tumors and certain medicines, according to the National Institute on Deafness and Other Communication Disorders.

"This is a very important study, which showed that in deaf guinea pigs it is possible to restore some degree of hearing by expressing a gene that is key to the hair cell development," said Zheng-Yi Chen, an assistant professor of neurology at Massachusetts General Hospital and Harvard Medical School. "The current study is a major step forward that shows the new hair cells can help with functional recovery from deafness."

Chen believes this discovery will open the way to new treatments for deafness. "Because of the striking similarity between human and rodent inner ears, there is a strong reason to believe that a similar approach may result in certain hearing recovery in profoundly deaf people," he said.

More information

The National Institute on Deafness and Other Communication Disorders has more on hearing loss.